CELEBRATING OUR DIFFERENCES

LIVING TWO FAITHS IN ONE MARRIAGE

By Mary Heléne Rosenbaum
& Stanley Ned Rosenbaum

Foreword by Martin E. Marty

Ragged Edge Press
and
Black Bear Productions, Inc.
Boston, Kentucky

Celebrating Our Differences: Living Two Faiths in One Marriage. Copyright © 1994 by Mary Heléne Rosenbaum and Stanley Ned Rosenbaum.

This Ragged Edge Press publication
was printed by
Beidel Printing House, Inc.
63 West Burd Street
Shippensburg, PA 17257 USA

In respect for the scholarship contained herein, the acid-free paper used in this book meets the guidelines for permanence and durability of the Committee on Production Guidelines for Book Longevity of the Council on Library Resources.

For a complete list of available publications please write
Ragged Edge Press,
Division of White Mane Publishing Company, Inc.
P.O. Box 152
Shippensburg, PA 17257 USA

Book design and editing by
Black Bear Productions, Inc.
775 Simon Greenwell Ln.
Boston, KY 40107

Library of Congress Cataloging-in-Publication Data
Rosenbaum, Mary Heléne, 1944-
   Celebrating our differences : living two faiths in one marriage /
by Mary Heléne Rosenbaum and Stanley Ned Rosenbaum :
foreword by Martin E. Marty.
   p.   cm.
Includes index
ISBN 0-942597-69-9 : $19.95
   1. Interfaith marriage. 2. Marriage—Religious aspects—
Judaism.
3. Marriage—Religious aspects—Christianity. 4. Judaism—
Doctrines.
I. Rosenbaum, Stanley Ned, 1939-   . II. Title.
HQ1031.R65 1994
306.84'3—dc20   94-8447
                                                            CIP

PRINTED IN THE UNITED STATES OF AMERICA

Also by S. N. Rosenbaum
Amos of Israel: A New Interpretation

To our parents:
living and dead,
in blood, in law, and in faith.

ACKNOWLEDGMENTS

We are grateful for the inspiration and assistance of Paul and Rachel Cowan, Olga S. Pottker, Jan Pottker, and the people—known and unknown to us personally—whose insights and experiences we have drawn on for this book. We also thank our children: Ephraim Rosenbaum, William Rosenbaum, Sarah Rosenbaum, and Craig Wilkinson; they're the reason for all our celebrations. Maria Mack has been unfailingly helpful and supportive in our attempt to distill the experiences of a lifetime into readable, useful form. And finally, thanks to James Klein, who started it all when he introduced us December 23, 1961.

Any mistakes or oversights in the following are my spouse's fault.

Mary Heléne Pottker Rosenbaum
Stanley Ned Rosenbaum

CONTENTS

FOREWORD iii

A THREEFOLD CORD SHALL NOT BE BROKEN 1

THE BASICS
1   Religion: Another World 7
2   Culture: A Different World 27

GETTING MARRIED AND STAYING MARRIED
3   The Wedding: Your Dream World 42
4   The Marriage: Your Real World 54

GETTING TOGETHER AND GETTING ALONG
5   Sex: How, Why and to What End 66
6   Identity and Crisis 77

FAMILY TIES
7   Starting a Family 90
8   Building a Family 105

TIES THAT UNBIND
9   Divorce: Severing the Cord 123
10 Death: The Third Strand of the Cord 129

TYING IT ALL TOGETHER
11 Spiritual Life and Intellectual Life 139
12 The Seasons 163
13 The Holidays 170

PRACTICAL POINTERS
14 Food for the Body 198
15 Food for the Mind 205

CONCLUSION 215

INDEX 216

FOREWORD

The market for a truly helpful book on interfaith marriage should be huge, and I hope that *Celebrating Our Differences* finds a good share of it. Marriage across the lines of religion and of most but by no means all of "everything else" is growing. Our society is too mobile, too fluid, too unprotecting to make it possible for people to stay out of acquaintance and out of love. The shtetl and ghetto walls, the boundaries of urban wards and rural valleys, do little to shield the marrying kind from meeting people who are "other," so far as faith traditions are concerned. They need not only the cautions and warnings implied and uttered on these pages, but also a manual of action (I almost said a "manual of arms") with which to follow up on their decision to wed. This book is it.

The verb "celebrating" in the title of this book may seem misleading. The authors could as well have written: "Anticipating the Pitfalls and Pratfalls that Go with Mixed Marriage." Turn the pages for the first time, as I did, and it may well occur to you to think that the message to couples contemplating marriage across lines of faith is simple: "Don't."

Since Mary Heléne and Ned Rosenbaum know that few who consult this book to learn about pit and prat and other falls will take such wise but negative advice—love, if it does not conquer all, can at least delude many—their message might be translated from "Don't!" to "Since you will, here's how!" Or, at least, "Here is how one couple does it."

As someone who twice, once after widowerhood, has married a spouse of the same faith, I have on occasion had to engage in acts of empathy to understand What's the Big Deal with "mixed marriages." Of course, all marriages are mixed, and opinions about faith and its contexts are diverse and controversial in same–faith marriages such as my own. Still, there has been in such marriages some context which, as the Rosenbaums make clear, two–faith marriages lack.

Before Vatican II, one remembers and tries to describe for the young, there was more difference and tension within the rules of the game for Christians in Protestant and Catholic camps than there is today for a Christian and a Jew in our multiculturally edgy era.

Chicago Cardinal Joseph Bernardin has said he bet much more on a wedding between, say, a committed Catholic and Presbyterian than between uncommitted or noncommittal types who all but have to scramble to find out what each other's, or even their own, faith was or was supposed to be. The Rosenbaums, contravening the standard wisdom on the subject, agree. But they also help readers envision problems the young often do not picture couples having.

I read the book with at times a kind of grim and grinning fascination as it led me further into the labyrinth of complexities. It elicits and demands empathy and then satisfies the curious. The casual non–Jew might begin by understanding why Jews are so very wary about "losing" one of theirs through the conversion that often happens when the partner is non–Jewish. (Rosenbaums offer considerable advice on converting or nonconverting, one of the touchiest subjects.) It has to be remembered that the world has 1.8 billion people called Christian—that's one thousand eight hundred million folks—while Jews have perhaps 12.8 million, fewer than there are Southern Baptists in the United States. And Mary Heléne represents an atom of the billion–strong Roman Catholic church which has historically had so many canons and taboos against mixed marriage. Every thoughtful couple, busy enough working out the microcosm of marriage, is also acting against a macrocosmic background that only complicates things.

One will learn from these pages why Rosenbaums think—rightly, I believe—that conversion is always problematic; that uninformed and casual and superficially tolerant faith on the part of one or both partners in marriage is rarely as helpful as informed and committed versions; that dreamed–of problems are not easily addressed, and undreamed–of ones will plague most of all. The authors are not for Least Common Denominator religion as an aid to marriage. If their testimony is representative, one might advise to avoid a mixed marriage if she or he would avoid religion and theology. The Rosenbaums keep running into far more religious issues that demand response than will the single person or the couple nestled in a single tradition.

There is advice for readers who are not in mixed marriages, as well; I liked their suggestion of how to invent and observe a version of the Sabbath, something our family did to its great profit. The talk about baptism and confirmation, about divorce and death, is practical, but the passion with which families debate them is also evident in the telling here.

I hope I have not made it sound as if this book is of interest and use only to couples who are about to mix it up in marriage or who are mixed up after marriage. It turns out to be intrinsically interesting. One gets to anticipating the italics and bold type of their individual anecdotes, the further to get acquainted with two people who experience things well and write about them with depth and finesse alike. They are both reflective sorts who deal with experiences which find analogies and resonances elsewhere. And they are both first–rate storytellers. The story they tell is their own, or one that happens to acquaintances. They do not claim to have principles, dogmas, or canons to solve the issues they address. But hearing the stories of what they and others have encountered and thought and done will hold attention for its own sake, even as casual readers learn more about the lives of many fellow citizens.

The authors of this book suggest: "Celebrate!" But, quickly now, turn the page to see why and how.

Martin E. Marty
The University of Chicago

A Threefold Cord Shall Not Be Broken

The Bible is first of all about the relationship between God and human beings. The marital bond, however, is the primary one between humans. As God says in Genesis, "Therefore shall a man leave his mother and father and cleave unto his wife, and they shall become one flesh." Many people, especially people writing about interfaith marriage, put the third point of the Eternal Triangle, the one that touches the Divine, out of the picture. We think this is a mistake.

While a certain surface stability may be achieved by one or both partners' ignoring the part God plays in their lives, they're missing a chance to weave a strong, beautifully patterned web. As it says in Ecclesiastes: "Two are better than one. . . .and a threefold cord shall not be broken." Recognizing the sacred character of marriage will give your relationship strength for the long haul.

Though "God is love" is a Christian formulation, it describes an attitude vital to Jewish understanding of the Divine nature as well, as the apostle John himself points out elsewhere in the same epistle. We have found that the bond between the love of God and the soul of the believer clinches the bond between wife and husband. We're writing this book because we believe this to be true even when the wife God/husband-God connections are braided of strands drawn from different religious patterns. In fact, we think it may be more vital for a mixed-faith couple to keep ties to their individual faiths strong than for those who can take religious unity for granted.

This isn't the conventional wisdom on mixed marriage, and for good reason. Keeping two faiths strong while not weakening the marriage bond is hard work—it needs concentration and effort. But we think the results are worth it. And we know there are lots of you looking for the kinds of pointers our experience can give.

One recent study indicates a 75 percent failure rate for interfaith marriages—50 percent higher than for American marriages overall. This may be due to the fact that, as we've observed, many young couples marry without really understanding what their own unexamined assumptions can do to the fabric of a marriage. Adding the tensions of different faiths to all the other pulls increases the odds of ending up with tatters—unless you learn to pull together.

Of American Jews who marry, almost half marry non-Jews. In the past generation, according to a survey by B'nai B'rith Women, the intermarriage rate for Jews has increased fivefold for men and twelvefold for women. Two generations ago, "marrying out" often reflected a desire to reject Jewish* identity and/or gain social status.

*See Chapter 15 for our usage of asterisked words

Nowadays, especially since the Six Day War (1967), intermarried Jews tend to be proud of their heritage but confused about how to express its importance to their equally bewildered Christian partners. As a minority community, Jews feel threatened by burgeoning intermarriage rates. A 1991 Council of Jewish Federations survey reveals that the Jewish population of the United States has barely changed since 1970, although the general population has increased by twenty percent. Though in this age of delayed marriage, parents would increasingly prefer to see an older child marry a gentile* than remain single, they still withhold approval for intermarriage of younger children. Jewish parents would prefer intermarrying children to be married by a rabbi, but the wish so far has not widely become reality. It's still difficult to find a rabbi who'll participate in a mixed marriage. In many communities, even open discussion of the subject is taboo, although the Reform establishment has recently declared the offspring of mixed marriages Jewish if they are being raised within Judaism.* This move, however, has created controversy in the Jewish community, to say nothing (for the moment) about leaving many Christian partners feeling disenfranchised.

Meaningful statistics on intermarriage rates in Christian denominations are harder to come by. There are so many sectarian divisions, many with differing definitions of intermarriage: some don't count any marriage with another baptized person as interfaith, no matter what the denomination; some consider any marriage outside their particular version of Christianity "mixed"; some don't keep records of such marriages; some lump together numbers of marriages between their adherents and other Christians and marriages between their adherents and non–Christians. Suffice it to say that, although as the majority religion Christianity is less threatened by intermarriage than Judaism, its leaders are still concerned about the phenomenon and its implications.

For Christians, the problems of interfaith marriage fall into two broad categories: religion and culture. If they're committed to their faith, Christians wonder whether they shouldn't be trying to convert the Jewish partner—and whether they're spiritually shortchanging their children. If they're not religious, they're puzzled at the cultural strength of Jewish identity and history, and wonder why their nonobservant partners find it so important.

The Catholic* Church used to be the most negative of the Christian denominations about mixed marriage, but these days many Protestants* are feeling defensive, too. Both mainstream groups worry, rightly, about the differences in both belief and practice between interfaith partners, especially when it comes to children.

What will the next generation believe? How will it preserve cherished traditions?

And on the Fundamentalist end of the spectrum, of course, it's considered a positive duty for the Christian partner to convert the non-Christian.

At the same time, both Jews and Christians are discovering a new interest in traditional identities and structured belief systems. Not only do statistics show an increasing trend toward rediscovering religious roots, our own experiences with young couples indicate that more and more of them are wrestling with questions their parents may have dismissed as outmoded or irrelevant.

They reflect a concern expressed by the Prophet Micah over 2,500 years ago: "What does the Lord require of you?" Micah's answer—"Do justice, love mercy, and walk humbly with thy God" (Mic. 6:8)—looks deceptively simple. In practice, it's a difficult enough dictum to carry out when you're both on the same path. When you have different ideas about which road is the right one, walking together can become tricky.

In this book, we'll be sharing our experiences** in making an interfaith marriage work without losing touch with our own religious roots.

NED
I was born into a highly assimilated Reform family that had only a tenuous Jewish identity; now I am Coordinator of the Judaic Studies Program at Dickinson College where I am Professor of Religion and Classics. But my interest is not only academic. As the Talmud* says: Study is more important than practice, because study leads to practice. I have become steadily more observant over the years, to the point of now keeping mostly kosher and declining to ride or drive on the Sabbath. In this development, Mary Heléne has assisted, encouraged, and often pushed me along the way to finding my religious home. In Yiddish* story writer Chaim Grade's words, she "shouted at me as though I were a dark cellar and [s]he was calling to someone hiding in me." Jews especially, but gentiles as well, need to be aware of what religious yearning may be hiding in each of us.

MARY HELÉNE
I am a practicing Roman Catholic, a lector* and teacher in my church. When I felt disaffected in the wake of the sweeping changes brought by Vatican II, it was Ned who prodded and

**Ned's stories are set in italics, Mary Heléne's in boldface.

4

challenged me to redefine myself as a Catholic and return to the fold. Today, when I get discouraged at the institution's attempts to creep back to the rigid certainties of the 50s, he cheers me on to persist in fomenting renewal from within the establishment. For me, the links with tradition combine with the Catholic insistence on the link between soul and body, spirit and flesh, to integrate daily reality with religious feeling and intellectual theology. This is a major way in which Catholic and Jewish approaches to spirituality run in tandem. Where Catholics use sacraments* to link the sacred and the profane, observant Jews use the wide-ranging ethical and ritual structure developed from Torah and tradition to bind the visible world to the invisible.

Our interreligious marriage has been going strong since 1963. We have successfully negotiated the early years of "voluntary poverty" and round–the–clock diapers. We've also weathered our own and each other's religious ups and downs and come out stronger as individuals and as a couple. We maintain that each of our particular religious commitments has helped strengthen the other, and created a whole that is greater than the sum of its parts.

We have both written articles, given lectures, and conducted workshops on Christian–Jewish marriage. Out of this experience comes our book.

In the first chapter of this book, we outline various religious routes that can be taken: Conversion, Compromise, Secularization or "Love Conquers All," and our route—maintaining both religions. We don't pretend it's the easiest way, but we explain why we feel it's the most rewarding, despite the widespread opinions of others who don't have our experience.

In the second chapter, we look at the ways relationships with families—one's own and the in–laws—can cause conflicts in the marriage. Here is where culture and religion start to snag, and unravel the intermarried couple. And where families are concerned, everyone's emotions are engaged. We examine techniques for using these kinship webs as safety nets rather than traps.

Next, we give advice and practical suggestions on the wedding ceremony itself: who performs it, how, and what different traditions you may not be aware of.

In the fourth chapter we explore the cultural differences that frequently blindside couples who assume that if they've figured out how to arrange the wedding ceremony they've covered it all. We explore relationships other books on intermarriage ignore: those with friends and colleagues. There are possibilities for friction and alienation at work and play that we help the reader anticipate and deal with. We also unravel the strands of ethnic identity, and suggest ways you can constructively weave them together.

With this groundwork laid, we're ready to tackle the thorny subject of sex. Both in principle and practice, Jews and Christians can have radically different ideas that they may not even have realized, much less examined: it may seem disgusting to the Jew, for instance, to have intercourse during the menstrual period; to the Christian, it may be a matter of indifference, or even an advantage to a Catholic who observes church strictures on birth control.

The heart of our book is the section on children and family life. This is where the major pitfalls lie in wait for the unwary interfaith couples, even the ones who think they've plotted their course through this morass of emotions, traditions, and practical problems. We look first at the rites of passage of Christianity and Judaism, and how they impact the interfaith family. Then we return to the subject of culture, this time in the context of your own new family's habits and how to keep them from becoming a constant source of friction or discontent. Our family includes three twentysomething kids, none of them confused, alienated, or otherwise beset by neuroses the doom–sayers warned us of when we married. Nevertheless, we've had to work very hard at navigating with two compasses; we've plumbed these waters, and give you a chart of the dragons and delights along the way.

Next comes a chapter dealing with things we haven't experienced: death and divorce. The latter is something statistics show mixed couples are most likely to encounter. Increasingly, people are wrenched, even more than in the average divorce, when there are conflicting Jewish and Christian claims on the spiritual lives of children. How they will be raised, and who is able to raise them that way, is a question being debated in courts all over the country.

Many of the same problems occur when one partner dies while children are still at home. And all couples have to deal with death and dying eventually. Not only are there practical problems with finding appropriate burial sites and securing the assistance of clergy, there are profound differences between Jews and Christians in mourning practices and in the understanding of the meaning of death itself. We try to help you foresee problems and discuss solutions in advance, and to be prepared for the strong possibility that no preparation will really be enough in these milestone traumas.

Concluding on a positive note, we share with you the religious insights and strengths that our controversial approach has gained for us, and we review resources—books, magazines, and our own "think again" checklist as a basis for discussion—the mixed couple can explore. We also provide practical advice on such common problems as the "December Dilemma": to Tree or not to Tree; we even include a unique guide for the Christian cook trying to keep a kosher* kitchen.

The book's bad news is: We're not in favor of interfaith marriage in principle; the good news is that, in practice, we've been happily married for thirty years. During that time we've piled up enough experiences, our own and other peoples', so that we think we can tell you what you (or someone you hold dear) is in for. The pattern of your relationship will not be exactly the same as ours so it would be wrong to assume that because we've made it through three decades of marriage you can too. Conversely, don't think that you won't have the problems we had because . . . whatever your situation, you can be sure it's neither unique nor problem–free.

Both our general observations and our particular suggestions are based not only on our own experiences as an intermarried couple, but also on conversations with dozens of similar couples of all ages and from all walks of life. We're sure you'll find your situation mirrored at many points by what we've assembled here.

Let's emphasize one thing again, though: Proceed with caution! It may sound strange to say that "you can't get here from there," wherever you are, but we trust you noticed what we said above: three out of four mixed marriages fail. This book will therefore be mainly concerned about the work required to solve the problems in intermarriage.

Many engaged couples have ended conversations with us less confident of their ability to deal with intermarriage than they were before. This is as it should be; if we make you think of aspects that hadn't occurred to you, better you should deal with them now rather than after you've been joined at the hip . . . or the ring finger.

We have hard questions and we don't have easy answers. In our view, the many books that suggest you can be happily intermarried by outpourings of simple good will are, to say the least, inadequate. They usually haven't been written by people like us who know what intermarriage feels like on a day–by–day, year–to–year basis. If they promise you a rose garden, remember that roses have thorns. And if you're going to try to weave both faiths together, remember: the more complex the design, the more time you'll spend at the loom.

THE BASICS

Chapter 1
Religion: Another World

"Therefore a man will leave his father and mother and cling to his wife and they shall become one flesh." Genesis 2:24, the Bible's first description of marriage, is more than a license for lovers to ignore their parents. It instructs us that the marital relationship takes precedence over any other. The ancient Israelites knew that effecting a spiritual union would be hard enough; they didn't want the newly-weds' loyalties to remain with the families from which each had come, but envisioned the creation of a new family unit.

But what the ancients thought about intermarriage can be found all over Scripture: they were unequivocally against it. If a same–faith marriage can be seen as a kind of hybridizing of two families, an interfaith marriage is more like grafting one species of tree to another; the graft doesn't always take.

It may seem ridiculously obvious to say that the first question you need to deal with in marrying someone of a different religion is your different religions. But we've been amazed at how many couples discount religious belief or affiliation as unimportant in comparison to practical problems of arranging the wedding ceremony. They either ignore their religious differences or pick an approach to them that they may not have thought through.

For instance, we've talked to many couples who blithely assured each other that good will and a sense of humor would be sufficient to keep them practicing each of their own faiths. Good will and a sense of humor are certainly necessary, but not sufficient. Often these couples haven't thought about what process they'll use to resolve differences that can't be compromised—whether to circumcise a child or baptize it, for instance. You can't do both under religious auspices, and no amount of good will is going to make a partner with a strong emotional or intellectual commitment to one tradition or the other feel better about giving way.

As the following pages show, there are basically four approaches to interfaith marriage: Conversion, Compromise, Love conquers all, and Our way—keeping both faiths alive. Naturally, we think our way gives interfaith couples the best chance at success. But remember: none of these ways guarantees success; and—what's even more important—solving the religious problem can be a long–term affair.

THE HOME TEAM APPROACH: YOUR GOD SHALL BE MY GOD

If your partner is already more religious than you are, or belongs to a stricter or more exclusive religion than yours, you may be tempted to convert just to make things easier. But will they be easier? The community that you now enter may not be too receptive, especially if your conversion is only for the sake of the marriage.

In France, conversion to Judaism for the sake of marriage is not allowed by the French rabbinate (though they allow civil marriage and life together without expelling the Jewish partner). And it was not too long ago that Jewish conversion to Christianity was considered invalid throughout Europe.

According to the 1989 *Faithful to Each Other Forever: A Catholic Handbook of Pastoral Help for Marriage Preparation* issued by the National Conference of Catholic Bishops, "An interreligious marriage may be the occasion, but must never be the cause of any conversion," though they cite some positive statistics indicating a correlation between conversion and marital stability.

Even if conversion smooths some obstacles, how comfortable are you going to feel in five years, or in ten, having given up your belief in God for someone else's? We'll return to this subject shortly.

Conversion has been fairly common in gentile–Jewish marriages. On the average, 21 percent of Christians now married to Jews have converted to Judaism either formally, or through adopting its practices; only 3.3 percent of Jews married to Christians converted to Christianity. (Interestingly, most Jews–by–choice are women; of 1,591 converts to Reform in 1983, 75 percent were women whose average age was 29: 44 percent of them were Roman Catholic, 38 percent Protestant; most of the Jews who converted out were men: 43 percent Conservative, 41 percent Reform.) However, as of late 1991, conversion to Judaism associated with intermarriage had fallen to 5 percent in new marriages; twenty years ago it was nearly one third.

Statistics show more of these conversion marriages succeed than those in which there was no conversion, on paper at least. Conversion can make questions of marriage ceremony, child raising, and family affiliation seem easier, and can also remove superficial conflicts.

Paul and Rachel Cowan, whose book *Mixed Blessings* analyzes a number of intermarriages—including ours—arrived at this position before Paul's untimely death. After some years of marriage, Rachel converted to Judaism. She is now in fact a Reform rabbi, and even before Paul died, theirs had ceased to be a mixed marriage—their convictions had met in Judaism.

Another person we talked to was raised Catholic, abandoned the church, and is now in the process of becoming Jewish like her partner. She said, "Before I made the decision to convert, both Judaism and Christianity seemed unimportant—I didn't feel particularly identified with established religions and thought I didn't need one. Now I feel as though a hole in my heart I didn't know was there has healed." A great testimonial for adult conversion.

If you, however, convert for convenience, not from conviction, you may well be letting yourselves in for deeper trouble later on. In the first place, you may have to conceal your real motive for converting from the clergy conducting the process. This may make you feel hypocritical.

And how will you feel toward the person who "made" you do this? If you don't feel the least bit resentful at the moment, will you later? Will you feel that he or she "owes" you a big one? We know a woman, originally Jewish, who began having second thoughts about her conversion to Catholicism—after fifty years of marriage.

Still, many people you meet will see conversion as the obvious solution to your problem. Which one of you they think should do it may depend on their own affiliation or on their ideas of gender roles— their unexpressed attitudes may range from: "you should convert because your religion is wrong"; to "the woman should convert because she should follow her husband"; to "the man should convert because household religion is the mother's business [sic]."

MARY HELÉNE

We were living in Jerusalem in a small Orthodox–Jewish neighborhood. There was an oldfashioned greengrocer at the corner of our block with whom I'd developed a lively friendliness and mutual respect over the course of a year.

Then one day the father of a friend, an American Jew who spoke no Hebrew, came to visit us, bearing a box of strawberries he'd bought at the corner shop. He had been significantly overcharged, and the fruit under the top layer was moldy.

Next time I went to Baruch the greengrocer I said (in Hebrew), "You know, that American you cheated on the strawberries this morning, that was a friend of ours."

He was aghast. "A friend of yours? I didn't know. If I had known! I thought, *has v'ha'l'illah*," (an Arabic interjection meaning "God forbid") "that he was a Christian."

"What did you say?"

"I thought, *has v'ha'l'illah*, he was a Christian!"

"*Nu ?* So what if he was a Christian?"

Baruch, born in Morocco and never to his knowledge having met a Christian, explained, "What do Christians know about good food? Jews eat. I wouldn't waste my fine fruit on a Christian."

"*Adon* (Mr.) Baruch," I said formally, "you didn't know that I am a Christian?"

"But," he sputtered, "you're a good woman! *K'mo b'nai adam!*" (Literally, "like the sons of Adam," i.e. a real person.)

"Nevertheless, I am a Christian," I answered.

Well, he pressed goods on me, hustled about my order, and waved away my money even as he accepted it, to show that this revelation would make no difference between us.

But a week or so later he drew me aside, as I had known he would. "Lady," he said, "you have such a husband . . ." rapturously kissing his own bunched fingertips. Then, pointing at me, he crisply commanded, "Convert."

"But I'm a believing Christian," I said. "My religion isn't just a matter of convenience: I really believe."

He clicked his tongue, tilted his head, waved his hand. "So believe," he said. "But convert."

Baruch's attitude—choose the religion that makes things easiest for you, not the one you believe in—has been paralleled by that of many American Christians who think Ned should convert for the sake of "family unity," regardless of what he believes.

We don't, obviously, agree with this attitude. If you really don't care what religion you belong to, we suggest you not belong to one.

Even if you are sincerely attracted to your partner's religion, and would still convert if you weren't marrying a member of it, your path may not be smooth.

There are special problems involved in converting to Judaism. Judaism has not been a proselytizing religion for the last 1,500 years, and never had the goal of making the world Jewish. Jewish religious rules are mandatory for Jews only; everyone else is bound merely by some basic moral tenets, in the Jewish view. Because of this philosophy and because in the past harsh penalties have been levied on Jews who converted Christians (or Muslims), conversion to Judaism is not made easy.

As a proselyte in most forms of Judaism, you would have to convince a rabbi of your seriousness in order to begin to study the religion, then enter on the course of study and pursue it until the rabbi was satisfied that you knew what you were doing. Next you would appear before a specially appointed board to prove your grasp of

Jewish principles and laws and your own determination to adhere to them. If you are converting into Conservative or Orthodox Judaism you will also undergo a ritual bath and, if you are male, circumcision* or the ceremonial drawing of one drop of blood if you are already circumcised.

And if you convert into Reconstructionism or Reform, you would not be automatically accepted as Jewish in more traditional congregations.

Don't be surprised if your partner is not much help in showing you what being Jewish means. Partners may be people who never had much Jewish training—after all, they're marrying you, aren't they—and may be more interested in mollifying grandparents than in sharing a faith. In fact, we know an originally unobservant man who resented and resisted his convert wife's attempt to keep kosher. (Now, some fifteen years later, he's the one who won't eat meat in our house because we're not strict enough in our observance. Go figure.)

Then, too, psychologists tell us that members of persecuted minority groups often resolve the inner conflict generated by good "in–group" and bad "outsider" images by projecting the negative ones (stereotypes we'll discuss in Chapter 2) onto the opposite sex of their own group. That is, instead of a Jewish male feeling, "We Jews are pushy and materialistic, as the gentiles say," he may unconsciously adopt the notion, "We Jewish men are okay; it's Jewish women who are bossy and greedy." A Jewish woman might think the converse. There are many Jews who collude in the popularity of self–hating JAP—"Jewish American Princess/Prince"—jokes on college campuses and elsewhere.

Or a gentile might escape from stereotypes of WASP* coldness or Catholic superstitiousness by ascribing those qualities solely to coreligionists of the opposite sex. Such an individual might unconsciously be looking for a resolution of this conflict by intermarrying. If the spouse then converts, becoming a member of the very group that the other partner was rejecting, the original problem reappears. That is, if you married a gentile (or a Jew) so as not to be bound to a "JAP" (or to a "mick," or whatever), and then your partner converts, your psychological "escape route" has been closed off.

Some people will continue to regard you as an outsider no matter how enthusiastic you are. Our son–in–law, for instance, is aware that other Jews are conscious of him as a convert because he doesn't have an identifiably "Jewish name." Although Jewish law insists that the convert is a fully competent member of the community, as "reborn" as any evangelical Christian might be, we have met more than one convert who feels discriminated against in Jewish company. This happens to converts of any faith, but there can be an emotional content to rejection of converts by individual Jews that's hard to overcome.

For example, one rabbi tells of a father who could not accept a converted daughter–in–law because of the psychic scars left by his experience in merely liberating concentration camps after WW II. The Conservative Rabbinical Assembly issued a statement in 1985 calling on its members to "correct the impression converts are not welcome." This is all to the good, but as Ned says, "prohibition presupposes previous practice"—that is, if they're bothering to issue directives, there must be a problem.

The intertwining of religion and culture in Judaism can work the other way, though. One of our acquaintances, originally a Protestant, converted to Judaism while married to another Protestant. Evidently, her conversion was prompted by an intellectual acceptance of the tenets of Judaism in the context of a hitherto successful marriage. However, as she became more involved in the lifestyles and folkways that are virtually inseparable from Jewish practice, the link with her husband strained and then snapped. She has since remarried—a rabbi. Time will tell how his congregation will accept her as a Jew. (Her first husband has remarried—a Jew! We predict another conversion down the road.)

Don't underestimate the emotional reaction of your Christian family and friends to one who converts to Judaism. After all, some of them will believe that you're Damning your Soul to Hell. If members of your family believe that salvation can be achieved only by profess-ing faith in Jesus, they will be bewildered and frightened at your rejecting what they see as an obvious truth. We know a man who didn't tell his Catholic parents of his plan to convert to Judaism until he was sure he wanted to take the step. His thinking was that there was no point in upsetting them unnecessarily. Unfortunately, what he thought of as tact and consideration left them feeling they'd never had an adequate chance to present their "side" until it was "too late." He, in his turn, was taken by surprise at the persistence of their unease; remember that your Christian family, however tolerant when it comes to outsiders, may not be able to accept a difference of belief as simply a matter of opinion when it comes to their own kin.

Less strictly religious Christians may feel that you are slightly deranged, a masochist or a misguided martyr, for giving up your place in the majority for a place among those that majority has often persecuted. Even some Jews feel this way; the idea of anyone's deliberately taking on the social burdens of Jewish identity is often incomprehensible.

Still, many people obviously think the rewards of becoming Jewish outweigh the problems. According to sociologist Dr. Egon Mayer, there are about 100,000 Jews–by–choice in the United States today. About a third of interfaith marriage conversions occur after the marriage, and the originally non–Jewish partner is usually "more Jewishly inclined" than the born Jew. That can cause its own problems, as we pointed out above.

Converting to Christianity can be a more or less complicated process, depending on the denomination. Roman Catholics, at one end of the spectrum, require a course of instruction before baptism* and confirmation, while some Fundamentalist Protestants, at the other end, only require a declaration of faith.

The major problems for the Jew taking the conversion route are social and psychological. Socially, many people will never cease to identify you—and treat you—as a Jew, especially if you have what is perceived as a Jewish name. In some circles, you may be laughed at behind your back and suspected of switching allegiance for material advantage. A neighbor of Ned's did this in the 1930s, but even after he became an elder in his wife's church, people referred to him as a Jew.

Or, what may make you even more uncomfortable, Christians may see you as a "good example" for all your poor benighted brethren who haven't seen the light and expect you to missionize other Jews. How will you respond?

Psychologically, there is the burden of history: the sense you may have of having abandoned your ancestors, who suffered and died to preserve what you're rejecting, and that at the hands of members of the very group you're joining. You'll be accused of "self–hatred" by people who may compare you to the leader of Chicago's American Nazi Party at the time of the Skokie incident, who was born a Jew. You may think the comparison unfair, even irrational, but be unable to shake it nonetheless.

It will be especially hard to shake if your family and friends are constantly throwing your decision up at you—referring to dead ancestors allegedly "turning over in their graves," or live ones being brought to the brink of them. A Jewish friend of ours was adjured by his parents never to tell his aged grandfather about his gentile wife— "It would kill him"—even though the young man hadn't converted. When the old gentleman in fact lay dying, he asked matter–of–factly, "Is Harvey still married to that shiksah*?" It's not uncommon for parents to use the "this will kill your grandparents" gambit; we suggest talking directly to the grandparents. However, be prepared for the possibility that they will in fact be deeply distraught at your "marrying out"—and devastated at your conversion to Christianity. A relatively small percentage of Jews married to Christians do convert, a further indication that this step requires an extraordinarily high degree of commitment to the Christian faith. While Judaism is essentially an ethical system without a detailed belief structure, Christianity depends first on a faith experience. Because of this, most Christians would say that a Jew should convert only out of conviction—though some simple people may take a less complicated approach.

MARY HELÉNE

Tonina and Pete, childless themselves, were like extra grandparents to me. When Ned and I became engaged, I just had to go tell the old Italian couple my great news. Whoops of joy, hugs and kisses, and then when Pete disappeared into the basement for some homemade wine—what had teasingly been called "black milk" in my childhood, now to be offered me as a coming–of–age rite—Tonina drew me to sit beside her at the table.

Happy tears still silvered the wrinkles of her face, her mouth was still drawn into a close–lipped, nostalgic smile, but her brow was furrowed and her eyes anxious. She reached across and pressed my arm, leaning toward me confidentially. "Maria," she murmured, "this boy, he's a Jew'sh?"

I stiffened. "He's Jewish, yes," I said warily.

"Okay, it's okay," she said hastily, patting me. "A Jew'sh, he's make a good husband. He's good to his wife, he's give her what she want." She drew the last three words out, conjuring visions of fur coats, diamonds, sparkling kitchen appliances: the material trappings of the immigrant's dream. "And he's don't drink, a Jew'sh he's never get drunk. But . . . he's a gamble. You gotta watch out, he's a gamble."

She wagged a finger, while I filed the observation for oblivion. (Yet it surfaced years later, when Ned lost $10 we couldn't afford, playing gin rummy with a neighbor. He later won it back and then some, while I knew my own Italian grandparents loved nothing better than an evening playing briscola or blitz for money with their friends, but the dictum still echoes uneasily in my subconscious: you gotta watch out, he's a gamble.)

Meanwhile, Tonina had gone on to more serious matters, hitching her chair closer to mine. "Maybe," she said, peering at me sidelong, then using a pet name for me, "maybe, Marriucc', he's turn Cat'lic."

"But Tonina, I wouldn't want him to do anything he didn't believe in."

She threw herself back, hands upflung. "No, no, no, no, no! Not if he don't believe!" She tapped the table magisterially. "<u>But</u>, if he believe, is good, becose sometimp a best Cat'lics is convertibles."

Well, I've often told Ned he reminds me of a 1947 ragtop Studebaker, but that's as close to "turning Catholic" as he's likely to get.

Tonina's idea of conversion might not be the most sophisticated theology imaginable, but it reflects an attitude you may run into, especially from older members of your family. Like Baruch the Jewish greengrocer or Tonina the Catholic housewife, they may shrug off the intellectual content to faith and see only the cultural implications.

If you genuinely have leanings towards your partner's religion, by all means look into it, preferably before the wedding. Otherwise, take all the time you need. We know several people who have converted after two or three years of marriage. As one of them said, "Either I'm converting to Judaism or I'm not and either I'm marrying Mike or I'm not. The two are not connected." In the event, she married and then converted. Now, fifteen years later, the union is still flourishing. Conversions are often successful, significantly increase the chances of the marriage succeeding, and are most likely to be accepted as viable by the world at large.

If you are committed to your own religion, or if for other reasons conversion doesn't appeal to you, then expect to be challenged at unexpected moments by unexpected people, with very few snappy retorts at your disposal, as the following story illustrates.

MARY HELÉNE

We were married, with two little ones, living in a small apartment. A brace of nuns appeared at the door.

"Are there Catholics here?" the elder asked tentatively.

"Yes, sisters, I'm a Catholic, won't you come in?" Then I could have bitten my tongue, for the place was a mess and their flowing black pre–Vatican–II habits seemed to fill up every space not actually occupied by toys and newspapers.

They politely pressed me to subscribe to *St. Anthony's Messenger*. I politely stonewalled. We exchanged chitchat: names, family size and so on. All the while, the eyes of the one not speaking to me at the moment darted here and there.

Suddenly they spotted the menorah* on the bookcase, with its decorative Star of David*, and froze. Did the younger nun actually nudge the speaker? I can't be sure—I was feeling pretty paranoid—but I do know that a second later the elder said hesitantly, "'Rosenbaum'. . . . That's—that's not a Catholic name, is it?"

"No, Sister. My husband is a Jew." They looked as taken aback by my use of the naked monosyllable as by the information it conveyed. ("Happens to be of the Jewish faith" is a favorite circumlocution among educated Christians, while among the well meaning but less worldly you can still hear "of the Hebrew persuasion.")

The leader mused, "You said you had . . . children?"

"Two so far. The younger was baptized right here at St. Luke's." Manifestly reassured, they began to take their leave. We turned from the living room, where I had put up the Hanukkah menorah because it was so pretty, toward the tiny vestibule. On the wall there was a crucifix* which Ned had promptly hung in the interests of "equal time." Made of wrought iron by an artist friend, it was very abstract in design. The sisters gazed at it for a moment before deciding that yes, that's what it really was.

The older of the two took my hand and fixed me with a profound look. "Well, dear, who knows" she said in a voice throbbing with significance. "Perhaps . . . someday . . . with your good example. . . ."

"Sister," I returned, "we try to be good examples to each other."

"Oh," she said, nonplussed, and the good ladies left.

Now, that's never going to make the *Guinness Book* for the world's punchiest comeback, but for what it's worth, you can have it. In a mixed marriage, you're going to need all the verbal ammunition you can amass.

And conversion to your partner's religion will not make you immune to well meaning or intrusive inquiries about your background, motives, and intentions. Our advice: Don't do it unless you really want to.

THE MEET–YOU–AT–THE–CORNER APPROACH: THERE'S A PLACE FOR US

There is another conversion option: we call it the Lowest Common Denomination. Both of you could convert to a third religion. Obviously, if you both believe strongly in some faith that's not your original one, you've already thought of this. But we're talking about something else: a compromise in which you both adopt a faith neither one of you has particular feelings, negative or positive, about.

In this gambit, you shop around—by reading, attending services and talking to clergy and laity—for a denomination you both can live with. Some people find a compromise choice satisfactory. We find this a bit puzzling since, for us, religion involves passionate commitment, not just the ability to sit still for an hour on Sunday morning, but it suits some people's emotional and spiritual needs.

Unitarianism is a common choice in this situation. Ned's own great–grandfather, in rebellion against an Orthodox upbringing, joined a Unitarian church shortly after immigrating to America, and attended it all his life—though he was buried in a Jewish cemetery at the end of it.

Unitarians have, not a formal creed, but a general ethical, humanistic approach that may or may not be theistic, depending on the individual member. They do not believe that Jesus was other than human. Their services vary from congregation to congregation, but tend to have a high intellectual content rather than emphasizing liturgy and ritual.

We know a couple, a nominal Jew and a disaffected Catholic, for whom this has been a very satisfying choice. They are comfortable with Unitarian thinking and practice, and don't miss the more structured religions of their childhoods.

But your cradle religion may have left you with a taste for ritual and theological definition. Our middle child, at the age of thirteen, outlined a philosophy that sounded a lot like Unitarianism to us. We gave him a book to read on the subject, and he said "Yes, this is what I think." So we arranged for him to attend services in a nearby town. After a few weeks, he lost interest. "When I go to services or mass with you guys," he explained, "I might not agree with everything—but at least I know what you believe. I can't tell what Unitarians believe."

Now, this is a thirteen–year–old's assessment; John Haynes Holmes and other Unitarian luminaries would have plenty to say about what they believed. The point is that for our son, raised in the more highly spiced atmosphere of our religious traditions, there seemed to be something too bland about Unitarianism. If your most positive memories of your childhood religion involve the drama of the Consecration* or the resounding *shofar**, then you may want to look for a religion with more pageantry.

Another possible difficulty with Unitarianism as a compromise choice is more subtle. A friend of ours from a Jewish background once became Unitarian enough to be ordained as a minister. But he eventually decided it was not for him. Though he was comfortable with Unitarian tenets intellectually, he felt its social atmosphere was alien to his; the discussions were too decorous, the refreshments too "white bread." As he put it, "Unitarianism is for gentiles who don't want to be Christians ... their style is gentile, and their attitudes. Jews who don't want to be Jewish are more comfortable in something like Ethical Culture." (He has since married a Kurdish Jew, moved to Israel and become very enthusiastic about his Jewish identity.)

Ethical Culture, as its name implies, is not so much a religion as an idealistic but secular way of interacting with society. It combines social duty with a nontheistic transcendentalism. As a movement, it was originally most popular in urban areas, with the heaviest Jewish cultural influence occurring in New York City. Today, its focus has shifted, as have many Jews, to middle class suburbs, and you might have a hard time finding an active group near you.

Other Lowest Common Denominations might be considered. We once invited a Seventh Day Adventist couple, a minister and a physician, to Friday night Sabbath dinner. They shook their heads at our religious mix–and–match and suggested their faith as a tension–reducing compromise. They pointed out that Adventists have rules and rituals, and theology which gives them a Christian orientation, but they celebrate the Sabbath when the Jews do, on the seventh day— Saturday. However, they don't dance, drink or eat meat, so it would seem to us conversion to Adventism requires a greater commitment than a simple desire for compromise.

The Church of Christ Scientist has appealed to people of both Christian and Jewish backgrounds. Paul Cowan's *An Orphan in History* retails the fascinating interactions of Christian Science and Judaism in his own family, reporting that 60,000 Jews joined in the movement's first 30 years of existence. The attraction for Jews is that no formal conversion is necessary. Christian Science does involve other commitments, however, the most notable being avoiding conventional medical treatment. We met a Catholic whose marriage to a Christian Scientist was happy and workable—till they started talking about health care for children.

The religious phenomenon that many Christians think of these days when the subject of Christians and Jews comes up is "Messianic Judaism" or "Jews for Jesus" and similarly named groups. These are people of Jewish birth or inclination who believe in Jesus as the messiah and yet wish to retain some sort of Jewish identity. They may do this by including Hebrew in their services, by adopting Jewish practices, or by simple assertion—I'm a Jew because I say I am. The problem with this as a compromise choice is that it creates more tension than it alleviates, especially in terms of responses from the outside world. Christians may be quizzical, most Jews will be hostile.

To understand why, please let us digress into history for a moment—it's the only way to catch the resonances of this controversy.

Certainly, Jesus and the original apostles were Jews who lived according to Jewish law. It was only with the teaching of St. Paul that it even became possible for gentiles to become Christian. But the situation quickly reversed itself, to the point where only a minority sect, called the Ebionites, still lived and practiced as Jews within the Christian Church. At the beginning of the fourth century, they were banned as heretical by the Church, which had become an adjunct of the state. For centuries thereafter, Jewish practice was forbidden to Christians. The Inquisition, contrary to popular belief, was not originally directed against Jews per se, but it did focus on spotting indications that people forcibly converted to Christianity were "relapsing" into Jewish ways; you could be tortured and killed for putting on clean linen on a Saturday.

The atmosphere has lightened considerably in recent years. In 1965 the Second Vatican Council reevaluated Judaism in an encyclical that acknowledged the Jewish roots of Christianity and encouraged Catholics to explore and understand those roots. Protestants and Catholics alike are now encouraged to celebrate some sort of Passover supper on Holy Thursday and otherwise to adopt practices that would have gotten them burned at the stake a few hundred years ago. However, the Bishops' Committee on the Liturgy of the National Conference of Catholic Bishops in 1988 issued guidelines on the presentation of Jews and Judaism in Catholic preaching. In that booklet, they emphasize, "It is wrong, however, to 'baptize' the seder* by ending it with New Testament readings about the Last Supper or, worse, turn it into a prologue to the Eucharist. Such mergings distort both traditions."

That moment when Pope John XXIII descended from his throne to greet an American Jewish group with the words, in Hebrew, "I am Joseph, your brother," was a great one in Catholic history, and no doubt very moving to the Jews present. But we're reminded of a line from Leonard Cohen's song, "The Story of Isaac": "And if you call me Brother now, forgive me if I inquire/ Just according to whose plan?" To many Jews, it seems that Christians not only have their own dominant religion but want to coopt the Jews', as well.

The anger is exacerbated in the case of groups who call themselves

Jewish Christians. To people with a strong sense of the injustices that Jews have suffered historically in the name of Christianity, that's like calling yourself a Nazi humanist. They are also made suspicious by the fact that most of these groups are financed by missionizing Christians. Members of such groups are seen as people with shallow or incomplete Jewish roots, who were without defenses against the "body–snatching" tendencies of evangelizers. Jews, in our experience, are more hostile to such hybrids than they are to people who convert into a traditional Christian denomination.

If a nominal Christian is marrying, say, a Conservative Jew, a less controversial possibility than any of the above is for both of you to move toward the middle and meet in Reform or Reconstructionist Judaism. This will certainly not require formal conversion for the Jew, and might not even for the Christian. In 1982, the Society for Humanistic Judaism (which is non–theistic and so to the left even of Reform) confirmed their conviction that a married Jew and her/his non–Jewish partner are acceptable members of their congregations. In a sense, it's another Jewish counterpart to Unitarianism.

We regard this as a compromise option rather than a conversionary one, since each partner would be leaving "home base" to meet somewhere in center field. However, this is not a complete solution. Orthodox Jews will still flatly reject you, many Conservatives will view you with a jaundiced eye, and the Christians won't be thrilled, either.

Do you get the impression we don't really recommend the Lowest Common Denomination? You're right. We're both too impassioned about religions in general and our own in particular to go for the compromise idea intellectually. We think that the "tension" between our religions can be constructive. We don't see faith as an appropriate area for compromise; you might think yours is true, or you might have doubts in some areas, but you don't say something like, "I'll give up believing in the Assumption of Mary if you'll stop believing God doesn't want you to eat Spam." At least we don't.

But if your convictions on the subject aren't fixed, it's worth looking into the possibility that, as Maria and Tony sang in *West Side Story,* "there's a place for us": a neutral religious "somewhere" in which you both may abide. Just remember that they didn't succeed in finding it.

THE THIRTY*SOMETHING* APPROACH: WHO CARES, AS LONG AS WE LOVE EACH OTHER

An acquaintance who'd just had twins explained why she'd named them Corin, after a character in C. S. Lewis' Christian fantasy of Narnia, and Caleb, after the Old Testament figure: "They're names from two beautiful myths."

If you see Christianity and Judaism in this romantic light, your marital problems may consist of determining how to meld your respective traditions to produce the prettiest picture. Lee Gruzen, in *How To Raise Your Jewish–Christian Child,* takes this tack. At first glance, it may seem the ideal setup for a mixed marriage. If religion is only window dressing, what's the problem? He's not religious, she's not religious, let's just be civilized and take it all with a grain of salt. As long as they love each other. . . .

Well, if "love conquers all," what's causing all those divorces? Surely those couples loved each other at the beginning. The problem may be lurking beneath the surface. Before you embark on that modern, laid–back, aesthetic course, examine your own deeper thoughts and feelings.

You may have had a stained–glass sort of polite, formal religious training that stopped at the age of thirteen or shortly thereafter. Your ideas about religion may be confined to memories of colored oleographs of a sissified Jesus, or simple stories about a fatherly God with a white beard explaining the dangers of trichinosis to Moses. If so, consider: have you learned anything important since then about Iraq? Oat bran? The opposite sex? Why should religion be the one important topic you can get along in with an eighth grader's perspective? Because religion is just a matter of opinion, you say. Well, so is a stance on supply side economics, but smart people at least try to garner a few facts and listen to some expert opinion on the subject before investing in junk bonds. Still and all, most of us aren't subjected to boring classes and incomprehensible presentations on economic theory every week throughout childhood. Many of us were subjected to superficial Sunday School classes whose relevance to our daily lives was never clear; that doesn't mean we'll never come to an adult appreciation for religion.

Or you may be a victim of religious overkill. Maybe your parents sent you to Industrial Strength Bible Camp and kept you so holy in the off–season that all you want from religion now is Out. In that case, you may in fact need a cooling–off period. But keep in mind that you probably got more at that camp than poison ivy. Your early religious training may blossom or it may fester, it may even lie fallow for years, but it won't disappear. If you're reacting against a strong religious background, you're going to have to deal with the conflict sooner or later, and it won't be any easier if your future spouse can't understand what you're carrying on about.

NED
One couple we know were attracted to each other partly because of a shared distaste for religion. He'd had a washed–out Jewish background and gotten nothing from it. Psychology, his profession, had given him all the answers he needed. Religion was okay for children or emotional cripples, but healthy adults shouldn't lean on it. She had been raised Catholic and had gone to parochial schools. She reacted against the repressive atmosphere she had experienced. Her attitude toward religion in general, as she told me, was that she didn't see "why anyone needed it." I was a little surprised, then, that after several years he came to our college's High Holyday* services. After the usual pleasantries, he asked to see me privately. When he came to my office, the reason for his new interest in religion quickly became apparent. His wife had become "born again" and joined a Fundamentalist Christian group. She not only refused to see merit in any religious position but her own, she wouldn't seriously study religion, feeling that factual knowledge attacked the basis of her new–found faith. Instead, she filled their house with other proselytizers, who tried to convert him. He found this intolerable, but he didn't have sufficient religious background to defend himself against it. When we had that talk he'd already moved out. Mary and I couldn't be much help to either of them—the rift had gotten too wide too quickly. They are now divorced.

Sudden discovery of religious roots can happen to Jews, too.
Some years ago at a Jewish scholar's convention, I found myself in company with another man my age. We were wearing those ubiquitous lapel tags, and I noticed that his Hebrew first name and European–Jewish last name were coupled with a college that had been well known for discriminating against Jewish students. I re-marked on this and we both laughed.

The conversation then turned to "Jewish geography": Where are you from and Who do you know sorts of things. Rosenbaum's Postulate is: Any Two Jewish People Know a Third. In the course of casting about for common acquaintances, it came out that we had both gone to Tulane University.

Suddenly, I realized why he seemed familiar. "I know you," I whispered—I didn't want to blow his cover in a room full of other professional Jews. "Your name used to be [a common American one] and your wife is a Protestant."

"My ex–wife," he replied. When they'd met, twenty years before, they were both graduate students, she in music, he in philosophy. He'd been born in Europe, she was from the Midwest, but both were into universal brotherhood, so their differences hadn't kept them from marrying. When I'd met them in the early 60s they already had a child, a little girl, whom they laughingly referred to as their "demi–shiksah." They all slept on a mattress on the floor—my first experience with Beatniks; I was impressed.

Then in 1967 Israel pulled off an astounding victory in the Six Day War, a war that everyone but the Israelis thought they would lose. During that anxious week, the husband's buried religiosity went off like a time bomb. He Hebraicized his name and began to explore his neglected Jewish identity. In short, he returned to Judaism.

This was a trip his wife couldn't take. That marriage also broke up.

Your religion may be an unexploded bomb, buried so deep as to be invisible—now. That doesn't mean it will remain that way the rest of your life. This is especially true for Jews because their ancestors lurk in every corner of European history while contemporary events, e.g., the Gulf War, are always reminding them that there are those who will always seek to destroy them. (Something to keep in mind if you're thinking about conversion, too.)

Even without the traumas of the wider world, events within your own may trigger the detonator. In the words of sociologist Joel Crohn, intermarried couples' "nebulous compromises collapsed at times of stress, e.g. birth of children."

We loved the TV series *thirtysomething*—but its tendency to "solve" religious questions with soft–focus photography, bland dialogue, and even misleading plot resolutions was a serious flaw. Remember Hope and Michael's argument over circumcising their little boy (more on this subject under childrearing)? Hope's objections were never answered, they just sort of disappeared. Worse, the episode ended with a *mohel*, a Jewish ritual circumciser, performing the religious ceremony on the child of a non–Jewish woman with the participation of gentiles and without a commitment that the child would be raised as a Jew. If you know where such a *mohel* can be found, please let us know.

The incident did point up the essential emptiness in Hope and Michael's "love conquers all" approach. Just what did either of them think was being accomplished by this Jewishly invalid gesture? And why was it so important that it be made or not made, as it obviously was to them, if neither of them feels actively attached to their parent religions? The trouble with "love conquers all" is that it leaves out the apex of the Eternal Triangle: love of husband for wife, love of wife for husband . . . and love of both for God. If a relationship with God is important to you, in however nonsectarian a way, don't think you'll never feel uncomfortable "cheating" on it.

And don't feel "safe" even if your background is thoroughly secularist. We've seen a number of cases where people were indifferent or downright hostile to religion and then suddenly become enthusiasts. Remember the woman who spoke of the Bible as a charming myth? She's now a Jehovah's Witness, and has cut off contact with anyone she knew outside that group.

Our Approach: Having It All Means Doing It All

As you're already aware, we actively practice our respective faiths. For us, religion is a vital influence that is at once the source of problems and of resolutions in our relationship. The problems stem from our attempt to come to grips with the Big Questions such as What is true, What is important, and What shall we do about it? We have somewhat different (though not opposed) answers.

As Ned puts it: "The gap between us is deep but it is not wide— we can hold hands across it." But we know that doesn't make it go away. Instead we try to strengthen each other in our respective identities, while constantly challenging each other's intellectual and theological commitments. The result is that we are stronger in our respective religions than we were when we began.

MARY HELÉNE

My father was a Lutheran who agreed, in tune with the tenor of the times when he and my mother married, that the children should be "raised Catholic." In addition, I grew up in my mother's hometown rather than my father's, a town that not only contained my Catholic grandparents but also had a population majority of Italian–American Catholics.

On the other hand, my sister and I were not sent to parochial school—in the tradition of my grandparents, who were fierce champions of the American public education system. And Mom was not the sort of Catholic to accede passively to anything someone in a habit or a cassock said. I grew up with the conviction that to be a Catholic meant to take responsibility for one's own religion; that I was as much "The Church" as any nun or priest.

So by the time I met Ned I had done some exploring. I had read the Bible (a practice frowned upon for Catholic laypeople at that time) in English and was learning a little Hebrew. I had attended

Jewish and Protestant services (another pre–Vatican–II no–no) and chewed over religious questions endlessly with friends of various faiths.

But marrying a Jew challenged my faith in a sense I had not foreseen. Whatever I did, I felt to a certain extent I was doing as a Catholic before a non–Catholic onlooker. This not only inspired me to be a better Catholic, it made me think about Catholic issues in a new way.

And Ned actively aided me in this development. When, like a lot of other Catholics, I was confused and disaffected by the upheavals of the Vatican II reforms, he kept after me to define what it was that was bothering me. He helped me discover that the kernel of my religion was at the core of my being, and to put the more transient aspects of the institutional church into perspective. When I encounter bigotry in the hierarchy, he reminds me that I have to resist individual evils in the church, not abandon the whole business in disgust. When I feel tired or out of sorts and disinclined to fulfill religious duties, he tactfully encourages me to seek spiritual satisfaction by getting my act together. Without Ned, I might have drifted—or stormed—out of the church long ago.

NED

Without Mary, I doubt that I'd ever have found my way back.

My Bavarian ancestors began coming to America in 1825, after their government passed a law prohibiting Jewish families from settling more than one married child in the parents' home town. Five generations later, our assimilation into American culture was so complete that I grew up with virtually no identifiably Jewish influences at home. My mother was taught as a child in Reform Sunday School that it was her duty as a Jew to minimize the differences between Jew and gentile, to assimilate.

So when I met Mary Heléne I had been in a synagogue only a handful of times in my life, far fewer than the number of times I'd been to church. I was so unfamiliar with Hebrew I thought she must be wrong when she described the system of vowel transcription. I flatly didn't believe her when she told me there were religious Jews who believe in an afterlife.

Suddenly here was someone who knew much more than I did about Judaism and challenged other callow, preconceived notions, e.g., that religion was outdated or at best a crutch for the emotionally crippled and that Catholics, especially, were unable to think for themselves. At the same time, I audited a course in "Old Testament" at the Divinity School of the University of Chicago, where I was a graduate student in American History. That sparked a scholarly interest in the study of religion. My life, personal and professional, took a new direction.

Fifteen years later I had earned a doctorate in Judaic Studies; I now teach the Hebrew I never learned as a child and other Jewish subjects in college; I keep more–or–less kosher, observe the Sabbath, and frequently lead religious services in our little community. In all these developments, I have been aided, abetted, and encouraged by my Catholic wife. In fact, I now find myself involved in a peculiar anomaly: she has helped me become so Jewishly committed that, if we were to meet now, I wouldn't be able to marry her in her church, maybe not at all—the internal contradictions would be too great!

Some people consider this attitude hypocritical. "You did what you wanted, now you tell other people they shouldn't," is an accusation I sometimes hear, most recently when Mary and I were on the Sally Jessy Raphael show. What Sally confused was the difference between hypocrisy and paradox. My wife caused me to recover my heritage, God bless her: I've been very lucky. You can't count on meeting a Christian who will care more about your Judaism than you do.

In fact, we've both been very lucky—and have worked very hard at being supportive of each other's religious convictions. If your spouse won't be willing or able to make the effort, you'd better find that out now, and start talking about which of the other approaches you can take together.

Practicing both religions in an intermarriage is not a popular option. An article called "Intra–Marriage, Mitzvah*–Marriage, Mixed Marriage, Inter–Marriage and the Family: Toward Reworking Definitions" by Reeve Robert Brenner in the Winter 1990 edition of *Response* attempts to develop terminology for the variants of interfaith unions . . . and doesn't even mention the dual–faith possibility. And for good reason. It's a lot of work and takes a greater concentration on religious issues than most people are willing to give them. But, as with many difficult achievements, the rewards are very great.

Our first conversation was about religion and we've been discussing it ever since. Our marriage is not a monolith, a great stone held in place by gravity; it is an arch, where balance is achieved through dynamic tension from both sides. This is not an easy posture, but it is effective—for us. We'd like to think that, if you can't be persuaded to make a nice stone wall by marrying within your faith, we've created something you can walk through.

Chapter 2
Culture: A Different World

The part of your partner's personality you can see is like the proverbial iceberg tip: it's founded in weighty layers of unseen accretions under the surface. Marriage is the wedding not only of two individuals but of their families, who they are and where they come from. This is true even when the families don't speak to each other or to the newlyweds—their silent presence can resound louder than any number of arguments.

Before you can develop your own new family style and culture you need to understand the shape and composition of all that ancestral underwater ice—your own and your partner's.

A fascinating scholarly look at this end of the subject is provided by Joel Crohn's "Ethnic Identity and Marital Conflict: Jews, Italians, and WASPs." Crohn examines general differences in behavioral norms and roles: Jewish families tend to be relatively chaotic and tumultuous: children often challenge parental authority, men and women exchange roles or fight over issues of control, and the rules of behavior are often ambiguous. Italian families, he found, also foster an environment where frequent emotional catharsis is the norm. Conflict among same–generation family members, however, is less open than in the Jewish families studied.

Also, in Italian families, gender roles are more sharply defined, so battles for control are more covert. Conflict between the generations is also less tolerated—parents were authoritarian, fathers "were respected as the heads of household, even where mothers ran the show." In WASP families, you will not be surprised to find, emotional expression was simply avoided.

Also not surprisingly—and this is a biggie—he found differences in conflict resolution. For instance, there was a difference in the uses of silence and separation. WASPs use the former to express disapproval, and need the latter as a normal recurrent state. Both Jews and Italians see the silence as tacit approval, and are threatened by separation. These patterns carry over into expected relations with kids, naturally.

Interestingly, we recently mentioned this last point to our son–in–law, whose background—though Catholic—is French/English rather than Mediterranean or Irish. The subject sparked an impassioned argument over which perception (silence means Yes or silence means No) is "right." The discussion took us as far afield as comparisons of

English common law with the Napoleonic Code. Finally, we just agreed always to try to say explicitly whether we agree or disagree with a proposed plan of action, without regard to whether the other party "should" have understood our meaning. And we agreed, as Jesus put it, to "let our yes be Yes, and our no be No"—no fair waffling later about what we really meant.

Many in Crohn's study identified their religious differences, but underestimated ethno–cultural ones. They knew they didn't believe the same things about God, but they didn't realize how their hopes about, for instance, their children's future might be conditioned by their differing backgrounds.

For example, Jewish achievement/togetherness agendas create conflicts in marriages to either Italians or Irish. Italians and Irish—usually Catholic, of course—value family bonds over achievement. Jews, even with close family ties, expect them to be sacrificed in favor of advancement by the children—as long as ethnic identity is not sacrificed. Early Jewish immigrants had no desire for their children to pursue the same difficult or dangerous jobs that they themselves had been forced to take in order to survive. There was, in other words, no pride in following Dada down the mine as in *How Green Was My Valley*. The WASP emphasis is also on advancement and ethnic identity (in this case, with the superior social status it involves) over family, but without the Jewish expectation of intergenerational bonds.

You might feel Jews and Italians will naturally have resemblances, and of course they do. But, Crohn cautions, "the agrarian tradition of the southern Italian is quite different from the intellectual and mercantile experience of the European Jew. Among white ethnic groups in America, Italians have made the slowest progress in socioeconomic terms, Jews the most rapid." Among his intermarried subjects, although ". . . some had worked out satisfactory solutions to these issues, none felt that the years they had spent together had erased them."

Crohn's study also found that Jewish in–laws tend to reconnect with intermarried children even if they initially disapproved of the wedding, while non–Jews often remain distant, even if they didn't openly oppose the match. This may be partly due to the closer kinship bonds among in–laws in traditional Judaism. Hebrew has titles for in–laws—*machuten* and *machutenayste*—that are etymologically and psychologically separate from the terms for mother and father; your spouse's parents are in a new, unique relation to you.

If your intermarriage crosses these religio–cultural lines in a way that seems geared for conflict, you will have to be even more careful in sorting out your actual religious differences from your cultural

29

ones, rather than blaming every disagreement on religion. You'll also have to agree on a common style, one that at least doesn't engender constant disputes between you on childraising, whether you've chosen a single religion for them or not.

WHITHER THOU GOEST, I WILL GO: BUT I DO THINGS MY WAY

Everyone who follows football admired the great coach Vince Lombardi, and grieved when he died . . . of what? It was weeks before the word leaked out. The word was (whisper it) CANCER. Italians have two verboten subjects, cancer and money. Jews talk about both freely, maybe too freely. (The question of what Italian Jews do we'll leave for another book. We're going to be making some sweeping ethnic generalizations in this section, something we are ordinarily particular about avoiding; please don't be offended. The subject is cultural identity, and can't be approached effectively without temporarily setting aside a necessary and proper reluctance to make broad characterizations. We'll try to avoid caricature.)

Unless you work for the Mob or the CIA, you'll probably discuss your job and salary with your spouse. Questions of who works at what, how much money there will/could/should be, and who controls it and in which circumstances, are issues to be resolved in any marriage. This won't be easy if you come from two divergent traditions that handle the issue in markedly different ways.

In Jewish–Christian unions, there are often cultural elements intertwined with religious attitudes that tangle the financial-attitude undergrowth and complicate the problem even further.

Both sets of our parents were comfortably middle class. They lived in the same town and had similar social lives. Still, their attitudes about money—which had naturally influenced our own—were worlds apart.

NED
My family has been up and down financially. Their attitudes still tend to be typical of those associated with "old" money. They expect, for instance, that the older generation will be the conservator of the family fortune, such as it is, and will naturally administer it to the benefit of the as–yet–unestablished younger members.

Add to this the traditional Jewish family intimacy, especially the assumption that parents will still be actively involved in almost every facet of the lives of grown children, and you have a setup in which, for instance, it seemed perfectly natural to me to turn to my mother (who at that point was quite financially secure) to augment our income when we were juggling jobs, school, and two small children.

MARY HELÉNE

I was appalled. In my one–generation–from–immigration family, the pattern was the opposite; each succeeding generation was expected to be more successful than the last, and if any assistance were required, it would naturally flow the other way— from child to parent. That wasn't necessary (or possible) in the case of me and my parents, but I still would have considered it an admission of failure to take any sort of financial assistance from them. When Ned casually informed his mother that things were a little tight and he could use a temporary monetary boost, I was bewildered and frightened. It seemed irresponsible; it also seemed to be a declaration that we were not really adults. He in turn was taken aback and, finally, offended by my reaction.

This basic divergence has persisted throughout our marriage. It is also reflected in our parents' attitudes towards each other: mine tended to think of his as manipulative and interfering; his have thought of mine as stingy and uncaring.

We've had to develop a strategic noninvolvement with each other's parents on this subject.

I learned to keep out of money conversations with his mother, and allow him to interact with her in the informal, intimate way that made them both comfortable. Ned, for his part, refrains from pressing me to approach my parents as he does his; he realizes we are more comfortable talking about money in a formal, business-like context . . . if at all.

This sort of communications glitch can occur in marriages with other mixes, of course. But in our experience, it's particularly common in Jewish/Christian matches (though it's more often the Jewish family that's been financially secure for the shorter period). The trick is to recognize the problem for what it is—an expression of different cultural patterns, not of right–or–wrong values.

How to handle charitable contributions is another such issue that's bound to arise. Religious giving in the two groups is generally organized differently: Jewish institutions are independent of any universal sectarian body, and they claim, as institutions, no moral necessity for the Jew to contribute to them (though charity in general is very much a Jewish imperative). The Christian structure is the reverse, with financial support of the religious institution being closely identified with the moral responsibility of its members.

There is a potential for conflict here. The Jewish partner may be content to discharge charitable obligations by contributing to nonsectarian umbrella organizations such as United Way, and feel alienated by the Christian's need to give to the church. But the Christian may be put off (as are many Jews) by the Jewish practice of charging often–onerous synagogue dues and restricting attendance at High Holyday services to members or ticketholders.

One woman says that the last straw in her disintegrating intermarriage was when her husband came home and announced he had spent several hundred dollars she felt they couldn't afford on a temple membership. He felt this was necessary if they were to be effective in raising their children as Jews, which she had agreed to.

Or you may have a conflict over whether to give financial support to Israel, or to Christian missionizing groups.

If you each have an income accounted separately from the other's, you can agree to contribute to your own charities separately. If the family money is single–source or shared, you'll need to work out compromises on charitable giving: not in the context of a fight over who's spending too much, please.

Be aware that there may even be cultural differences between you regarding where to spend your daily budget: small–town loyalty to local business conflicting with big–city I–can–get–it–for–you–whole-sale.

You will also need to work out your approach to including children, if you have them, in the financial picture.

MARY HELÉNE

I never had any idea how much my parents made. When I applied for financial aid to college, I was not allowed to read the form I was signing. And they in their turn get embarrassed and change the subject if I get too specific about Ned's and my finances.

One result of this reticence was that I was married before I bought an article of clothing on my own. Though I'd had jobs all through high school, the money went into my college fund. I had no experience with budgeting or with long–range financial planning.

My only idea as to why this should be a particularly gentile pattern (as our experience talking to other couples seems to indicate) is the speculation that it relates to Christian uneasiness with the proximity of "filthy lucre." Avarice is one of the Seven Deadly Sins; to avoid even the appearance of it, pretend money doesn't exist.

NED
My divorced mother shared all too much of our financial situa-
tion—I was under the impression we were on the verge of starvation
much of the time. Eventually I came to realize that our financial
situation was not so dire as constant harping on it had made me
believe. Perhaps the "Jewish connection" here is that, even in so
attenuated a tradition as my family's, there was some vestigial feeling
of warding off the "evil eye" (in the form not only of ill luck but of
unwanted attention from envious gentiles) by crying poverty.

Driving Miss Daisy, featuring a socially assimilated Southern
Jewish lady, struck many chords for me—it might almost have been
about my grandmother, whose husband was bred in Macon, Georgia..
But I had a particularly immediate sense of familiarity when the
obviously well–off Jessica Tandy character rounded on Morgan
Freeman (the chauffeur), indignant because he'd called her "rich."

Money comes right after sex as a fertile field for marital disagreements. And, in a Jewish/Christian match, it's not just a case of the
woman's family expecting the man to take care of her. An interfaith
lesbian couple we talked to had exactly the same culture clash: the
gentile partner is "completely not used to" her Jewish partner's
mother's propensity for spending money on their household—she's
getting used to it, but it still makes her uneasy. (Interestingly, the
Jewish family—though not happy about their daughter's lifestyle—
are more shocked by the fact that the Catholic family has severed
relations with their own daughter.)

In our case, we had to realize that though our parents were on about
the same rung of the financial/social ladder, Mary Heléne's had
achieved the level recently; Ned's had seen better days. They had
different hopes and fears, for themselves and for us.

It also helps to keep a sense of humor, as we found when we first
experienced an effect of this "class" distinction between relatively old
and relatively new prosperity.

The first year we were married, we went to the local country club
as the guests of Ned's grandmother, Hazel. As we entered the dining
room, Ned kept turning toward the tables, greeting friends and
acquaintances among the guests, largely Jewish businesspeople;
Mary was turned in the other direction, greeting friends and acquaintances among the staff, many of whom were Italian neighbors. We
thought it was hilarious, but we're not sure Hazel was amused. In your
intermarriage, you may find it's the Jewish side that's less prosperous,
or less secure in its prosperity; and you may find differences in what
each side considers amusing, as we'll detail later in this chapter.

In addition to money, food is a powerful symbol that permeates life and relationships, and can clearly illuminate the cultural and religious differences of a couple.

MARY HELÉNE

I was nervous and excited when Ned's grandmother Hazel invited me to a dinner at her home celebrating Ned's mother's birthday. It meant they were recognizing our relationship as a reality, and including me as part of the family.

The night was warm, at the end of June. We ate on Hazel's spacious screened porch: a whole cold poached salmon with Russian dressing, salad, hot rolls—delicious, elegantly presented on green glass plates. When they were cleared, I expected the rest of dinner to appear. I was taken aback when the next (and last) thing to be served was the cake and ice cream.

This was a celebration dinner? I said something about it to Ned, afterwards. He was puzzled in his turn. "You could have had seconds if you were still hungry," he said.

"You don't understand," I said, and for the first time glimpsed differences between us that were not simply intellectual abstractions.

NED

Two weeks later, Mary's grandmother invited me to a family dinner. It took place on her porch, similarly screened and spacious. Nonni served up what I learned to call vitello tonnato—cold veal in a tuna and caper sauce—with salad and hot rolls. I felt right at home. When we finished, I rose to help clear. "Oh, don't bother," said Mary's mother. "Wait till we're finished." Finished? Here came the soup—egg drops in chicken broth. Then the lasagna. Then the turkey and vegetables. Then a chocolate whipped cream charlotte. Then a big tray of assorted tortes and cookies. Finally we got to the fruit and nuts, four hours after we'd sat down.

"That," said my bride-to-be, "is our idea of an important meal." You may be sure I've come to see the light on this one. Meanwhile, I'm forty pounds heavier. . . .

This sort of mutual discovery can be fun. But in an interfaith marriage, eating differences can take on value differences that stick in the throat. We have to keep in mind that our respective patterns of celebration derive from the relative lengths of time our families have been able to take having enough to eat for granted.

Perhaps a more usual situation in America would be the reverse of ours. The Jewish side of the family would be the one for which the specter of famine is so close it needs pushing off farther by gigantic meals, and the gentile side more interested in effectively presenting a special meal than in piling up everyone's plates half a dozen times.

This is the sort of thing that can leave a couple feeling dissatisfied and frustrated without being sure why. And words won't cure it—you can't eat words. Talk it out, certainly, as always, and understand what's going on. But when it comes down to the guts of the matter, someone who thinks the reason for reclining at the Passover table is so you can fit more food in is not going to be happy with a seder consisting of a cup of consommé and half a cornish hen. While the person who's used to debating whether we really need mashed potatoes as well as sweet potatoes and rolls and stuffing and corn for Christmas dinner (and deciding in the affirmative) is going to feel lonely when that strip of boned turkey breast surrounded with carrot straws and green peppercorn sauce appears.

Compromise, accommodate: and maybe the person who is so interested in the bigger meal should cook it. Also, if there's going to be a big combined family meal, remind the host family not to say grace in a language the other half won't understand (such as Hebrew) unless they add a running translation, or not to use phrases (such as "Jesus Christ Our Lord") that will make half the table choke on their "amen."

Recreational activities, as well, can be culturally linked. Bowling versus golf have obvious class/status differences, largely because of the latter's requirement of long stretches of daylight leisure time.

But what about hunting? That cuts across socioeconomic lines but often not across ethnic ones. We are, again, an exception—Ned's father was a hunter. He himself isn't interested in the pursuit, and neither is the majority of America's urban–oriented Jews. (There may also be a residual repugnance toward eating game even for nonobservant Jews. Venison, for instance, is kosher in itself . . . but it's pretty hard to kill a deer with one knife stroke simultaneously severing windpipe and jugular, as required in Jewish ritual slaughter, unless you're very fast on your feet.)

If your partner is from a fairly Americanized family, some other recreational stereotypes may not hold, either.

MARY HELÉNE
I thought, when I married a Jewish scholar, that I was leaving behind forever the raucous sound of baseball announcers on Sunday afternoons. One of the early disillusionments of my marriage was that I was wedded to, not only a baseball fan, but a Cubs devotee!

It's hard to live with a man who spends most of every summer in a deep depression. Even in Israel, he had a picture of Wrigley Field taped over his desk . . . only to rip it down at the end of the season; it was 1969, and the home team blew it in the last six weeks. I could only shake my head.

NED
I don't understand this woman. Her grandparents were championship bowlers; an uncle played AAA ball before the Second World War and a cousin had a basketball scholarship. She can't differentiate between Bo Jackson and Mahalia Jackson. No doubt about it, sports fans, ours is a mixed marriage.

Recently, Jews haven't been as conspicuous in one minority escape route from poverty—sports—as they were when the likes of Benny Leonard and Dolph Schayes were big names in boxing and basketball. But they continue to rise through the entertainment industry, the other great social leveler of our society. The relative absence of major Jewish sports figures may be explained by the traditional Jewish emphasis on learning (one form of riches the gentiles can't confiscate) and suspicion of sports as focusing inappropriately on the body at the expense of the mind. Yes, Ken Holtzmann (Cubs) beat Sandy Koufax (Dodgers) in his last game because both had refused to pitch on Yom Kippur—an event with some of the same emotional resonance for American Jews as the signing of Jackie Robinson has for African Americans—but they were two of a tiny percentage of Jewish athletes. Besides, Koufax married a gentile.

We've talked about gambling—a recreation both sides of our family indulge in, but one side of your interfaith one may disapprove of. Old Tonina's folk observation evidently had some truth to it: in 1982, with Jews two percent of the US population, they comprised twenty–five percent of the membership of Gamblers Anonymous.

The converse is true of drinking, though alcoholism is no longer a problem strictly for gentiles. And casual drug use has skyrocketed as high among Jews, evidently, as it has in the larger society. But your feelings about any or all of these practices may have religious aspects you're not aware of, that can make discussions about how to spend an evening heat up and boil over.

NED
I have been asked whether there wasn't some secret, sneaking element of social climbing in my choosing a gentile wife. My sarcastic rejoinder is, "Yes, now I can get into an Italian Catholic country

club." Mary has other ethnic strains in her background, but choosing that one seems to make the point best: marrying her did not improve my social standing. If anything, the reverse was true—at least in my family's mind.

I loved and respected Mary's Italian grandparents (I never knew the German ones), who came here with nothing and won security and freedom for themselves and their descendants. That's what America is all about, I think. But I knew their relative lack of formal education and "nouveau" status would influence my relatives' attitudes.

My grandfather was a founder and charter member of the exclusive (Jewish) Standard Club in Chicago. My grandmother objected to one girlfriend of mine because she was of Eastern European Jewish extraction, rather than the more prestigious German Jewish. After I met Mary, Hazel wished she'd kept her objections to herself—"At least the last one was Jewish," she lamented.

My grandmother herself attended Smith College; she was a cultured, educated woman with little emotional or intellectual involvement in Judaism. But this didn't keep her from saying to me, quite seriously, when she learned of our engagement, "Some day she'll throw it up to you. No matter how happy you think you are, you'll be arguing and she'll insult you because you're a Jew."

Actually, Mary and I agree that anyone reduced to ethnic slurs has automatically lost the argument, whatever the subject. We have never been tempted to use that feeble weapon, but the point is that Hazel was convinced no gentile would resist it.

When our two grandmothers met, one said, "I'm not too happy about this, you know." "Neither am I," responded the other. The air cleared, they shook hands and were great friends from then on. If your in–law problems can be resolved as cordially, you'll be lucky.

Have you found any of this book so far amusing? What do you think is funny, and how do you express it? One of the most frequently expressed desires of people looking for mates is "someone with a sense of humor." And one of the qualities most obviously influenced by cultural/ethnic background is what evokes laughter.

Since Jewish humor is often self–deprecating, it doesn't mind deprecating others. Remember this from Fiddler on the Roof?

"'Rabbi, is there a proper blessing for the czar?'

"'A blessing for the czar? Of course. May God bless and keep the czar . . . far away from us.'"

Puns are a favorite form of Jewish humor, going back to the Bible itself. In rabbinic times, one rabbi termed Christian preachments (evangelion in Greek) evan gilyon, Hebrew for a "stumbling block." The Christians weren't amused.

NED

When I came to Dickinson College to teach, my departmental colleagues were all gentiles of northern European ancestry. They got off on things I seldom found funny. Their jokes had punchlines I could see trundling up for blocks. Maybe that's preferred in some cultures, but I like jokes with unexpected endings or zany nonsequiturs. I've never enquired of my colleagues what they think of my intrusive puns, one-liners, and wisecracks.

More to the point, consider how you will use humor in family relationships. In mine, humor was sardonic, snideness almost a virtue. We used it as a safety valve in crisis situations—the more egregious the situation, the wrier the twist.

For instance: my mother, a woman who conscientiously kept her figure until well into her sixties, had a particularly hard time getting over the cosmetic aspects of her mastectomy. Once she sobbed to me on the phone, "Who has any use for a woman with one breast?" Without thinking I replied, "A man with one hand?" It cracked her up. In part, I think, because we share the same Jewish perspective on life: things could always be worse than they are.

Many adult friends who've known us for years misunderstand my idea of humor. When Mary's sister lived with us, she cried herself to sleep—we learned much later—thinking I meant the things I offhand-edly joked as serious criticism. A friend once asked Mary, "How long did it take you before you understood he was joking when he said those things?"

MARY HELÉNE

I always seem to have understood what Ned meant. But it did take me a while to catch on to all the nuances of Rosenbaum family humor. During our engagement I made the misstep of joking to his grandmother, "Hazel, with my looks and your money, we'd make a great team." ERROR. They talk about money; they don't make jokes about having it. The frozen silence told me I'd goofed, but I didn't know how to retrieve the situation.

Then Hazel twisted her ankle and I paid a call, hoping to redeem my precarious standing. She used the occasion to read me the Riot Act, finishing with, "My grandsons know they can joke with me, but they are never disrespectful: I will not brook impertinence."

As I sat there quavering before her regal presence, her ankle swathed on a chaise longue, Ned came in. "Hi, Hazel, ya big lummox," he said cheerfully. He couldn't figure out what she, and after a stunned moment I, was laughing about.

If you want a handle on Jewish humor, we suggest you get hold of Leo Rosten's *The Joys of Yiddish,* or our friend Moshe Waldoks' *Big Book of Jewish Humor.* If you don't understand when your partner is joking, you're in deep doo–doo.

NED

That reminds me. Do you know why the Israelis were reluctant to follow the former president's advice on the Middle East? It's because the last time Israelites listened to a bush they spent the next forty years in the wilderness.

Even ordinary conversational patterns can differ across cultures. Our daughter used to date a young man whose WASP, military parents were very courteous and correct in their habits of speech. They took the kids out to dinner one night, and Sarah struggled to keep the conversation going against what she felt as a wall of silence. Later she asked, "Were your parents upset about something? They never said anything all night." Her date answered, "Well . . . they were waiting for you to stop talking."

In our family, anyone who waits until the speaker comes to a full stop literally never gets a word in edgewise. Fortunately, we don't have a cultural mismatch here. For various geographical, historical, and societal reasons, our styles of enjoying ourselves are similar. We had identical reactions (disbelief followed by terminal boredom) when we spent an evening early in our marriage at a party that consisted of the two of us plus some fifteen WASPs sitting primly around a living room and each speaking in turn!

We think of our boisterousness as vaguely Mediterranean. You may think of it as obnoxious. The point is, you need to be able to appreciate what the other one finds amusing, making whatever adjustments and compromises are necessary along the way.

For starters, we'd suggest that you mothball your supply of ethnic jokes, even those directed at third parties. (What if you hear a really, really rich one? We've been known to tell such with the phrase "a member of the ethnic group of your choice. . . ." Yes, it takes some of the punch out, but it makes the point—especially to the kids.)

All the above areas—family structure, generational interaction, household atmosphere, money, class, food, recreation, and humor— are fields for any new couple to explore. But the Jewish/Christian couple should take extra time and make an extra effort to understand each other's backgrounds.

If your partner's family is so hostile they won't let you learn about them by relaxed socializing, encourage your partner to share impressions and memories with you: How were allowances handled? How were holidays celebrated? How was anger expressed? What about other emotions? Was sex a taboo subject?

If you're not sure what your unexamined expectations are, try flushing them out. Maybe you could each sit down and free–associate for a while: what do you think of when you hear the words "Jewish," "Christian," "Catholic," "gentile," "Italian," whatever? Write down your responses and then compare and discuss them.

For instance, if you're a Jew who associates primarily with gentiles, notice whether your responses to "Jewish" word cues are all negative, then consider whether you're expressing self–hatred in your choice of mate. If you suspect that to be the case, you don't have to break off the engagement on the spot, but it would be wise to get some counseling and work on your self image before proceeding further with wedding plans.

Perhaps, on the contrary, your social circle has been almost exclusively Jewish and your associations with "Christian" word cues are the negative ones; you think of your partner as the exception. In this case as in its converse—the Christian who thinks of the Jewish partner as "not like the rest of them"—the cure may be as simple as broadening your circle. Spending time with people different from yourself may help you internalize the fact that religious and cultural differences, while real, are broad and vague, not very helpful in interacting with any actual human individual. To look at the other side of the coin: if you're a gentile, are your associations with Jewishness unrealistically positive, as compared to negative assumptions or experiences concerning your own group? A friend of ours entered a relationship with a Jewish man assuming that his ethnic identity included liberal political and social beliefs, unlike the elitist and exclusionary ones of her WASP upbringing. When she discovered that he was prejudiced against Blacks and Puerto Ricans, thought bright colors were for "primitive" people, and displayed other narrow–minded, repressive attitudes, she wasn't only dismayed at his differences from her; she was disillusioned about what she had thought she knew about Jews.

A relative of Mary Heléne's, a warm, generous–spirited, well–educated person, expressed dismay on returning from Israel because, contrary to expectation, it wasn't "a whole country full of Neds." Aside from our conviction that Ned is one–of–a–kind, we were astonished that anyone otherwise so sophisticated should imagine that a common religion would result in similar personalities.

You may find it hard to grapple with all this as a couple without getting defensive about your respective backgrounds. Reading

Joel Crohn's monograph made us aware of a resource we hadn't encountered: ethnotherapy groups. They may help you sort out the tangles described above, or at least identify for you which of your differences are religious, which cultural, and which simply the wrinkles any two people have to learn to iron out between them. Ask around–it sounds to us like a worthwhile expenditure of time and money.

If you can't find an ethnotherapy group near you, you might try to understand your partner's roots by analyzing their expressions in popular culture. Read *Marjorie Morningstar* (Jewish) or *A Tree Grows in Brooklyn* (Irish Catholic) to start getting a fix on why your in–laws may do the things they do in the way they do them. Or watch a modern movie about a family (*Ordinary People*, for instance, is about a dysfunctional WASP one, which throws the underlying patterns into sharp relief) and discuss the ways in which your own and your partner's approaches are similar and different.

"THINK AGAIN" CHECKLIST

You should seriously think again about marrying out of your faith if:

1. You secretly hope maybe someday s/he'll convert.

2. You feel an affectionate (or not) contempt for anyone who could really believe that guff (otherwise known as your partner's religion).

3. You tell yourself, "S/he's not as bad as most of them."

4. You figure that how you raise your kids will work itself out, and besides, maybe you won't have any.

5. You think what your parents think doesn't matter.

6. You think what society thinks doesn't matter.

7. You think religion doesn't matter to you—and never will.

8. Talk about religion makes you nervous, bored, embarrassed, or angry.

42

Chapter 3
The Wedding: Your Dream World

YOUR "PLACE" OR MINE? THE RELIGIOUS ASPECT

So, enough theoretical stuff. You have an immediate problem: who's going to perform the ceremony, and where, and how? This may very well be your first religious stumbling block. You don't want to stomp on anyone's sensibilities, or hurt their feelings.

It will be easiest to pull this off if at least one of your families is not deeply involved in their own denomination. But even then, you'll still have cultural differences to contend with—and they can be more ingrained than mere questions of truth, eternity, and the nature of the divine.

Paul Cowan, in *Orphan in History,* remembered his own wedding: she was not Jewish, he was not observant, but he broke a glass as part of the ceremony because it was "the only thing Jewish" he could bring to mind that was appropriate for weddings.

Our own wedding in 1963 didn't even have a symbolic Jewish gesture. We were married in a Catholic Church because, at the time, neither denomination would consider a joint ceremony (with a couple of rare exceptions among American rabbis) and the repercussions of an out-of-the-faith wedding were much more concrete for a Catholic than the psychological discomforts for a non-observant Jew, as Ned then was.

In our parents' generation, the atmosphere was such that in 1932 a priest refused to include the bestowal of a ring in his marriage of a Catholic to a Protestant, on the grounds that such a wedding was not a sacrament. Even more recently, Catholic-Protestant marriages were conducted outside the altar rail or even in the priest's study, for the same reason.

The Catholic Church is far less sticky on mixed marriage these days. Still, an Apostolic Letter of 1970 reiterated the conviction that the wedding of a baptized person to an unbaptized one is not a sacrament, and therefore shouldn't be conducted in association with a nuptial mass, a situation that still obtains. On the other hand, Father Henry Fehren, in the September 1988 *U.S. Catholic,* underscored the ancient doctrine that the sacrament of marriage is actually adminis-tered by the couple involved—the priest's presence is merely sym-bolic of the church's facilitation of their vows (which constitute the important part). He also said, "[F]orcing Catholics to do all in their power to baptize and raise the children Catholic is not very ecumenical." Don't get too excited, though. The *Ladies Home Journal* two months later has an article by Eileen Ogintz, a Jew married to a Catholic. His priest, she says, "practically threw us out of his office, telling us that our marriage was doomed to fail" when they declined to promise to raise the children as Catholics.

And you may also have a problem getting married in the Catholic Church if you've been living together. In 1987, Bishop Fiorenza of the Galveston-Houston Diocese issued a pastoral letter to the effect that couples who insist on cohabiting during the marriage preparation period have chosen to appear already married, and therefore should only have a small, simple wedding more on civil lines rather than a full-bore church "do."

If you do marry in the Catholic Church, you will have to attend a series of premarital counseling sessions called "pre-Cana" after the site of the wedding where Jesus performed his first public miracle. If this makes the non-Catholic partner uncomfortable, it may help to think of it as an opportunity to ask questions and work out solutions rather than as an alien intrusion into your private relationship.

Always, though, the goodwill of the people involved is the key to a ceremony in which neither side is offended or alienated. Some clergy may close their eyes to official rules of the denomination in order to avoid estranging the couple completely. If you're lucky, your rabbi, minister, or priest may be one of these. (Just don't assume every one you encounter will be.) In our case, the priest conducted a wedding service that was virtually nondenominational—there was no mention of Jesus, no sly references to "Holy Mother Church," no sign-of-the-cross blessing.

MARY HELÉNE

I'd heard horror stories all my life about mixed marriage ceremonies in which the priest went out of his way to make the non-Catholics feel uncomfortable. And, though my Lutheran father was always heroically polite about intolerant priests (my mother, a fire-eater, was less so), I knew that he had often been made to feel benighted at best, damned at worst.

But I was reassured by the fact that our priest, the Reverend James Shea (may his memory be for a blessing), whom I'd known since childhood, was an exceptionally sensitive person who combined firm Catholic piety with broad practical tolerance. For years, Ned and I gave Father Shea full credit for our non-divisive ceremony.

Then, after his death, we were reminiscing about him and lauding him for having been so far ahead of his time over the wedding. "Well, yes," Mom said, "but I think my phone call had

a little to do with it, too.''

Phone call? It turns out that, unbeknownst to us, she had called him some time before the wedding and pointed out that half the people in the church that day were going to be non-Christians. If the marriage were to succeed, it would be advisable not to alienate the in-laws at the outset. It is to his credit that he agreed— and to Mom's that she insisted.

So the combination of an assertive parent and a sympathetic priest, plus a then-lukewarm religious identity on the Jewish side, gave us a wedding that left no bitter aftertaste. If you have a similar setup, you're lucky. Chances are, though, that your problems will take more solving than a little goodwill can provide.

For the Christian, the situation is likely to be easier than it once was.

Ned's Jewish mother was married to his Catholic stepfather by a priest and a rabbi co-officiating in her own home—something that would have been unheard of before Vatican II. Jacqueline Grennan Wexler, then president of Hunter College, could attest to that—she's a former nun and still a devout Roman Catholic, her Jewish husband Paul was then president of the National Council of Christians and Jews. In 1969 they were married by a priest and blessed by a rabbi. Today, Catholics for whom marriage as a sacrament is less important may even be married at an entirely non-Catholic ceremony, if the priest will file "Dispensation from Canonical Form" papers.

Many Protestant denominations will also allow clergy to cooperate in making an interfaith marriage a meaningful ritual for both parties. This may be especially true for those that don't consider marriage a sacrament, established by the Bible. Or it may not: Southern Baptists are non-sacramentalists, but they're not happy about intermarriage nonetheless. In contrast, Unitarians are especially accommodating—they allow even non-members to conduct weddings under their auspices.

And, just to round out the possibilities: some Episcopalians require a declaration that the couple will lead a "Christian life"; Mormons can marry outside the faith but not in the temple ceremony that signifies an eternal bond (but there's still no divorce); Eastern Orthodox will reluctantly allow intermarriage to other Christians if they've been baptized in the name of the Holy Trinity (not all Christians have)—they consider marriage to a Jew equivalent to self-excommunication, which is why Michael Dukakis can't receive Orthodox sacraments since he married Kitty; Moslems allow marriage to Christians or Jews, because all are believers in the God of Israel (and because so many of the world's Moslems live in Buddhist/

Hindu cultures, they'll make accommodation for that, too); Hindus don't advocate intermarriage but will allow it in certain circumstances—check with a Hindu priest. A Buddhist monk will bless a couple before or after marriage, though the wedding itself is considered a civil, not a religious, event.

But this book is primarily aimed at those contemplating marriage between Christian and Jew. For you, the major snag will be finding Jewish clergy who will either participate with a minister of a different faith or officiate alone at a wedding between a Jew and an unconverted gentile. There are more now than there used to be: 50 percent of Reform rabbis responding to a 1986 questionnaire said they would conduct an interfaith ceremony, 31 percent of those would co-conduct one with non-Jewish clergy, and 32 percent of those who wouldn't conduct it themselves would refer the couple to someone who will. However, the 1990 survey by B'nai B'rith Women yielded a lower result—only 40 percent of their Reform-rabbi respondents said they would participate.

If you want a joint ceremony—and can afford the fees—you'll probably have to hunt for one of these rabbis. Things could be worse: a British couple recently flew to America because they couldn't find a single rabbi in Europe who would participate in their intermarriage, which eventually took place in no less a landmark than St. Patrick's Cathedral. But even here you may find locating a sympathetic rabbi harder than you expect. That lesbian couple we mentioned in the last chapter asked a Reconstructionist rabbi to officiate at their joining ceremony, which they called a *brit ahavah,* "covenant of love." The rabbi refused—because one of the young women wasn't Jewish!

If you are on a college campus, you may find your Hillel rabbi accommodating; the one at Brown University participated in a *huppah** ceremony with the campus Protestant chaplain in 1986. But he was publicly excoriated for it by the acerbic Professor Jacob Neusner who, though himself a Reform Jew ordained as a Conservative Rabbi, maintains that a Hillel rabbi has a responsibility to represent the entire Jewish community by upholding traditional Jewish law.

If you go to the rabbi who's known you since you were a pup and get cold water thrown on your romance by a flat refusal to perform your wedding, don't be hurt or angry. Understand that the reasons most branches of Judaism do not recognize or condone mixed marriage are profound and complex—you may not agree with them, but you are not being personally rejected on some frivolous basis.

As Conservative Rabbi Jeffrey Wohlberg of Washington, D.C. puts it, " . . . I have to decline such an invitation, but it is almost never without difficulty or pain. The couple, which feels that it has 'compromised' by making such a request in the first place, does not understand my religious inability to do so . . . it is not the people but their plan that

I reject. . . ."
So why reject the plan?
The first reason is biblically based. Interreligious marriage is explicitly forbidden to Jews in several places in Scripture and implicitly in many others. In the earliest, most authoritative statements found in the Torah (the first five books of the Old Testament, or Hebrew Scriptures, as you might as well learn to start calling it), the prohibition is grounded in the fear that marriage with a non-Jew will lead the Jew astray into idolatrous practices.

Although most Jews today do not consider Christianity a form of idol worship, they still are alive to the threat of losing their people to a religion based on what they hold to be an untrue premise. In later biblical writings, the concern about interfaith unions seems to emphasize the social angle: Jews who marry out will assimilate to the culture of the partner and be alienated from their own. In our melting pot society, this is not seen as such a problem . . . or is it?

In any case, it's hard to see how anyone who considers the Hebrew Scriptures to be divinely revealed can simply ignore its direct strictures.

Then there is the matter of definition: what is a Jewish marriage? To understand this we have to look at how Judaism sees marriage as an institution. For Jews, marriage is a legal contract and a social institution. It is a very solemn and important one, one in fact divinely ordained as a duty for all individuals for the purposes of companionship and procreation (celibacy is not considered a superior or even acceptable state in Judaism). Its major elements of *ketuba** (contract) and *huppah* (canopy) are emblems of the formation of "a new Jewish unit," as Susan Weidman Schneider puts it. But though there are mystical elements in theological interpretations of Jewish marriage, it is a rite that primarily affects the society in which it takes place rather than primarily transforming the souls of the individuals involved. Christianity, on the other hand, tends to view marriage as a sacrament—that is, as a spiritual transformation that not only represents the union of divine and human nature, but actually enacts it in the person of the "mystical body of Christ," the Church.

Historically, Jewish weddings require no rabbi. All that is needed are two competent witnesses, a valid contract and cohabitation.

You may think this means it should be easy to set up a marriage between any two partners along Jewish lines. The problem is, if it isn't between two Jews, then it simply isn't a Jewish marriage by the definition of the community. It may be a valid marriage, it may even be a good marriage, but you can't make it a Jewish marriage any more than you can make a person a Jew by pointing a finger and shouting, "Zap, you're a Jew!" Just as a non-citizen, however educated, dedicated, or devoted to the welfare of a country, can't vote in its elections, so a non-Jew is technically not competent to act as partner in a Jewish wedding.

NED

I have often been asked by students to provide a Jewish presence at a mixed marriage. It will seem hypocritical, I know, but I usually decline. I don't want to seem to be authenticating such unions as Jewish when I believe a Jewish wedding is a wedding between two Jews. But in one special circumstance I did participate—along with a Catholic priest. The groom, an art historian, had a strong Jewish identity: his father was president of their synagogue. The bride, a biologist, was from a devout Catholic family only a generation removed from Spain. Neither family was particularly happy about the wedding, but each was able to put a good face on the situation.

The priest and I were asked to minimize the religious content of our remarks so that we wouldn't discomfit either side. In fact, the couple themselves had written their own ceremony, including in it such religious elements as they could agree on.

When my turn came to speak, I looked at them and said, "You two represent the coming together of two ancient and honorable traditions . . . " I paused, feeling the tension grow in the congregation, and finished the sentence, ". . . Science and Art." It's the only time I've tried to get laughs at a wedding ceremony, and I succeeded. The tension was broken. I went on to make a series of remarks about Leonardo DaVinci and his scientist contemporary Andreas Vesalius, but everyone in the room knew that these two were metaphors for the religious division.

The ceremony was a success and both families came away from it, I think, feeling they had been properly represented.

If what you want is a Jewish presence or flavor at your wedding, then the kind of ceremony described above, in which some Jewish person says something or some Jewish references are made or Jewish customs observed, may satisfy your needs and your families'. But don't kid yourselves—this doesn't make it a Jewish wedding according to Jewish law. If you don't care a stale bagel about Jewish law, okay. If you sort of do, you'll have to find a rabbi who will participate in your kind of ceremony.

Rabbi Samuel Silver of DelRay, Florida, one of the first and best-known rabbis who will officiate at such marriages, makes the following hair-fine distinction: "I don't do intermarriages. I give a Jewish ceremony to a religious mixed couple." He does not, however, co-officiate with Christian clergy.

Perhaps he would agree with Rabbi Harold Schulweis, who found a vivid way of showing the underlying problem for rabbis asked to "do intermarriages." He asked a couple requesting his participation alongside a priest, "If it's okay to have a priest and a rabbi, why not let me be the priest?" That is, if there isn't any difference between being married by a rabbi, married by a priest, or married by a rabbi and a priest, what's the difference between the rabbi and the priest in the first place? This brought home to them the logical extreme of blurring denominational lines.

And injecting a Christian element may raise the hackles of even the most cooperative rabbi.

NED

When my mother married my Catholic stepfather, the rabbi—a Humanist so far left he asked to be addressed as "Doctor" rather than by the traditional title—seemed perfectly comfortable at co-officiating with a priest.

The two alternated blessings, readings, and administering of vows with every evidence of nonsectarian ease. Then suddenly, at what seemed to be the end of the ceremony, the priest concluded "In the name of the Father and of the Son and of the Holy Spirit," and people all around the room crossed themselves.

I was taken aback, and interestingly enough the rabbi evidently was, too. He immediately interposed a blessing in Hebrew, a language my mother had stipulated and he had agreed was to take no part in the ceremony. Then the priest quickly added an obviously extemporaneous "final word." I don't remember who was, in our kids' phrase, "last-hit Harry," but the total effect was rather comical. If either of the marrying parties had been more religious, it might have been decidedly unfunny.

Although you might favor the dual clergy approach, keep in mind that the sort of rabbi who would do a mixed marriage may not be observant enough or will not use a conservative enough ritual to satisfy your spiritual needs. Rabbi Silver says that most of the Jewish partners in interfaith couples which he encounters come from traditional homes. Why might this be? Those from more conservative backgrounds may be more concerned about having a religious presence—the more secularized may not bother.

In a letter to the editor of the *Philadelphia Inquirer,* Rabbi Simeon J. Maslin of the Reform Congregation Keneseth Israel of Elkins Park, Pennsylvania makes an interesting observation. In this country clergy are empowered by the state as instruments of the legal contract of marriage at the same time that they administer the rites of their religions. In many other countries, the civil contract is separate from the religious one, and involves a separate ceremony: the couple go to the equivalent of a justice of the peace to satisfy the interests of the state, and only then proceed to religious rites if they want that sort of union. Rabbi Maslin suggests that this keeps the distinction clearer in everyone's mind without coopting the clergy for the functions of the state.

A civil wedding does have a lot to recommend it for the two-faith couple. It doesn't have to be, you know, just some bloodless mumbling in a clerk's office and back on the street in fifteen minutes. You can make it as elaborate as you like, with all the traditional trappings of white gown, black tie, and the Wedding March (but make it Mendelssohn if you're marrying a Jew—that side of the family may have negative feelings about the music of the antisemitic Wagner). You can even have Jewish elements, if you want to: a canopy, wine-sipping, glass-crushing; a Jewish friend, relative, or teacher to say a few words, maybe in Hebrew; chair-lifting and hora-dancing at the reception . . . whatever.

Reconstructionist rabbis may be particularly receptive to this approach. A recent resolution of the Federation of Reconstructionist Congregations and Havurot (Fellowships) on intermarriage states that, while "[t]he traditional rites of the Jewish wedding ceremony *(kiddushin*)* should be reserved for the marriage of Jew to a Jew," and "Jewish officiation should never take place as part of a joint interreligious wedding ceremony," still, "[w]here an intermarrying couple is committed to establishing a Jewish home . . .," rabbis may attend the civil ceremony and offer welcoming remarks at its conclusion.

This injection of Jewish flavor can be done under Christian auspices, as well. In Waukegan, Illinois, in the early 80s, a Jewish woman married a man of Irish descent in a Catholic Church. The ceremony began with the bride's brother, serving as groomsman, reading "the Jewish Wedding Blessing" which, according to the story in the *News-Sun,* had been provided by the bridegroom's aunt, a nun. Then the bridegroom's sister, acting as bridesmaid, read from the New Testament. The priest performed the actual ceremony under a wedding canopy. (And yes, the groom crushed a glass. For a ritual whose precise meaning has been lost in the mists of time, that one sure seems to have an unquenchable appeal.) He finished off by singing the Sabbath Song from *Fiddler on the Roof.* At the reception they played "Hava Nagila" and "a medley of Irish tunes." The bride's parents are deceased, so one can't know what their reactions to this extravaganza might have been, but the groom's people were evidently delighted.

There is a difference in the ways Catholics and Protestants traditionally view marriage, as well. Patricia Hunt, chaplain of Mary Baldwin College in Virginia, put it this way:

[For Protestants,] Jesus is a personal lord and savior, and sexual ethics, whether conservative or liberal, are personal. They have little appreciation of marriage as a social institution functioning to meet social ends. Protestants invented serial monogamy and "denominations." When one's spouse or church is personally unfulfilling, one finds another.

Roman Catholics have believed in finding God not through a personal relationship but through belonging to the church. Marriage was viewed as primarily a social institution (albeit ordained by God), not as a personal relationship. No matter how difficult the relationship with spouse or church, one stuck it out, not out of stoicism but out of an understanding of the social nature of the arrangement.

The Catholic Church has had a high tolerance for infidelity, both in marriage and in retaining people in the church who had lapsed morally. It has had a low tolerance for divorce. Divorce/remarriage and leaving the church have both been heavily penalized. Excommunication was the ultimate punishment that threatened salvation itself. The preservation of the institutions of church and marriage has been highly valued.

Protestants have had a low tolerance for infidelity within marriage and within the church, but a high tolerance for "divorce" from spouse and church. They tend to value individual integrity over the welfare of the institutions of marriage and church, individual good over societal and institutional good.

What we need is a theology of sexual relationships and of God and church that takes into account the Protestant insight that we are individuals and the Catholic insight that we are social creatures living in a web of relationships to each other and the planet.

What Hunt characterizes as "the Catholic insight" could just as easily be called "the Jewish insight"—one resemblance that, in our view, gives Jewish-Catholic marriages an edge in similarity of theology, though Jewish-Protestant marriages may benefit from the relative lack of centralized authority structures in most Protestant and Jewish denominations.

These may seem very dry and abstract speculations to you, but we think you'll find these underlying assumptions grow in importance as your marriage matures. Meanwhile, back to the wedding. . . .

WE'RE NOT IN KANSAS ANY MORE: THE SOCIAL ASPECT

You will have details to work out. The day of the week, for instance. We suggest Saturday evening. Many Christians prefer not to marry on Sunday, and choose Friday night or Saturday as most convenient for out-of-town guests. But most Jews disapprove of marriage on the Sabbath (sundown Friday till after sundown Saturday) both because the Sabbath is an important festival that people should not be distracted from by a rival celebration, and because a wedding is considered a business transaction.

And it's for that latter reason that traditional Jews don't go in for double ring ceremonies. The giving of the ring is the "bride price," the object of value the groom gives in exchange for the privilege of marrying the bride. If she gives him one back, they're even—no contract has been entered into. For the same reason, a traditional Jewish wedding ring is always plain metal, with no gem to confuse the issue of its value. Some people have only the bride receive a ring during the ceremony, and the groom simply starts wearing his afterwards. Maybe the charming, and sensible, Orthodox tradition of giving the bride and groom a few minutes alone directly after the ceremony affords a good moment for the new husband to be given his ring by his wife, in private.

Then, where will your ceremony be held?

When a relative of ours and her fiancé, both atheists, were looking for an asthetically pleasing venue for their civil wedding, they considered a beautiful local church—if the pastor would agree to take the crucifix down! The bride's mother declined to make the request, and the wedding was held at the Officer's Club of the local naval base. If you have military connections, you might consider doing likewise. Or if you live near a college or university, you could check out its facilities—academic chapels, commonly used for ecumenical services, often have fewer or less obtrusive religious symbols.

Orthodox Jews favor outdoor weddings, for symbolic reasons— the canopy is then more vividly a "dwelling" for the new couple. It's a lovely custom, if you can stand the meteorological tension.

MARY HELÉNE
Our daughter married a convert to Judaism in a Reconstructionist ceremony. The wedding was outdoors on the Dickinson College campus at 9:00 on a Saturday evening.

It rained for a week beforehand; then the Day dawned cool and sunny. On Saturday afternoon, the groom's uncle—a Dominican priest—said a mass for those of us Catholics (a majority of the combined families). One of his prayers was, "We thank Thee for necessary rain." His sister (the groom's mother) and I simultaneously hissed, "Not tonight!"

Somebody heard us. The evening was perfect.

However, if you're doing a dual-faith ceremony, remember that some bishops don't allow outdoor weddings.

And whether it's a dual-faith ceremony or one at which there are many people of two faiths, we suggest an explanatory program (which also makes a nice souvenir for guests).

For example, if you adopt the Jewish custom of having both parents of both bride and groom come down the aisle with them, and stand together under the canopy if there is one, guests may be intrigued by the symbolism of the joining of the two families, rather than the more standard Western "giving" the bride from one man to another. (Abby Van Buren actually wrote in a column of this as a "remnant of the biblical notion of women as chattel." The Bible in fact does not consider women chattel, and the custom derives from feudal Christian practices. If a woman like Abby, who was born Pauline Esther Friedman, doesn't know this, maybe your guests won't, either.) Our own daughter and son-in-law opted for the Orthodox practice of having the two mothers walk with the bride, and the two fathers with the groom, rather than each set of parents with their own child, to emphasize this coming-together-of-families theme for our largely Christian clan.

It's a wonderful feeling to be an integral part of your child's wedding, and we hope our sons and their brides want to adopt this custom, no matter what auspices their weddings are under. If your parents don't want to participate, they're missing something precious.

You might also tell them that Rabbi Steven Carr Reuben, author of *But How Will You Raise the Children? A Guide to Interfaith Marriage*, says he has never known a case where parental refusal to participate or even to attend stopped a wedding from occurring.

Try to make sure everyone is comfortable, not only at the ceremony but at the reception. Don't serve pork or shellfish if one side of the family keeps kosher; don't serve alcohol if the other side religiously abstains.

If either Jewish or Protestant family members disapprove of dancing with the opposite sex or dancing at all, try to accommodate them. Remember, a wedding is an event that takes place in and for society—it's not just about two people in love. You'll have your whole lives to dance, if you want to. We once attended a lovely wedding between two Protestants; the grandparents of the bride disapproved of social dancing. At the reception, a chamber group played classical music. The feeling was as festive as any we've experienced, and we didn't have to scream over a deafening dance band. Most important, that couple began their marriage with an understanding of the vital part consideration for others plays in a relationship.

In contrast was a wedding we heard of between a Greek Orthodox young woman and the son of a reserved, WASP couple. The groom's parents didn't disapprove of dancing on religious grounds, but the riotous exuberance of the reception was so far from what they felt comfortable with that they left the celebration early.

You should also talk to your families about pictures. On one side, some people have religious objections to being photographed; on the other, be sure no one who doesn't have such objections gets left out. You'll also want to tell the photographer in advance if there are religious symbols involved in the wedding that one set of parents wouldn't like to be captured on celluloid standing in front of.

With tact and determination, a wedding can be devised that doesn't make anyone feel alienated. If you have fixed ideas about what your wedding has to be like in every detail, you're going to have trouble. Remember what Miss Manners says: the "series of tableaux" that constitute most modern American wedding ceremonies, from white dress and orange blossom to tossing the bouquet (or—vulgar practice—the garter) is largely the invention of 20th century Hollywood. The only really ancient wedding custom attested in most societies, she points out, is the only one never seen any more: the display of the bloody sheet the next morning (talk about vulgar!).

Instead of immutable fixtures, think in terms of the flavor you want to impart: "taste and see how good the Lord is," for instance. And searching for just the right flavor to suit the palates of the two of you and your families can be your first important exercise in mutual sensitivity. It will also give you practice in sorting out what's really important from what only seems important—practice you're going to need if you're going to live happily ever after.

Chapter 4
The Marriage: Your Real World

When Armalona Greenfield married Little Sun Bordeaux, hereditary chief of the Teton Sioux and descendent of Chief Crazy Horse, the
rabbi had no problem performing the ceremony—the couple were
both Jewish. But we'd bet a buffalo nickel they still had cultural
differences.

And cultural differences go deeper than simple disagreement
whether to have danish (New York) or cucumbers (Jerusalem) for
breakfast. In this chapter we'll delve into two important aspects of
your new life together—where you live and who your friends,
neighbors, and colleagues will be.

WHERE IS MY PLACE, ANYWAY?

When you're just starting out, your choice of a place to live is often
dictated by what you can afford. But as you acquire the means that
allow you to choose, you have to consider potential problems beyond
the ordinary if you're "mixed."

Everyone wants to live in a "nice neighborhood," but if one of you
is Jewish, there are nice neighborhoods and nice neighborhoods—in
a dimension that doesn't affect Christians.

Close to where we grew up there were three towns in which Jews
could not buy property; the local folks had illegal real estate compacts
that screened potential buyers and simply kept Jews out. The law's
being better enforced these days, but there are still places we wouldn't
feel comfortable in. How comfortable would you feel in a neighborhood where your partner wasn't wanted?

Jewish neighborhoods don't have traditions of formal exclusionary policies, but the tight social weave can keep a non-Jew from
penetrating the fabric of local life quite effectively.

For instance, if the non-Jewish partner is the one who does the
shopping: will you feel conspicuous having to ask about the "right"
food for a holiday at the neighborhood store?

MARY HELÉNE
When we lived in the Orthodox Jewish neighborhood in
Jerusalem, I got accustomed to being good-naturedly laughed at
for not knowing, say, that I needed to buy plenty of greens at
Passover because matzo is binding to the digestive tract.

There were cultural differences that weren't strictly religious
as well, like the time I asked Leibl the butcher for veal. Red-faced,
he lunged across the counter and admonished me, "What, your

husband is Rothschild? You'll eat goulash like everybody else."
"But I'm having company," I quavered. "I wanted to make a schnitzel."
"Schnitzel, is it?" he said. "I'll give you boned turkey breast—your company will never know the difference."
They didn't, either.

It's not uncommon for Jewish neighborhoods to have this sort of close-knit atmosphere, which a gentile may find intrusive or intimidating.

The homogeneity of Jewish communities varies from place to place, of course. At one end of the spectrum is the one in which an I LUV JESUS bumper sticker was seen in the synagogue parking lot. Please don't do that, folks, it's poor taste at the least. If that's ultraviolet, perhaps the infrared end can be expressed by Rabbi Jacob Hecht of the Lubavitch sect of Hasidic Orthodoxy, who feels Jews should not eat nor socialize with gentiles. A more humane position is expressed by Rabbi Alexander Schindler: "If a member is a thief or an adulterer, he may remain a member [of the Jewish community]. Are these not greater sins than intermarriage?"

We lived in two sorts of Jewish neighborhoods in Israel: Orthodox and secular. In the first, we were the objects of curiosity—a neighbor's first question to Ned was, "Is it true your wife's a gentile?" We were careful not to obtrude our different practices, but there were inevitable clashes. Our daughter, then five years old, was once sent home from a playmate's because, in 90-degree heat, she was wearing a sleeveless dress. (We told her that our own choice would be to stay home and be cool, but she should make her own decision. She put on a blouse and went back.) Interestingly, we met far more overt prejudice in the non-religious Moroccan neighborhood we lived in later; it was the only place in Israel where we ever heard anti-Christian taunts.

Now, in a Christian town, we get smirked at by checkout clerks when we buy food or candles with Hebrew on the labels, and our kids were always being singled out in school to "explain" Jewish holidays.

A heterogeneous, mixed neighborhood is the obvious answer. But that won't solve all your problems. If you are an observant Jew, you may find it difficult to obtain kosher meat or to live within walking distance of a synagogue. If you are a traditional Christian, you may find the secular attitudes and values of your neighbors inimical or threatening.

Even places without an obvious religious character can have deeply ingrained biases. In the town where we live now, populated largely by Protestants without much experience of people of other religions, all the public school children had to sing Christian hymns in music class or leave the room and take a zero. A newcomer from Philadelphia expressed concern to a principal about this situation. His response was to cancel the Christmas program "because a Jewish mother complained." The situation exploded in the private sphere, with one member of the Jewish community maintaining, "We've never had trouble before," while another shouted, "You'll be saying that when they take you to the ovens!" And it escalated in the public sphere, too, with deputations to the school board and letters to the editor. The situation was never actually resolved, but a combination of a lessening of the aggravation and weariness of the people involved served to defuse it.

On reading this, many Jewish people will simply shake their heads and say, "So send the kids to a day school." (Presuming you live someplace with a large enough Jewish community to support one.) Day schools are Jewish parochial schools, like the Solomon Schecter schools of the Conservative movement. They are fine schools and teach a full secular curriculum as well as giving daily Jewish instruction. But if you're a mixed couple you won't want to send your kids there unless you've already decided to raise them as Jews—they probably wouldn't be accepted, anyway. Neither would they be welcome in Protestant "Bible schools." And though Catholic schools do accept non-Catholics, a child with one Christian and one Jewish parent who is not being raised Catholic will be subject to all sorts of pressures, social at the very least.

The town where we grew up in the 50s was an affluent community shifting from a fairly equal representation of the three major denominations to a majority Jewish population. Though the high school was virtually deserted on Jewish holidays, there was always a Christmas program featuring such bravura religious pieces as "O Holy Night" and the "Hallelujah Chorus." No one we knew minded. In fact, when a new director made a little speech about classical music having a secular value apart from its sacred content, the choir didn't know what he was talking about. (Yet no one was forced to participate.) At the same time, no one ever raised the question of whether it was appropriate in Christian terms to use sacred music for secular purposes. The attitude was that no religious issue was particularly important, and religious practice was largely a matter of aesthetic preference.

Maybe that seems to you the way it should be. And it was, in the 50s and early 60s. If you're lucky, you'll find such a situation.

But don't think things will stay the same forever, for you or your partner. Albert Einstein said, "If my Theory of Relativity is accepted, Germany will claim me as a native son and France will proclaim me a citizen of the world. If it is rejected, France will call me a German, and Germany will tell me I'm a Jew." After Einstein came to America, he became active in the Zionist movement.

The question for you is, what sort of community will make you most comfortable: Christian; Jewish; Gentile secular; Jewish secular; Mixed secular; Mixed religious? (The last situation is hard to find.) Will your partner feel the same way?

Here is a suggestion that may seem odd at first glance: if one of you is decidedly more religious than the other, choose if you can a community that's not your own "kind." Let the strength of your faith make up for lack of daily contact with coreligionists, while avoiding making your partner feel like a stranger in a strange land.

No matter where you live, or how little choice you had in finding a community, try to find benefits in the situation.

For Jews in a gentile setting, be flexible about the aspects of your practice that can be adapted. If you can't find kosher meat, maybe you should consider vegetarianism. (That's been called the first dietary law in the Bible, anyway—see Genesis 1:29.) If you're not in walking distance of a synagogue, try to find ten Jews to come together in someone's home for an informal prayer group. Jewish friends of ours who emigrated from the US to Israel were surprised to find that, in a majority Jewish society, they missed the feeling they'd had in America of being part of a small, encapsulated group; if you're a Jew living in a non-Jewish neighborhood for the first time, try to explore those resonances.

If you're a Christian in a Jewish neighborhood, you have a rare opportunity to explore the historical and scriptural roots of your own faith by learning about your neighbors'. If you're used to group devotional activities, be open to the different insights and strengths to be garnered from individual spirituality.

You may discover you actually prefer religious practices adapted to your individual situation. And you may discover your own faith deepening as you learn to center yourself in it without either depending on or being hostile to the people around you.

WHO INVITED ALL THESE TACKY PEOPLE?

You still may have to deal with the hostility of those people toward you, though.

Antisemitism: it's not dead by a long shot. There are still people—maybe among your partner's family—who think Jews are damned and damnable. Still others may be convinced they're always loud and pushy. And in a 1982 Gallup Poll, 30 percent of the respondents believed American Jews are more loyal to Israel than to the U.S. (with 27 percent "Don't Know," less than half didn't believe it).

This doesn't mean, however, that your only troubles are going to be with gentiles.

NED

As a graduate student at Brandeis, I was once called in by the temporary chairman of my department, Near Eastern and Judaic Studies, who challenged my presence in that academic program. He told me he didn't think I could be serious in my pursuit of Jewish scholarship and still have a Catholic wife.

The regular chairman, on his return, told me he thought the questioning of my personal life had been an outrageous invasion of privacy . . . but he didn't say that he himself had no question about my personal situation's affecting my professional one.

We have encountered this attitude again and again. I have lost job opportunities because of my marriage, and my college has at least once lost money because a potential donor would not support a Judaic Studies program led by someone who was such a poor example to students.

An Orthodox rabbi in our area whom I have never met has made it known that he will not participate in any program of which I am a part, in any capacity, no matter what the subject.

This sort of thing hurts one's emotional equilibrium, to say nothing of what it might do if you lost your job because of it. Consequently, your professional life is an area in which it's absolutely vital to your marriage to be open about what's going on. Not, of course, that you should recriminate each other for having "caused" the problem, but that you should share your feelings of rejection or discouragement, and your worries about how discrimination beyond your control may limit your professional prospects.

If neither of you is a "professional Jew" your marriage may not affect your career so directly. But a "professional Christian," or even a Christian who is a professional, may find discrimination even more blatant. The experience of Rebecca Brown, who was fired as a teacher at the (Protestant) Baymonte Church School in California in 1983 for marrying a Jew, has been repeated all around the country. A particularly egregious 1991 case involves a <u>Protestant</u> teacher in a <u>Catholic</u> school who was fired for marrying a Catholic. . . in a civil ceremony! Many of these cases are in litigation, but the emotionally and economically charged definition of the lines between church and state, freedom of religion and right of privacy, ensure that such incidents will keep cropping up. Be ready for trouble.

The workplace isn't the only arena of discrimination. When the Zionist Organization of America presented awards to Lew Lehrman and Sam Rothenberg, Meir Kahane attacked the organization on the grounds that these men had non-Jewish wives. (Lehrman, incidentally, whose wife is a practicing Christian and whose children have been allowed to make their own religious choices, said as candidate for governor of New York that he thought it was fair to raise the question of his marriage in the context of his campaign. Would you view the world's disapproval of your personal life intruding into your professional one with as much equanimity? Lehrman has since converted to Christianity.)

On the gentile side, plain old-fashioned social antisemitism is still more common than one might hope. As recently as 1982, Dr. William Bell was told that his Jewish guests were not welcome at the toney Long Island South Shore Ocean Club. Are things getting better? In 1991, the Kansas City Country Club admitted its first Jewish member, Henry Bloch, only after pro golfer Tom Watson resigned over the club's initial refusal. Open antisemitism seems to be more socially acceptable now than it was a decade or two ago; there were more incidents in such posh areas as Montgomery County, Maryland during the early 80s than there had been in many years before.

NED
We had a dispute with a local painter over substandard work he had done on our house. When we asked our decorator whether we would be justified in withholding part of the payment, she replied casually, "Oh, sure, jew him down."

At our reaction, she protested that the phrase "doesn't mean anything" and that she "hadn't thought of it as insulting." That was probably true, so far as it went—it was against her own interest to offend people who were employing her. But her remark had the effect of leading us to pay the painter his full bill. We felt that any attempt to reduce it would in fact be seen by him and the community as an example of Jewish money-grubbing (most casual acquaintances assume we're both Jews).

Christians, too, may find themselves the objects of social prejudice in Jewish circles.

MARY HELÉNE
Ned and I recently presented a joint program on Jewish American literature at a Jewish home for the elderly. We spoke to separate groups, then we switched and each spoke to the other group. During my morning session, I had no occasion to mention my religious affiliation. The group assumed I was Jewish and therefore concentrated on what I was reading to them rather than on me.

During lunch, one delightful lady said to me confidentially, when the general subject of interreligious relations came up,

"Let's be honest. Do you like every Jew you meet? No. I know gentiles I like better than some Jews." She said this ingenuously, not knowing I'm not Jewish.

However, during his morning session, Ned had occasion to mention my non-Jewishness to his group. When I met them during the afternoon, their response was very different from that of the earlier group. They glanced sideways at each other at my pronunciation of Yiddish or Hebrew words that cropped up in the readings, the question period was dominated by their "explaining" elements in the stories to me, and they kept reverting to my personal situation rather than the subject of the session.

Later, we heard there had been negative comments on Ned's having "put one over" on the program organizers by suggesting I take part without "warning" them about me.

These people didn't care about Christianity one way or another; it was the marriage that scandalized them. Often, in Jewish circles, it will be the intermarriage itself rather than Christianity specifically that is the focus of intolerance. We once walked into a roomful of Jewish strangers who were discussing intermarriage. We joined in the general conversation. All at once, one of the women hooted derisively, "That's nothing! You've got that guy in Carlisle (our town) who's married to a <u>Catholic</u>!" When we told her we were the couple in question, she tried to cover her embarrassment by an enthusiastic display of interest and a declaration that she wanted us to address a group she headed—a proposal she never followed up. She displayed no anti-Christian feeling per se; it was the fact of our intermarriage she was scorning—that a Jew would marry not only a gentile, not only a Christian, but a Catholic Christian (which many Jews think of as parallel to Orthodox, as compared to Reform, Judaism).

This was the most comical incident of our "passing"—since then we've made a point of coming out of the closet as soon as possible, to avoid embarrassing people. But the attitude that intermarriage is in itself scandalous, even if risibly so, is a common one among Jews. Still, we've never once attended a Jewish service in which Christianity as a religion or Christians as people were criticized or even mentioned.

Unfortunately, the opposite is true of our experience among Catholics. While individuals in social situations seem unthreatened and at most curious about our intermarriage, in ecclesiastical situations we hear sermons criticizing Jews and Judaism and perpetuating historical misconceptions about them with monotonous regularity. In addition, while on the social level our marriage itself doesn't seem to bother Christians, we do hear remarks and intercept looks that seem to indicate only our presence is inhibiting the group from expressions of antisemitism. How will you, Christian partner, handle this?

MARY HELÉNE

I run into this often because, since I took Ned's last name, people are very aware of my "Jewish connection." Once someone at a Parish Council of Women gathering made an antisemitic remark. Before I had time to respond, someone else chided, "You shouldn't talk like that in front of Mary."

Another time, when I tried to get my local League of Women Voters group involved in combatting religious discrimination in our public school system, I was told, "We understand why *you're* concerned."

A priest I questioned about the Vatican's non-recognition of Israel, a news manager I challenged regarding discriminatory wording in classified ads—all sorts of people have responded with a knowing relief when they hear my name. They think they know why I'm making a fuss, and feel comfortable discounting my concerns.

All my life my parents have set an example of active crusading against racial and religious discrimination: to have my ideals discounted as special pleading infuriates me.

Then there are the people one encounters who disapprove of any religion other than their own, and seem truly unable to understand why anyone would choose not to join with them.

NED

I once opened the door to a white-haired little lady in orthopedic oxfords earnestly proffering the <u>Watchtower</u>, which I knew was a publication of Jehovah's Witnesses. "I'll be glad to talk to you," I said, "but I won't give you any money. I don't want to support your organization, since you're so virulently anti-Catholic."

"Oh," she fluttered, "oh, I don't think we're any more anti-Catholic than we are anti-the-rest-of-them."

Since then I've had many conversations with door-to-door evangelists, particularly Witnesses and Mormons. I feel obliged to show them, as gently as I can, that without scholarly training they don't really know what they're talking about. In their turn, they try to save my soul—often by repeating a litany of people who used to be Jews and are now members of their denominations.

They really seem to think hearing that other Jews have joined their group will make me want to do it too, as though I must necessarily be looking for a way out of being Jewish.

MARY HELÉNE

I don't have Ned's sense of mission—or his patience—when it comes to sorting out the misconceptions of strangers. "Oh, let me send you our expert on why radio-carbon dating is a myth," a doorstep missionary with a stake in believing the world was literally created in 4000 BC will say, for instance, and we'll have a tag team stopping by every Saturday afternoon for weeks till they give up. These days, when we get into one of those serial conversations with proselytizers, I go about my business and leave it to him.

Once, though, I came into the room while he was discussing religious dress codes with a couple of sincere young Mormons. Now, Ned has the peculiarity that he almost always wears a hat, in the house or out of it. On that afternoon, doing the dishes while talking to the visitors, he had on a particularly extravagant-looking Portuguese fisherman's cap, knitted of heavy natural wool, coming to a point with a pom-pom on top, and having large earflaps sticking out like wings on either side. A horrible thought occurred to me.

"You do realize," I said to the young men, "that he's wearing that hat because he's weird, not because he's a Jew."

Their mouths dropped open. "I did think," ventured one, "that Jews wore those little round skull caps, but. . . ."

They'd evidently thought Ned's headgear was some special insignia of Jewish rank.

It would be nice if all misunderstandings were so benign.

Like us, you will also have to learn to be sensitive to each other's discomforts when someone of your religion is slighting your partner's. Whether it's listening to a Lubavitcher Hasid* (member of an Orthodox Jewish sect) sneer at "idols" in churches or to a Fundamentalist Christian missionary blather ignorantly about "the yoke of the law" in Judaism; whether it's a Jewish professor who smugly attributes his enjoyment of life's pleasures to his being part of "a hedonistic people"—implying a contrast to joyless gentiles—or a Catholic priest who can't resist running on about the "hypocrisy" of the Pharisees*—implying that Judaism was spiritually bankrupt when Jesus came along—you will constantly be put into situations where you must speak out on each others' behalf.

Do make your objections to such pernicious nonsense known; you may even find that the speaker was sincerely in error, and will be glad to have the truth pointed out. Don't count on it, though. Try to keep your temper, and if the thought of face-to-face confrontations makes your palms clammy, write the clod a polite but firm letter later, giving the facts and your source for them.

Naturally, we would try not to countenance cant and bigotry regardless of our marriage. But having a spouse of a different religion makes the necessity particularly weighty, while the one whose group is being insulted will have to try not to be unduly touchy.

NED
I usually go along to mass when we're traveling, because it's often more practical in terms of our itinerary and because it's interesting to note regional differences. Once, in England, we approached a Catholic church and I read, with a cold chill, the sign over the door: "St. Hugh of Lincoln." The murder of a child called Hugh of Lincoln was the occasion of a bloody pogrom in the Middle Ages. But we were there, and knew of no other church in the area, so I bit my tongue and went in.

As it happened, we'd been told the wrong time—there was no service. When we came out again, Mary noticed the sign for the first time. Horrified, she gasped, "Why didn't you say something? I never would have expected you to sit in a church commemorating Hugh of Lincoln. In fact, I'd have been queasy about it myself."

We've since learned we'd fallen prey to a common confusion: the saint was a churchman, a near contemporary of the murdered child, but himself a man of rather remarkably tolerant views for his time. The point is that Mary and I were trying to keep from upsetting each other.

Sometimes a successful marriage is like that in O. Henry's "Gift of the Magi": she sells her hair to buy him a watch chain while he's out selling his watch to buy her a haircomb.

Other communication lapses may reflect deeper misunderstandings. Starting from the cultural assumptions we discussed in Chapter 2, a mixed couple can drift far down separate paths of perception before noticing they can't see each other any more.

For example, perhaps you've lived in a milieu in which Jews are considered smarter, cleverer, and more clan-loyal than gentiles. If you're a Jew, this may have made you proud. If you're not Jewish, it may have made you envious, admiring, and/or resentful. In either case, if you're carrying this piece of mythical baggage, get rid of it— it can only weigh down an intermarriage.

Conversely, either of you may think of Christians as more cultured, better mannered, and more sophisticated than Jews. This is possible even for people who also hold the contradictory picture of non-Jews as more physically aggressive, less tolerant, and more superstitious. We're all subject to unexamined prejudices; the trick in your marriage is going to be to identify and deal with them without alienating each other. You will constantly need to examine cultural assumptions—as well as to explain yourself and your religious practices to family and friends. Make sure you and your partner can share these with each other.

MARY HELÉNE

Someone exclaiming, "Jesus Christ! . . . Oh, sorry, Mary," incites me to mayhem. It seems to combine insensitivity with a casual contempt for religious people that is all too common in our society, among both Jews and gentiles. But I also get very tired of dealing with questions beginning, "How can an intelligent person really believe . . ." or "Do you really think that whatever the pope says . . ." or that perennial Jewish favorite, "What about the Spanish Inquisition?"

These know-nothing gambits are only too familiar to Catholics in mixed company. But when you're married to the mixed company, it goes on for years, and you can't get out of it by claiming you have to rush home and say a rosary before midnight or the pope will make all your fingers fall off.

NED

My biggest gripe is Christians who assume my religious life is unsatisfactory, prohibition-ridden, and incomplete. "Why don't you accept Jesus as the Messiah?" is typical of the more aggressive. There is also the intimate, affectionate style (usually from virtual strangers): "I want you for Jesus."

My response tends to be flip. To the first I say, "Why should he be the Messiah? Why shouldn't I be the Messiah?" To the second: "Let Jesus get his own friends." But my attempts at humor mask a real resentment at the presumption that I haven't considered the question properly, and at the assumption that they have no need to take my beliefs seriously.

If the other side is actually knowledgeable enough to want a conversation in depth, there can be snags even if you want to accommodate them.

It's very difficult for Christians to talk seriously about their beliefs to non-Christians they're closely involved with and manage to avoid the overtones of proselytizing. If you're a Christian who feels a responsibility to "witness," be prepared to help your partner understand your moral imperative and to deal with the resentment and defensiveness it may well arouse in your new relatives. (If you're thinking at this point, "What's wrong with proselytizing? Wouldn't it be wonderful to bring the people you love to Jesus," please don't marry a Jew.)

A comparable conversational situation for Jews in our day seems to be the Holocaust. Many a Christian has said to us, "Why do they have to keep harping on the subject? I feel like they think it's my fault. It's all so long ago—can't they just drop it?" Well, no, they can't. If you're a Jew who shares this common concern with the implications of that unspeakable slaughter, be prepared to explain it to your partner and to cope with the impatience and boredom of your new relatives. (If you're thinking at this point, "Too bad if they're bored. I'm going to rub their noses in it. It's about time they realized how evil Christian civilization has been," please don't marry a Christian.)

You can evade the subject of personal belief altogether, but that approach is not likely to foster understanding or even social ease. If religion is important to you, then years of silence may give a you choking sensation at family parties that has nothing to do with the hors d'oeuvres.

The best tack in dealing with this is to understand what you in fact believe. Don't find yourself defending Jerry Falwell or the late Meir Kahane when among fellow Christians or fellow Jews you'd be giving him the raspberry. Then learn to feel comfortable in it. If in fact you think every word from Rev. Falwell's or Rabbi Kahane's mouth is a Pearl of Great Price, don't try to hide that fact. Finally, remember tolerance and, yes, humor: "You think I'm wrong, and I think you're wrong, but at least we both know [Kahane/Falwell] is wrong."

All of these situations require study and discussion to resolve. We don't mean you should argue about these questions. We mean you should read and think about them, and share your reflections. Don't use religious differences to further other disputes or mask other agendas; if the issue is really power or money or sex, leave the theology till you're cooler, and talk about the real controversy. You might try setting aside a particular time or setting to discuss religion—Friday dinner, maybe. (Or maybe not; we realized early in our marriage that a pattern was forming of Friday Night Fights. We were too tired and cranky by that point in the week to be able to talk objectively. So we banned all conversation about problems or disagreements till Saturday . . . and were amazed to find how many of them had vanished by the late, lazy morning.)

Using a text as structure can help you avoid getting too emotional. Don't use the Bible: differing interpretations are too potentially explosive, especially if you don't have the scholarly background to analyze the text impersonally. Use a good modern commentary like Nahum Sarna's *Understanding Genesis,* or a social critique like Harvey Cox's *Secular City,* or a spiritual biography like Thomas Merton's *Seven Storey Mountain.* Read a chapter at a time, and talk about your reactions. Remember to notice where they're the same as well as where you differ.

Or take a class together. (Dickinson College has a wonderful Judaic Studies program!) Or go to a museum and compare your reactions to religious subjects. Or get together with friends for a discussion group that takes the heat out of one-on-one friction. There are many ways of communicating on religious subjects. The important thing in a mixed marriage is that you do it.

We've talked to many couples who don't like and aren't used to spending a lot of time and energy on such questions. They're not interested in religion/politics/sociology, or arguing makes them nervous, or they think "love conquers all" equals "love means never having to say anything significant." Our opinion is, you're stuck with the subject. The rabbi who supervised our daughter's conversion to Judaism (see Chapter 8), on hearing a bit of our ongoing religious discussion that is part dialogue, part free-for-all, said, "Do you people do this often? . . . That's depressing." If you find the prospect of recurring conversation on these and related topics depressing, please don't undertake an interfaith marriage.

Chapter 5
Sex: How, Why and to What End

Can we talk? About sex? More important, can you and your partner talk about it?

Who initiates sexual interaction, who directs its course, who signals its end? A lot of those ethnic jokes we told you to mothball come to mind again here. Like the definitions of foreplay—Jewish: three weeks of begging; Italian: "Marie, I'm home." (Just to balance things out, here's the WASP woman after sex: "Feeling better now, Dear?")

Do you think of sex as dirty; do "nice girls" want it; does a "real man" engage in foreplay? What about sexual aids, toys, unconventional positions? Do you have a common definition of and attitude toward "kinky" sex?

The grandmother of a WASP friend of ours was an early student of Freudian psychology, and also notably buttoned-up on the general subject of human passion. Trying to reconcile these two bits of data, our friend once asked her how she dealt with Freud's theories of pervasive sexual elements in the human psyche. Alluding to Freud's Jewishness, the grandmother responded, "Well, it's perfectly true of course . . . for the southern races."

Sexuality is one of the greatest possible areas of friction. If one of you takes seriously the guidelines on sex proposed by his/her faith you will both need to know what they are beforehand. The similarities may please you, but there are differences that will have to be discussed and, if possible, compromised.

HOW: INTERCOURSE

Both Jewish and Christian traditions stress the sacredness of the sexual act, its patterning of the relationship between humanity and God. For this reason, both traditions structure it according to a vision of ideal order and reciprocity. Sex is good; do it well: sex is important; do it right. For the observant of both faiths this means first that sex outside of marriage (or of betrothal, in ancient times) is prohibited.

St. Paul, speaking from his Jewish background, even implies that it's impossible—the sex act itself constitutes *de facto* marriage. It's true, St. Paul in his Christian persona also brought us "it is better to marry than burn," which—whatever eschatological implications it had at the time—has ingrained itself in much Christian thought as an indication that sex even in marriage is a spiritual compromise with our fleshly weakness.

Jewish extremists, like their Christian counterparts, can box themselves into the attitude that sex is solely for the purpose of procreation and therefore a duty to be performed with as little sensual pleasure as possible. This is reflected in classic Orthodoxy where continued "barrenness" after ten years of marriage is considered sufficient, or even compelling, grounds for divorce.

But even the normative, non-repressive theologies of both Christianity and Judaism hold that marital sex is subject to regulation. However, here as elsewhere, the strictest religionists are being influenced by the mores of the wider culture. A recent study by Queens College sociologist Samuel Heilman showed that 40 percent of those classified as "centrist Orthodox" did not disapprove of premarital sex between couples dating regularly, and over 50 percent did not disapprove if they were engaged. Those under 35 were more liberal than their elders—the trend encompasses the *"tefillin** date," in which a young man religious enough to use phylacteries* (tefillin) at morning prayers takes them along on a date . . . so he'll have them in the morning.

You may be confused by the word "chastity" as it's used by Christian theologians. People tend to think it means "celibacy," not having sex at all, so they are alarmed or incredulous when it is held out as a standard for married couples. It actually means having a proper sex life: celibate if you're not married, divinely structured if you are. Pope John Paul II inadvertently caused a stir among ill-informed people when he said that it was possible for married people to commit the cardinal sin of lust. He was not condemning lawful and natural desire, but the sort of isolated, self-indulgent prurience that makes the partner merely an incidental object rather than a co-seeker of spiritual growth through physical love.

Conservatives of both faiths, however, hold that activities increasingly acceptable in the larger society such as masturbation, pornographic stimulation, and oral or anal intercourse are sinful. Traditional Judaism, for example, uses the Biblical example of Onan to forbid "spilling the seed" anywhere but in the woman's vagina. However, Rabbi Seymour Prstowsky cites another tradition allowing "a kiss on any part of the body"—a fine distinction, but a real one, between forbidden and allowed oral sexual contact. Evidently, you can kiss each others' genitals, but may not bring each other to climax in that way.

Another murky area: we know a couple, now divorced, both college-educated and sophisticated, both secularized Jews. But the husband had an Orthodox upbringing—and as a result insisted that neither he nor his wife completely disrobe during sex . . . for almost two decades! There is also a rabbinical dictum against having the lights on during intercourse. Interestingly, the text referred to as a basis for this prohibition is "Thou shalt love thy neighbor as thyself" (Lev. 19:18). The feeling was evidently that a woman would naturally be embarrassed at being seen clearly during intercourse, so her dignity as a particularly near "neighbor" must be preserved.

Christian ethical writings typically don't go into such detail in this area, but both Protestants and Catholics can come from ethnic/religious backgrounds that inculcate much the same attitudes.

If you and your partner are about equally conservative or liberal on these questions, no problem—if not, better work out solutions as much as you can before embarking on a lifetime of interaction. And remember that intellectual agreement doesn't always guarantee emotional smooth sailing. It is fairly common for even nonreligious Jews to feel that sex during menstruation is repugnant (as it is forbidden to the observant) for instance, while a Catholic bent on avoiding contact during fertile periods may feel the opposite way.

Speaking of fertile periods. . . .

WHY AND TO WHAT END: BIRTH CONTROL, ABORTION, FERTILITY

Hebrew Scripture holds that the production of children is the primary function of marriage. The first commandment is Genesis 1:28's "Be fruitful and multiply."

Problems arise when different religious traditions arrive at different definitions of what this multiplication is and how best to achieve it. Even within rabbinic Judaism there are different schools of thought on this—one says that one boy and one girl are sufficient children to fulfill the commandment, another that a girl and two boys are necessary to ensure the continuance of the line. Orthodox Jews and Christian conservatives alike still read the Bible's equation as open-ended and have as many children as God gives. More liberal adherents of both Judaism and Christianity find this stance to be a dereliction from the command to exercise stewardship over the earth. If your intended is a traditionalist and you aren't, this is one of the problems you'll want to begin discussing early in the relationship.

The dimensions of this problem can go beyond the dictates of faith. One married couple we know, Jewish but not traditionally observant, had four kids because, as they put it, throughout history Jews have been forced to make a sufficient contribution toward Zero Population Growth already. Jewish population in the United States, however, is slowly declining because the number of children being born in Jewish families is insufficient to replace losses. That's not your fault, but it may be another reason why those close to the Jewish partner may be against intermarriage.

Our own feeling is that, though clearly both partners should try to come to an agreement on the subject, the final veto power has to reside in the woman as the one whose body is at risk or at least under stress during pregnancy and childbirth. If she wants more children than he does, and he feels this would put an undue financial burden on him, they should explore the possibility of her taking on more of that (though that will probably necessitate his taking on more of the child care). It's important, however, to be in the same ballpark from the beginning of a relationship—that is, to think the same considerations are important and to have the same ultimate goals as a family. Don't get too hung up on deciding right this minute exactly how many kids to have; have them one at a time, and reevaluate frequently. But you'll eventually need to come to an agreement on how or whether to limit and/or space your children, and the sooner you raise the issue, the better.

The Catholic Church has more rigid formal proscriptions against birth control measures than most other Christian denominations. (The Greek Orthodox Church and the Church of Jesus Christ of Latter Day Saints—Mormons—are the notable remaining hard-liners.) Since the first international birth control congress in 1900, contraception has become increasingly acceptable to the Christian community. In 1930, the Lambeth Conference of Anglican Churches became the first ecclesiastical governing body to approve the practice. This approval has now extended to include other Protestant denominations, which either consider the entire question one of individual conscience and take no official stand, or make the proviso that the practice of contraception be undertaken thoughtfully and responsibly.

The attitude in the Roman hierarchy has been different. Through the 19th century, the official attitude was that marriage was for the purpose of procreation—which, in fact, was the only justification for marrying rather than living in celibacy, a state considered spiritually superior. Rather puzzlingly, the scriptural authority called on is that same story of Onan in Genesis 38:6-11 which Judaism draws on to forbid masturbation ("onanism"). In fact, the sin involved seems to have been Onan's refusal to fulfill the levirate law by engendering an heir to his dead brother on the widow.

In the early part of this century, Pope Pius XI expanded the official Catholic understanding to acknowledge the claim of companionship as a valid reason for seeking marriage, and the deepening of the relationship as a justification of sexual intercourse. It was declared legitimate for Catholics to plan their families, to space or even limit the number of children they had, as long as their general intent was to produce a family, and as long as—here's the kicker—they used only "natural" means to effect the planning. These come down to abstinence (no sex at all) and rhythm (sex only when complex physical indications point to an infertile period in the woman's cycle).

Pope John Paul II has reiterated this ruling and stated in no uncertain terms that there is no prospect of its being altered. More recently, he has expanded on this theme by suggesting that habitual intercourse without the possibility of conception may lead to increasing objectivization and disregard of the woman, who in this view is reduced to an instrument of male sexual pleasure.

Note that, according to polls, as many American Catholics use "artificial" birth control methods as do Protestants.

If one of you is a Catholic who believes the pope's authority is final on this question and the other isn't and doesn't, you have a problem. If the Catholic feels that the pope's authority, while nothing to take lightly, has no bearing on your conscientious conducting of your sex life, you may still have a problem. Depending on the diocese, a Catholic and a non-Catholic marrying in the church may have to join in signing a paper that includes, among other things, a promise not to use birth control.

The traditional Jewish attitude toward contraception is complicated. There is an ambiguous text in rabbinical writing that allows the use of a pessary (an obstacle between the sperm and the cervix—for instance, a sponge) by a woman under certain circumstances. The allowed cases are those of a child bride whose internal organs would be damaged by premature pregnancy, nursing mothers because their milk will dry if they conceive again, and pregnant women because it was thought possible for a second conception to interfere with the first. The problem is whether this device, or any such, is allowable when those circumstances don't obtain.

More recently a leading Orthodox authority in New York ruled that birth control pills were not forbidden since they don't interpose a physical barrier between the partners, whereas an IUD is forbidden because it does. The Orthodox American Rabbinical Council in 1988 reiterated its opposition to the use of condoms, but a minority opinion held them allowable in this AIDS-plagued world as preferable to the risk of death.

The heterodox majority of American Jews, and non-Jews too, often assume the Orthodox are "against" sex, since they structure their lives so rigidly. Such secularists might be surprised to learn that sex for the pleasure of the married people has been a recognized legitimate function of marriage at least since talmudic times. For this reason, Orthodox Jewish men are commanded to have intercourse with their wives even if the women are infertile or above childbearing age or pregnant. In fact, a woman can initiate religious divorce proceedings if her husband fails in his conjugal responsibilities.

There is also an Orthodox position that newly married couples can use birth control if an early pregnancy would wreak havoc in the family economic structure, e.g. if the wife is in medical school or some other program that ought not be interrupted, or is supporting her husband-the-medical-student. It must be added, however, that this exemption holds only if the couple have a firm intention to have children eventually.

Conservative Jews allow birth control as a planning measure, given the intent to have children. Even among Reform Jews, who are most liberal about when and what kind of birth control is acceptable, it is widely felt that a Jew ought to have children sooner or later.

We had our first two children within three years of the marriage. Ned's mother drew him aside and said, "You're not Catholic. Why don't you use birth control?" We had an exasperated laugh about it. Needless to say, the use or avoidance of any birth control measures has to be a mutual decision.

An aside: when they do have children, the Orthodox have a further consideration that might cause trouble for a mixed couple. The Union of Orthodox Rabbis of the US and Canada has come out against fathers in the delivery room as immodest. However, other Orthodox authorities allow his presence if he doesn't look at "parts usually concealed" and doesn't touch her. Even if your husband isn't Orthodox himself, contact with traditional Jewish standards of modesty and abhorrence of contact with blood may make him even more uncomfortable than most men about birthing; if it's your wife who has the Orthodox influence, she may not want you there.

Abortion is another subject that can create dissension where two religious traditions are involved. Although no one we've ever encountered is "in favor" of abortion in the sense that they think it's anything but a last resort in a dire situation, various religions have specific parameters for making the decision that a mixed couple has to be aware of.

In Judaism, abortion with the consent of the rabbinical courts has been a constant, though infrequent, possibility. The ancient rabbis had the same arguments about when the fetus becomes a person that our society has today. They came to no unanimous conclusion. (As one joke has it, Jews consider the fetus human when it graduates from law school.)

The question is usually decided on a case-by-case basis, and not always along lines of thought we might expect. For instance, it was held that if a woman knew she was carrying a deformed fetus, she could attain an abortion on the grounds that she herself could not bear the idea of giving birth to it. She would not, however, be upheld if she argued that giving birth would be unfair to the child! The reasoning was that no individual has the right to decide what another will be able or willing to bear—but one may judge this concerning oneself.

Official Catholic teaching today, of course, holds that human personhood begins at the instant of conception. The opinion is not unanimous in church history—no less an authority than St. Thomas Aquinas believed the fetus should not be considered human till quickening, or movement. But the modern position extrapolates from the human-at-conception dictum to the conclusion that the potential human life of the embryo takes precedence over the present quality of life of the woman carrying it.

Some Catholic theologians have proposed the controversial theory of the "just war" as an appropriate model when considering abortion. The church holds that in certain situations the taking of even innocent life can be justified if the reasons are grave enough and the good to be gained in the end outweighs the evils collaterally done in the means. You can't set out to blow up an Iraqi bomb shelter for the fun of it, that is, but the knowledge that civilians are in it needn't stop you from destroying what you think is a military command post. Applied to abortion, this model would mean that, given these criteria and the approval of the requisite authority (presumably the woman's doctor), the terminating of a potential or even actual human life is permissible. However, this is far from an ecclesiastically accepted view in today's polarized climate. Abortions are in fact somewhat more common among American Catholic women than among those of other religions, perhaps because the prohibitions against birth control lead to their being ultimately forced into more desperate positions. If one of you is a pro-choice Catholic troubled at being told you have allied yourself with godless secularists, the above minority theological stance may give you a more positive approach.

Protestant beliefs can run along the whole continuum from the most conservative to the least, depending on the denomination. The Bible text most frequently pointed to by Fundamentalists in support of their position is Jeremiah 1:4.

NED

As a Bible scholar and as a Jew, this infuriates me.

The phrase begins with a Hebrew word [b'terem] that Jews have always held means "while," so that the passage in question has God saying to the prophet, "While you were in the womb I knew you."

For centuries, Christians disputed this reading and maintained that the word meant "before," making this a prophecy of the birth of Jesus and not something to do with Jeremiah at all. Only now, when it serves their purpose, do they suddenly start reading "while" and using it as a ploy to claim biblical authority for forbidding abortion in the civil sphere.

It's also wrongheaded, from a Jewish and a scholarly point of view, because the books of the prophets are commentary on the laws found in the first five books, the Torah, and don't carry quite the same weight as the laws themselves. Jesus, for instance, is quoted in the Gospels as referring to "the Law (Torah—more properly translated 'Teaching') and the Prophets"—clearly distinguishing the two and, incidentally, not mentioning the "writings" (Psalms, Ecclesiastes, Kings, etc.) as scriptural authority at all.

In the Torah, the relevant passage is Exodus 21:22-25. There it is established that a man who accidentally strikes a pregnant woman so that she miscarries "but no further harm is done" pays a fine; if the woman dies, he pays life for life. This would seem to an objective reader to determine that the fetus, whether "human" or not, does not hold the same legal status as the independent life of the woman.

Nothing daunted, so-called biblical literalists interpret "no further harm" as the death of the fetus. In other words, they claim the passage refers to a premature birth rather than a miscarriage. Of course, if that were the case, no harm has been done at all in legal terms and it's incomprehensible that even a fine would be levied, but logic doesn't seem to have much to do with these arguments—the literalists are just as subject to "it means this because I want it to" as the most "liberal" interpreters.

The point is, it's perfectly possible to be seriously bound by scriptural law and still be pro-choice, especially if you're Jewish. Even as traditional an authority as former British Chief Rabbi Lord Immanuel Jakobovits, though he considers abortion "a grave sin," adds that it is not murder. So if you have an interfaith marriage, here's another knotty tangle to sort out before you can weave your beliefs together harmoniously.

Abortion in general aside, there is a classic disagreement between Jews and Catholics about what should happen if the birth process endangers the mother's life. The church teaches that no action may be taken to end life, but the physical processes must be left to the will of God. This typically means that the mother will die, while the baby may possibly be saved. (However, before the birth process, surgical procedures may be undertaken to save the life of the mother that will inevitably result in the death of the fetus, as long as that is not the primary result desired—for instance, to remove a cancerous growth. Try that on your Catholic friends . . . we bet they won't believe you.)

Judaism, on the other hand, holds that the mother's life—the one already established—takes precedence over the more tenuous, uncertain one of the infant; the baby may be killed even partially emerged if that's the only way of saving the mother. Fortunately, modern medicine has made this a rarer eventuality than in the past.

NED
When we were first married, I told Mary Heléne that if it happened
in our family, I would unhesitatingly go the Jewish route and tell the
medical people to save her. She, of course, didn't approve. But I
figured if it happened and I chose her life over that of our unborn baby,
she could always get a divorce after she recovered.

Seriously, what I mean to point out by this is that no amount of
love, good will, and prior discussion will close all of the gaps that
divide you. With any luck, none of the theoretical possibilities that
would cause each of you to act strictly out of your own tradition or,
at least, against the tradition of your partner, will occur. But in a
mixed marriage, you have to remember that these dilemmas exist.

A newer source of potential conflict in an interfaith marriage stems from modern advances in fertility options.

Artificial insemination, *in vitro* fertilization, post-fertilization implants, surrogate motherhood—these are all procedures that have been flatly forbidden by the Catholic Church though generally accepted by mainline Protestantism.

Judaism, as usual, encompasses a continuum: some Orthodox condemn artificial insemination (from donors drawn from outside the marriage) and surrogacy as forms of adultery; they consider technological assistance in bringing about a conception genetically derived from both spouses acceptable. Still, there is another Orthodox position holding that artificial insemination is acceptable if the sperm is from a non-Jew! The thinking is that this eliminates the possibility of incest. The recent case of the Virginia doctor who allegedly used his own sperm to inseminate as many as seventy-five "patients" shows this is no idle concern.

The Chief Rabbinical Council of Jerusalem reiterated this in its statement that the possible religious problem is not adultery but ritual bastardy (a serious disqualification from participation in the community—not the same as Western "illegitimacy"). However, there is still the caveat that the sperm cannot be acquired by forbidden activity, i.e. masturbation.

As for surrogacy, Rabbi Howard Kaplan equates the practice with slavery, pointing out that Hitler used Polish Jewish women as surrogates for "Aryan" mothers. But Rabbi Seymour Siegel of Jewish Theological Seminary (Conservative) held, for instance, in the "Baby M" dispute between a Jewish couple and their gentile surrogate mother that the contract was valid in Jewish law. It seems that what transpired in the household of Abraham between his fertile servant Hagar and his childless wife Sarah, or between Jacob's wives Rachel

76

and Leah and their servants Bilhah and Zilpah, were ancient analogies to the modern practice. However, this reading ignores the fact that in the biblical instances, the women bearing the children had a legal and social ongoing relationship with the father, the child, and the clan-group; they were literally part of the family, not mere hirelings. Therefore, Orthodox Rabbi Moses Tendler forbids the practice not on the grounds of adultery but on the principle of *p'kuach nefesh,* the saving of souls, in that the surrogate is illicitly being asked to risk her life for mere monetary benefit.

Genetic engineering is generally acceptable to traditional Jewish authorities, for instance in the case of a husband whose treatment for Hodgkins Disease had damaged his chromosomes, but in 1983 then–Chief Rabbi Jakobovits stipulated that cloning is unacceptable, as are the use of host mothers and the freezing of semen or embryos for purposes of convenience. He did, however, give the nod to *in vitro* fertilization and freezing embryos as a genetic "bank" to ensure the success of that project. Israel Health Minister Mordechai Gur points out that Jews are particularly susceptible to the genetically linked diseases Familial Dysautonomia (whose victims survive if diagnosed early) and Gaucher's, as well as the more familiar Tay-Sachs, and so should avail themselves of gene modification in hopes of eradicating these hereditary scourges. Depending on your ethnic background, you might consider intermarriage a plus in avoiding these conditions, or such others as Thalassemia or Sickle-Cell Anemia.

Reform Jews generally give the nod to all the possibilities. Those in between hold positions in between. And the possibilities and permutations, along with religious opinions about them, are changing almost hourly. If you have fertility problems, you'll need up-to-the-minute information and informed rabbinical and ecclesiastical advice.

Whatever your personal solutions to these vital questions, we earnestly advise you to acknowledge the problems and continue to explore your own responses to them. Don't put the blame or the responsibility for your marriage practices in this regard on your partner.

Chapter 6
Identity and Crisis

As you read this chapter, you might be interested to know it was the hardest one to write, the one we revised most often, and the one we got most irritated with each other over. All of which may indicate that even in an extraordinarily happy marriage, as we consider ours, between people who've had decades of practice in discussing profound differences in attitude without getting bent out of shape, as we've had, a couple can have a hard time sorting out this set of issues.

The issues, as we see them, fall into two broad categories with two major overlapping approaches to each. The categories are (1) Sex, (2) Everything else. The approaches are (1) Generalize, (2) Don't generalize.

WHO DO YOU THINK YOU ARE?

Both Judaism and Christianity make presumptions about gender and sexuality—presumptions that are similar, but not identical.

Let's start at the beginning, with Genesis 3:16. The King James Version translates "Unto the woman [Eve] He said, 'I will greatly multiply thy sorrow and thy conception; in sorrow thou shalt bring forth children; and thy desire shall be to thy husband, and he shall rule over thee.'"

Part of the fallout from the first part of this verse has been that when chloroform began to be used to ease the travail of childbirth in the 19th century, many Christian religious authorities inveighed against it with the idea that this passage constitutes a <u>command</u> that bearing be painful.

Jews focus rather on the last clause, which in Hebrew actually refers to frequency of orgasm! Eve is being told that, though bearing children will be painful, she'll desire the activity that will make her pregnant again . . . but she'll have to wait till her husband, to put it crudely, can "get it up." Her sexual desire, in other words, will be greater than his physiological ability to fulfill it; hence, he will "regulate" (Hebrew *timshol*) her only because <u>he's</u> the "weaker vessel"!

St. Jerome, when he produced the Latin translation called the Vulgate in the 4th century, thought this passage indelicate and altered it, as reflected in most of its present English translations. So far as we can tell, every Christian denomination—whether they approve of the Vulgate or not—follows Jerome's twist and treats the passage as though it has something to do with who decides what kind of car to buy.

Still, even Jewish commentators tend to Biblical interpretations that relegate women to passive roles. They'll point to Michal laughing at her husband David dancing before the ark, and being cursed with barrenness for it, for instance, and not to Moses' sister Miriam, who did some ark-dancing herself in a role perhaps best described as high priestess. Jezebel, the foreign-born Israelite queen who led her husband King Ahab into sin; Athaliah, the Judean queen who murdered her grandsons to hold on to the throne: these are the women Jewish patriarchalism loves to hate. Deborah, the victorious general; Yael, the freedom fighter; Huldah, the prophetess: these figures get much less play when female models are proposed. The heroines presented tend to be the self-sacrificing daughter of Jephthah or the obedient niece, Esther. (Outside the strictly biblical, there is Lilith, Adam's legendary first wife. Sexually corrupt—she wanted to be on top!—her name has become associated with demons . . . and feminists.)

On the other hand, recognition of female sexuality is widespread in Jewish tradition. As we mentioned in the last chapter, one of the few causes for which a woman can get an uncontested divorce in Orthodox society is nonperformance of husbandly duty to give her sexual satisfaction. Maimonides, the great medieval Jewish commentator, instructed husbands to have intercourse with wives even in the late stages of pregnancy, if there were no medical bar—though she might be less physically attractive to him, she needed the release and solace of sex. In another situation, the sage was appealed to by a man who had such a strong sex drive that he required intercourse every night. The problem? How then could he sanctify the Sabbath, as commanded, by performing the marital act, when it was an everyday matter for him? Should he signify the holy day by refraining? No, responded Maimonides: On the Sabbath, do it twice.

The down side of this for Jewish women is that they can come to be regarded as only physical, essentially light-minded, and subject to the vagaries of the flesh.

This attitude was taken to a desperate conclusion in medieval Christian thought, which saw women as sensual snares. The Reformation rather enshrined the "nobility" of women's calling as wives and mothers, with men as the sex-driven animal natures. So the men of the Christian Middle Ages in effect said to women, "We have to keep you locked up because you can't control yourselves"; the men of the Christian Reformation said, "We have to keep you locked up because we can't control ourselves."

Though the effect on women of all three attitudes has been a dismally similar result, we believe that neither Christianity nor Judaism is irredeemably sexist—both have a deep-seated egalitarianism of the spirit, that can be recovered from early texts, glimpsed struggling toward the light through history, and rediscovered by women and men trying to grow together today.

What this has to do with intermarriage brings us back to the question of stereotypes, this time between the sexes as well as across religious and ethnic lines.

For men, sexual stereotypes have had more to do with ethnicity than with religion per se. The Jewish man has historically been seen by Western culture as a "hot-blooded" seducer of gentile womanhood, oversexed and sly. In this century, interestingly, the converse of this figure has come to dominate stereotypes. The Jewish male is seen as mother/wife-dominated, impotent, and whiny.

What about sexual stereotyping of Christians by Jews? In Jewish cultural mythology, the gentile male draws his characteristics from the marauding Cossack and the ignorant serf. Rape and/or bigotry are his attributes; he is to be both feared and scorned. As for the gentile female, she is Delilah, the unfaithful idolator—another sensual sinkhole—luring away the Jewish future in the form of its young men.

Christians, as the dominant cultural majority, are unlikely to have adopted—or even to be aware of—the negative images of themselves in Jewish circles. They have historically been more likely to see themselves as the beneficent givers of cultural superiority and theological truth in relations with Jews.

These presuppositions have many reverberations in the roles each partner expects each gender will have to play in a marriage—and they're the more confusing when mixed up with presuppositions that grow out of differing cultural and religious bases.

If we could tone down the mutual accusations enough actually to be able to hear each other, we might learn something about, for instance, how gender roles carry over when both partners are the same sex. In the popular mind, homosexual couples consist of a "husband" and a "wife." Many gay and lesbian couples indignantly or amusedly deny this—but both the stereotype and its repudiation imply that there are "husbandly" and "wifely" roles that might persist beyond the actual gender of the individuals involved.

We asked the lesbian couple we've mentioned before about this question. The one whose background is Catholic is in the process of converting to Judaism, so this won't be a mixed couple for long. Cultural and ethnic differences still remain. Yet they were interested to note that when it comes to conventional gender roles such as money-making, housekeeping, and tending to relationships, they each move easily in and out of each; who is "supposed" to do what just isn't an issue for them.

Let's hope that as time goes on, more "mixed"—male and female—couples will be able to say the same.

Many of the old patterns have already disappeared. In an article in the *National Jewish Monthly* (2/91), the Jewish Orthodox feminist and writer Blu Greenberg says that 70 percent of mothers of an Orthodox day school in the Bronx with children under six held jobs outside the home (this compares to 25 percent twenty years ago, 65 percent nationally). "And this in a community that does not make pariahs of traditional homemakers, in a community that values family life over everything," she points out. The same issue reported on that 1985 study by B'nai B'rith Women we mentioned earlier; it showed nearly half of Jewish women polled demonstrated a "high" degree of affinity for feminism, compared to only 16 percent among non-Jews.

Some of this "liberal" attitude even among the most religiously conservative of women may be traced to Jewish history. The biblical Book of Proverbs extols the "Woman of Valor," who not only "provides clothes for her household" and "assigns duties to her maidservants," but "thinks of a field and buys it; with the gain of her own hands she purchases a vineyard" and "fashions girdles for the merchant." This paean to female competence and financial independence is read to a wife by her husband in observant households every Friday night.

MARY HELÉNE

I'm glad Ned reads it to me—otherwise I might not know, when this "Old Testament" reading comes round in church every three years, how the compilers of the lectionary have bowdlerized it. Somehow, as read to Catholics, it has lost all the independent, vigorous attributes and left only those extolling domestic housewifely virtues. She spins and weaves and gives to charity; verses characterizing her as an independent businesswoman are excised, and gone are the passages about giving orders to her household, being clothed in strength and dignity, or giving kindly instruction.

If the selection comes up on a Sunday when I'm assigned to read, I type up the full-length version and read that, and leave the typescript in the book for other lectors to use at other masses that day. I don't know whether they do or not; I do know that, though I do this with my pastor's permission, somehow the typed complete text never survives till the cycle brings it around again.

If you saw *Yentl,* you know that long before industrialization the Orthodox Jewish male ideal had more and more become the constant scholar. It was considered laudable and correct for women to be the breadwinners so the men could spend the day in study. The hitch, of course, is that—like today's "superwomen"—they were also expected to run the home and raise the children. No wonder they seemed domineering and overpowering to people reared on post-Industrial gentile notions of the idle woman as status symbol. In fact, as the German Jews achieved economic parity with gentiles, they, too, began to consider it a mark of status for wives to be "non-working."

The whole complex of questions about gender roles and the nature of women and men is no less tangled for Christians. Many volumes have been written on the subject, touching on the conflicting scriptural pattern. The same St. Paul who said both, "There is no male nor female . . . but all are one in Christ Jesus," also said, "Let the women keep silent in the churches."

Historically, the value to Catholics of the Blessed Virgin has been that she stands as an exemplar who suffered much of what many women suffer: childbirth, poverty, the death of a child; and triumphed as a woman and as a perfected soul. The paradox is that the institutional church never seemed to notice that she did all this without—as Sojourner Truth pointed out—a man having any part of it. Even the divine conception was an engendering by the Holy Spirit: "spirit" in Greek is a neuter word, not a masculine one; in Hebrew, it is feminine.

Much study has also been expended on the overlapping layers of historical religion—abbesses in the medieval church were so powerful they frightened the men; the Reformation influenced people away from both the glorification of celibacy as an ideal and the veneration of Mary as embodiment of it.

We believe that stereotypes about what men and women can and cannot do/feel/believe/accomplish are destructive and don't correspond to reality. For religious people this adds another dimension to the complications of an intermarriage.

Most troubling to a Christian feminist married to a Jew will be the streak of antisemitism running through some recent feminist thought. In their delight at the discovery that Jesus was not a male chauvinist, they have fallen into the classic Christian trap of accentuating the strengths of Christianity by exaggerating the weaknesses of Judaism. From the real or imagined sins of the modern state of Israel to the desire to see Jesus as unique in his own time, some feminist Christians have developed a superior or even derogatory attitude. In the same vein as the old canard about Jews unbearably burdened under the "yoke of the Law," modern versions like to see them as bound by ancient divisive and repressive social models.

The tendency to contrast the teachings of Jesus to attitudes reflected in the Torah would be rather like calling the National Conference of Bishops feminist because they're so much more tolerant than St. Paul: maybe they are and maybe they aren't, but you'd be comparing attitudes separated by lifestyle, history, and

2,000 years—much the same difference between Jesus and, say, Abraham. Jesus is much more usefully compared, in his social attitudes, to the rabbinical commentators of his time, who insisted that women had souls and spiritual responsibilities just as men did.

Jewish feminists may find the most troubling circumstance in the movement to be the political anti-Zionism that not only demonizes Israel but that seeks to avoid threatening—or endangering—Arab and other Moslem feminists by ignoring or downplaying the extremely misogynistic practices endemic in their cultures. If you're in that position, you might quote Phyllis Chesler: "American feminists may put down Israel for its macho men and patriarchal religion, as I do, but if you were a feminist in trouble, where would you go for asylum, Israel or Saudi Arabia?"

If both of you are feminists (we hope you are), you'll still have to figure out how your backgrounds are affecting your images of your own and your partner's gender. Following are some suggestions (note: not answers—we don't have those) on how to approach that. If you're not feminists, you still might find it useful . . . maybe we'll convert you.

WHO DOES YOUR PARTNER THINK YOU ARE?

We've dealt with the subject of cultural differences in Chapter 2, but we'd like to put in a word here about gender-related dimensions of the problem.

In your cradle family, did the women take all responsibility for maintaining relationships—writing the thank-you notes, planning the get-togethers, composing the Christmas or Rosh Hashanah family newsletter, luring a troubled-seeming teenager into the kitchen for confidences over the tea towels? In this common American situation, as a friend of ours put it, the men stroll into the well-nourished, healthy personal relationships as they would into a swept and garnished house. But hand them a broom—or a situation involving exploring feelings—and they don't know what to do with it.

In our melting pot society, we're not aware of a significant difference between Christians and Jews in this tendency to consider the human dimension of life as situated in a woman's world. Where it has special impact on the interfaith family, though, is in the fact that the partners may have different ideas about what relationships need tending, and how.

For instance, a Jewish man might not particularly care whether his cousin gets a bread-and-butter letter after a family weekend, but expect as a matter of course that his wife will have phone conversations with his mother several times a week. A Christian husband may have the reverse expectations.

Or a Jewish woman might think it natural and laudable to go to her parents for advice over marital problems, to her husband's embarrassment; this might never occur to a gentile woman, to her husband's frustration.

A dual set of holidays throws this problem into sharpest relief: is one partner responsible for both onslaughts of greetings/gifts/entertaining?

Our suggestion is the same as the one for the converse situation, getting along with in-laws. In getting along with your spouse where in-laws—or friends and colleagues from one religious group or the other—is concerned, the one whose relationship it primarily is should take responsibility for maintaining it. If it's his cousin, he writes the bread-and-butter letter. If it's his mother, he has the base-touching conversations (Mom will probably find this variation from her norm weird, but acceptable). If it's the wife's parents, she can talk to them about marital affairs if that makes her comfortable (but she should make sure they understand they should be discreet and not display insider knowledge around her husband). If he's the one who wants parental advice, he can go to his own parents himself, with the same caveat about discretion.

This is no panacea. You'll still have to deal with practical questions regarding your relationship with each other such as who you each think "ought" to be in charge of balancing the checkbook. Of course, that's a question that has something to do with received notions about gender and money but a lot more to do with cultural assumptions about gender and power.

The article by Joel Crohn we drew on in Chapter 2 also contained some fascinating findings regarding gender and power. In the Italian Catholic families he studied, even where the woman was perceived to make the decisions, in fact it was the man; in the Jewish families, even where the man was the nominal authority figure, in fact the woman ran things.

Many readers will be nodding and chuckling in recognition—this conclusion fits our popular images. The silent, stolid Italian paterfamilias providing ballast for the emotionally tempestuous mamma; the Jewish Mother with a will of iron beneath a querulous exterior, manipulating the intellectual husband even while she props up his image to the rest of the family—these are staples of novels and movies.

Like other minorities, some Jews or people from other strongly identified ethnic populations have internalized these stereotypes; either one of you may consciously or unconsciously hold them, and that may be influencing your choice of mate. As we've said, if you've accepted a warped stereotype of the opposite gender in your own

group, you may be unconsciously seeking escape by "marrying out."
This cuts both ways. Remember old Tonina, and her "Jew'sh 'e's
make a good husband." If you marry a Jewish man because you think
that means automatic material comfort, or a Jewish woman because
you've heard they're not sexually demanding (or that they are,
depending on the source of your stereotype); if you marry a Christian
man because you think he's more macho than the wimpy Woody
Allen types you know, or a Christian woman because you have an idea
she'll be less bossy than the Jewish girls you grew up with—watch
out. You may be in for some nasty surprises.

What about expressions of emotion in general?
A lot of our seemingly gender-restricted behavior has to do with
the expectations of our particular cultures.

NED:
Early in our relationship Mary wrote a letter in which she called
me "a man strong enough to weep." Naturally, when I read it, I cried.
I also cry at weddings, funerals, when the American flag goes by and
during commercials featuring babies. At our twenty-fifth anniversary
party, I cried while trying to read a little piece of prose I'd composed
for the occasion, telling everyone present how happy I was. My
emotional openness was complimented by several female friends and
relatives, leading me to wonder if, perhaps, their husbands were
trying to preserve the fiction that "real men" don't cry.
That, in turn, caused me to reflect on the roles we unconsciously
assign each other: we expect certain behaviors from men and others
from women. Does this expectation vary if it's, say, a Jewish woman
and a Catholic man?
From what I've read of the "men's movement" there is a growing
group of men who are discovering that there's no shame in "letting
it all hang out." I think this is good in itself and has great potential for
breaking down artificial and obsolete gender barriers that our society
foisted upon us.

This is only one side of the gender/culture equation, however.
Many cultures—ancient Greek and modern Arab come to mind—
value emotional expression by and between men while repressing
women even more fiercely than ours does. If it's socially acceptable
for men to find emotional and even physical intimacy exclusively
among their male friends, women become more marginal than ever.
This danger is particularly acute where women have no economic
clout or financial independence. That perforce is changing in today's
American climate, but old attitudes die hard.
In Boston we lived above a newly-married couple, both of Greek

background, in which the young man's shouts of "I'm the boss!" could be heard clearly through the floor. His abuse, both verbal and physical (we eventually called the police) made us wonder why they had gotten married in the first place. It was apparent, in any case, that they were duplicating gender role patterns both had learned at home. When at last the police came by the young woman covered for her husband's behavior: "We were just yelling around," she said.

This was in the benighted 60s, before Tony Danza was born and well before Women's Liberation had become a household phrase. At the time our own situation was just as conventional, if less poisonous. Mary Heléne had left college after one year to get married. She held down various low-level jobs, while pregnant and nursing, and kept house while Ned labored through endless years of graduate school and began his teaching career.

Our reasons for replicating this dysfunctional and already crumbling social model are complicated and boring—we've improved on it since. The point here is that before you get married you need to determine whether your expectations of who will do what and when are congruent and congenial. Then be ready to throw everything you've so carefully determined out the window when reality sets in. However you start out, will you be open to change as the need for change arises?

NED
I first noticed a need for change with our youngest child's diapers. Mary has always done the household "wet work," even though she has a skin condition that makes it painful. One day as she was reading Redbook *magazine, she exclaimed, "I can write as well as any of these 'young mothers.'"*

"Do it," I replied, "and if they publish it, I'll change all the rest of the diapers." Well, she did and they did and I did.

Three years later, when I'd finished my Ph.D., we decided that Mary should go to my office while I stayed home and did the housekeeping for the summer. It was an enlightening experience for both of us, but especially for me because I quickly learned how much physical energy it takes to run a house and how little mental energy you have left over at the end of a day or a week of doing it.

MARY HELÉNE
Note: he did those diapers when he was home—I really couldn't and didn't leave the poor kid festering till five in the afternoon.

As for the role–reversal summer: for my part, I got to have the experience of coming home from a long, tiring day of writing to find the house in an uproar and dinner not ready.

I learned to deal with that; the real sticking point was when we had guests. I found it really threatened some important part of my self-image to have people offered what I considered inadequate hospitality.

All in all, it was a learning experience for both of us, and provided a useful precedent. Now that our children have left the nest, Ned has taken on the lion's share of domestic duties, a role reversal that is gaining popularity in this country. He figures that after Mary Heléne's twenty-five year stint as chief domestic, it's his turn. But we do have a (female) person who comes in to clean one day a week, there are no kids to feed (when they do come home, Mary takes over in the kitchen again), and both the shopping and the laundry are shadows of their former selves.

Gender stereotypes we certainly have, despite our best efforts, but we've tried to divorce them from religious stereotypes. You might try switching roles as we did—if you can't do it for a long period, do it for an evening, or a weekend. Notice how you feel as you enact your partner's patterns; notice how your partner's enactment of yours does or doesn't jibe with your own image of yourself. Videotape the experience if possible. Afterwards, share your conclusions as though you were critiquing a movie or a play—that is, objectively, without getting into personal accusations or defensiveness.

WHO DO "THEY" THINK YOU ARE?

You probably don't think of yourself as a villain, and we hope your partner thinks you're wonderful. So you may not expect to be cast in the role of a destroyer of family values.

There still are, however, Jewish families who treat a child marrying out as literally dead. They put obituary notices in the paper and go into mourning. Even if your family members, Jewish or Christian, are not this extreme, they may be devastated, taking your action as a defection or as a rejection of their ideals. The element of guilt may also enter in: they're really upset because they've failed as parents. DON'T TAKE THIS SITUATION LIGHTLY.

When you're twentysomething and in love, it can seem that if only you have each other, the world doesn't matter. Maybe: but try to cast yourself into the future. Will you begin to be resentful of your spouse if, ten years from now, you're still being excluded from family functions? Will your children understand why their grandparents are absent? Will there be unbearable tensions within your birth family if one or more of your siblings keeps up a relationship with you without the knowledge of your parents?

We have a friend who married a Jew against her father's wishes. He never spoke to her again; when he lay dying in the hospital decades later, she went to visit, and he became so speechlessly agitated that she said, "Do you want me to leave?" He nodded "yes." After dealing with the initial grief and shock, she was able to say, "Imagine how much he must have loved me, to still be so upset after all these years." Would you be able to cope as well?

Even if there is a surface rapprochement with parents, simmering resentments and unexpressed anger can bubble out in ways that cause pain. We know a child whose Christian grandmother took advantage of his visits to propagandize against the upbringing his parents were giving him. She taught him Christian prayers, ridiculed Jewish practices, and encouraged him by such remarks as "Nobody can make you be Jewish if you don't want to be." The parents were forced to threaten to suspend contact. Although this was no longer interfaith marriage (one partner had converted to Judaism), the grandmother's intolerance still caused tremendous strain.

In such a situation, the easiest way to keep control is to put physical distance between yourselves and the offending relative(s). But this isn't always possible. Another thing that isn't usually possible is putting distance between two sets of hostile in-laws if, for instance, they live in the same town. We've found that there is least friction if we are each responsible for interactions with our own parents. This doesn't mean we don't have affectionate relationships with our in-laws, but that in certain potentially explosive areas we let the one most attuned to the situation deal with it.

Children, of course, complicate the problem enormously. When you two are gazing into each other's eyes humming the love theme from *Les Miserables*, remember—those quizzical or hostile parents whose opinions you now discount are going to be your children's grandparents.

You'll have to make it clear that, for instance, if you allow them to celebrate with your children a religious holiday which you don't acknowledge, celebration does not mean conversion. They should choose gifts reflecting an independent tradition—no rosaries* or prayer shawls*—and, if possible, be encouraged to avoid huge, tension-laden family celebrations where your children will feel left out.

There is, however, a plus to intermarriage from the grandparents' point of view, as Susan Weidman Schneider points out: they will then become the primary or only transmitters of their religious tradition, which can give them an importance in their grandchildren's emotional lives they wouldn't have if the parents were doing it too. At the same time, they benefit by their distance from the nuclear-family pressure cooker; rebellious kids won't feel as touchy about them and their ways as about the parents'.

You might remember also that just as you've made your own

decisions about your religious identity, your parents should be allowed to stand by theirs.

Children aren't the only area of conflict between interfaith couples and their in-laws.

" . . . a very lovely girl," the rabbi said. "You know what that means, when they call someone 'a very lovely girl?' It means she's a shiksah."

"Shiksah," in case you never watched *Bridget Loves Bernie*, is a Yiddish* word, often derogatory, meaning female gentile. The male counterpart is a "shaygetz."

If you ever hear, or overhear, yourself being referred to by one of these terms in your spouse's family, your feelings may be mixed. Or they may be quite unmixed—an unadulterated wash of rage, say, or of hurt feelings . . . or of loneliness. A lot depends, of course, on the tone of voice and the intentions of the speaker, but it's never fun to feel like an outsider.

One defense against being left out is to camouflage: to adopt the cultural colorations of, for instance, ethnic Judaism till your proudest moment is when Aunt Eppie from Sioux City says, "You're not Jewish? You're kidding—I never would have guessed. . . . Such a lovely girl." But Aunt Irene from Chicago may be offended at your attempts to pass, sensing patronization: "'*Oi gevalt?*' What a quaint expression. Is your family German, dear?" They both have a point. Are you losing your identity? Or are you parodying theirs? Is this successful camouflage, or is it more like pasting a leaf on your forehead and pretending you're a bush? Pretense may have the effect of confusing only you. Think about it, before you use this defense.

Another possibility is to play up to the role of outsider: "I'll do these dishes. After all, that's what you have a shiksah for." "What is this I'm eating? Kreplach, you say? I though it was some kind of Jewish won ton." Aunt Irene from Chicago won't like you for this one, either. But Uncle Seymour from New York might think you're real cute. Is this what you want?

To the Jewish partner, the attitudes of The Others may seem less excluding and more exclusive. That is, among gentiles there can be the unspoken assumption that it's perfectly natural, even right and proper, for a Jew to want to associate with, ape, and otherwise suck up to, gentiles . . . but don't think it's going to work, Bub, we know who you really are. We're not talking here about virulent antisemitism, but about a sort of unexamined cultural condescension.

"You mean the men put on their hats to pray? How . . . interesting," is an observation Uncle Chauncy from Newport should be discouraged from making. On the other hand, care and tact will have to be exercised in explaining to Aunt Desolina from Detroit why you would rather she didn't bring prosciutto to the bar mitzvah without giving her the impression you think her food is wicked, poisonous, or—God forbid—low class.

What to do? Invite Aunt Eppie from Sioux City and Uncle Chauncy from Newport, or Aunt Irene from Chicago and Aunt Desolina from Detroit, to your house for an evening. Watch them for a while as though they were characters in a movie or a novel rather than people you feel defensive or superior or resentful or whatever about. You'll gain some fascinating insights, and be well on the road to understanding your partner's unconscious ethnic agenda.

FAMILY TIES

Chapter 7
Starting a Family

We had our first child nine months to the day after we were married. Since we were excruciatingly young and inexperienced, we spent a lot of that short period agonizing over what sort of parents we would be. Ned's grandmother reassured us; "Babies bring their own love," she would say. But we were also being influenced by child psychologist Bruno Bettelheim, who said, "Love is not enough." They were both right.

In an interfaith marriage, religious upbringing of children is likely to be the sticking point, both for prospective parents and grandparents. When the daughter of Mordechai Kaplan, founder of the Reconstructionist movement, married a non-Jew, he was willing to come to the wedding (he was too sick actually to attend) but he wrote asking that the children be raised as Jews. The Catholic Church, on the other hand, generally demands that children of Catholics be raised as Catholics.

In the next chapter, we'll be discussing various childraising options for the interfaith couple and their consequences. Please take time to discuss this section with your partner—and be prepared for some unexpected stormy weather . . . generated by each of you. The great majority of couples we've talked to and read about who thought religion didn't matter to them have discovered, to their dismay, that the religion of their children mattered more than they thought possible.

Often, non-religious interfaith couples feel that they don't want to "deprive" their children of the experiences and influences they grew up with. Since they think of religion as appropriate only for childhood, they similarly think of childhood as incomplete or impoverished without religion. The feeling is indistinguishable from the common approach to Santa Claus: "Sure, no adult believes it, but it would be a shame to raise kids without that sense of magic." But religions claim a great deal more significance than feel-good fuzzies for the little ones, or sops to elderly relatives. And even if you choose to ignore those claims, you still have to decide which of your fond soft-focus memories are going to be passed on to your offspring: Yours? Your partner's? Both? Neither?

It's a problem you can't put off in religions that involve ceremonies for infants. You shouldn't put off a decision in any case, but you'll be more tempted to if you don't have to make that immediate decision: baptism or circumcision? Still, in our experience many couples do choose one ritual or the other—or try to have both—without dealing with the long-term question of children's religious identity. Like Hope and Michael in that *thirtysomething* episode we mentioned in Chapter 1, they vaguely want the emotional comfort and familiarity of baptism and/or circumcision but not the discomfort of thinking about their implications.

Baptism and circumcision are not spiritually identical "welcoming" ceremonies. Rabbi Harold Schulweis points out that baptism symbolizes a surrender to the power of grace,* while circumcision signifies entering into a covenant as a partner with God.

The question is not whether you're going to get to use that heirloom christening gown, or whether Uncle Seymour will be offended at not being asked to serve as godfather at the bris.* The issues involved go to the very roots of the split in the Jewish/Christian marriage.

WATER AND THE HOLY SPIRIT: BAPTISM

When we had our first child, our thinking did not involve this sort of profound abstract distinction.

Remember, at that time only one of us—Mary Heléne—was actively religious. Ned not only had never practiced as a Jew, he was suspicious of "organized religion" and believed that a sort of rationalist pantheism ("When I take a walk and admire the beauty of the trees, that's my religion. . . .") was sufficient spiritual fare. Mary Heléne, for her part, felt that the standard American Catholic practice of conferring the sacraments of Confession, Communion, and Confirmation in childhood had deprived her of a chance to experience what should have been solemn, soul-shaking events from the perspective of an adult's ability to appreciate them.

We had decided to marry in the Catholic Church—that seemed the obvious choice since only Mary practiced her religion and marrying outside it would have cut her off from the sacraments. In the Archdiocese of Chicago in 1963 that meant we had to sign a paper promising to raise the children as Catholic. (More about this condition in the next chapter.) We had told the priest, Father Shea, that we planned to have our children baptized but to reserve the other sacraments unless and until they chose Catholicism. His concern, and ours, was whether this plan sufficiently fulfilled our obligations under the pre-marital agreement. None of the three of us seems to have noticed we were assuming that infant baptism—because in Roman Catholicism as in some Protestant denominations its efficacy is conditional on their renewing the baptismal commitment later in life—was little more than a sort of *pro forma* naming ceremony.

Accordingly, when our first child was born, our main consideration was sentimental: to have her baptized in our home town church, by the priest who had married us. Church etiquette demanded that we get the permission of the priest in whose parish we were then living, which we duly did. We had a pretty ceremony in the familiar old church and left feeling that our little Sarah had had her official welcome into the community.

If you think you want a baptism, you may feel the same way about it; that doesn't guarantee your spouse will. Even a marriage between two Christians can stumble over this one. Robert T. Reilly reports on a Presbyterian married to a Catholic who surprised himself by his negative emotions surrounding a family baptismal gown—to him it was a symbol of Catholicism. "I know it seems superficial," he said to Reilly in a *U. S. Catholic* article, "but there are lots of little bombshells. It's as if I'd been talking into a tape recorder all my life and someone suddenly pushed Play." That is, his own past suddenly began to speak to him.

The situation with our second child was more awkward than with the first. We had registered at St. Jude's, the church closest to where we lived, spoken to its pastor about our situation and found out when their group baptisms were held.

We arrived on time and began giving particulars to the officiant. We had gotten no further than our address when he said, "But you're not in this parish. That address is in St. Luke's parish." So we hustled our white-suited infant out, like a jilted bride, to the curious stares of the other parents.

At the other church we got glares. The priest there was in the middle of an assembly line ceremony, which he insisted on interrupting for us. He also had different ideas on our situation than the St. Jude's priest had (more about that under "Godparents" below). What with one thing and another, all the babies were crying by the time he got us caught up and slotted in.

Our youngest was baptized in Jerusalem, where the main difficulty was getting the priest to understand the name we had chosen. The first name, Ephraim, posed no problem, but the middle name Samuel seemed absolutely strange to him. The man's own native tongue was unidentifiable; the heavy accent was certainly not Arabic, but after pronouncing the name in every other language we knew it in, we found the Arabic "Samwil" did the trick. The only other harrowing moment was caused by the authentic, picturesque, but spartan practice in St. Saviour's church of using "living waters"—flowing through an ancient bottomless stone cistern and icy with the cold of centuries—on the baby's defenseless head.

MARY HELÉNE

At this time I was beginning—a little late—to rethink my position on baptism per se. I had shrugged off the practical problems and personal glitches as peripheral to the meaning of the sacrament, which they were, but they had had the effect of distracting me from the central issue: what did I think I was accomplishing in having my children baptized?

I had been shaken by an experience with that third baby. He was very ill during the first few days of his life, and when they let me hold him I could see how terrible he looked. The thought went through my mind, "I should perform an emergency baptism." The force of the feeling surprised me. I don't intellectually think that anything bad happens to unbaptized infants, but I knew that I would never sleep soundly again if that baby died unbaptized. The only thing that stopped me was not rational reflection but a counter superstition: to do an emergency baptism was to acknowledge that he might die, and admitting the possibility felt like inviting the actuality.

In later months I pondered this aberration. Was my idea of this sacrament of the church no more than an unreasoned warding off of the Evil Eye?

Then we had a conversation with friends—he Jewish, she Catholic—who had not yet had children. "But I won't have them baptized when we do," she said, "because if I did, then I would feel that I had a responsibility to see to it that they were Catholic, and I don't want to make that commitment on their behalf." This made sense to me in a way that our own previous practice did not.

If the sacrament does not involve a magical warding off of evil from the helpless infant, nor a solemn commitment on the part of the parents eventually to produce a Catholic adult, what is it for? Theologically, it is the means by which the soul is cleansed of Original Sin*—but what if you don't believe in Original Sin, at least not as a condition guaranteeing the damnation of any unbaptized soul?

As it happens, the church since Vatican II has promulgated a view not unlike our friend's. To the consternation of lip-service Catholics who grew up seeing infant baptism as a cross between vaccination and insurance, priests are now insisting that parents have some active commitment to the church and to the Catholic upbringing of the infant—that there is a reasonable presumption that this baby will, in fact, choose to ratify the implications of baptism later in life.

Theologically, this is logical. Practically, it has the effect of discouraging excesses brought about by the earlier, almost magical, approach. It was and still is the case that the Roman Catholic Church, along with the Episcopalian and the Lutheran, considers baptism a sacrament: that is, a physical act that in and of itself has a spiritual effect even on an unknowing infant.

Therefore, in some periods of history, forced or even surreptitious baptisms have been held to be valid once performed. A notorious modern (as the church reckons time) case was that of Edgardo Mortara, a six-year-old child who in 1858 was removed from his Bolognese Jewish family on the grounds that he had been secretly baptized by a Christian servant five years before when she had mistakenly thought he was dying. Despite international protest, the papal authorities kept the child in Rome, where he eventually became an Augustinian monk, professor of theology, and ardent conversionist. The ensuing controversy, however, sparked a ruling forbidding such baptisms (they have technically never been allowed, but the official attitude has ranged from tolerant to encouraging in some times and places).

In contrast is the 1984 case of the son of Barry Roffman of Miami. Although the fact that his divorced wife is Catholic meant that according to traditional Jewish law the child is a gentile, Roffman, a Jew, had raised the child Jewishly. But the mother persuaded the seven-year-old to be baptized without the father's knowledge. That baptism has since been annulled, a stunning and history-making move on the part of Archbishop Edward A. McCarthy, on the grounds that the "priest was not aware that the mother had told the child that the baptism would place a shield over him so that he could not go to hell." That is, she had misrepresented the purpose of the sacrament, which is the freeing of the soul from Original Sin but carries no guarantee of future indemnity. Even more important from the mixed-marriage perspective is the fact that the explanation goes on, "Nor was he [the priest] aware that the child considered himself to be Jewish." Here we have a diametric reversal of policy in a little over a century, with both decisions resting on identical understandings of the meaning and importance of the sacrament.

Which all goes to prove that not everything is what you vaguely feel it must be from your childhood experiences, and it will behoove you and your partner to find out exactly what you're doing before you enter into a religious covenant on your child's behalf. Read a current book on Catholic beliefs and practices (see the resource list at the end of this book), talk to as many priests as you can corner, and while you're at it talk to a rabbi or two about what they think of baptism (see also the section on circumcision below).

Baptism is a naming ceremony, but it should be clear by now that it's not only that. It represents a serious long–term commitment on the part of the parents to do their utmost to raise the child a Christian. It's also an immediate expression of belief in a profound theological tenet, that of the cleansing from Original Sin. If you don't hold with its premise, nor want to abide by its implications, don't do it to your child.

If you do decide to have your child baptized, there will be another element a mixed couple must deal with thoughtfully, that of choosing godparents.

Many of us think of a godparent as merely someone to be honored with a mark of affection and allowed to buy the baby a present. But technically, for Christian churches that practice infant baptism, the godparent is a religious sponsor whose responsibility it is to ensure the child's religious training if the parents are unwilling or unable to do so. This, as you can see, is a serious and potentially explosive situation when the godparents are not of the same religion as one of the parents. Although it's not terribly likely, in these days of increased religious activism it is just possible, that, for instance, a godparent might decide you weren't feeding your children strong enough religious fare and start trying to beef it up without your consent.

Religious disaffection and ordinary American-style mobility can create practical godparental problems as well. Our first child's godfather has completely fallen out of our lives.

When it came time to choose godparents for our second child, we discovered that we had no close contemporary male friends who were practicing Catholics. One priest said in that case a single godparent was enough. But this was the Case of the Shifting Parish Boundaries baptism. The other priest demanded we name two godparents, even after hearing what his colleague at St. Jude's had said. St. Luke's priest kept repeating like a broken record, "You have to have a godfather." Finally he fingered a bystander, a total stranger to us, and informed us that this was our baby's baptismal sponsor who would be responsible for his spiritual training in the sight of God. We were certainly relieved that the man made no attempt to interfere in our religious upbringing of the child; possibly the only humane, sensible thing to do in that embarrassing situation was exactly what he did—pretend it hadn't happened.

The priest also, incidentally, made a great to-do about the fact that the baby was eight weeks old, not in the nearly newborn state more common for American Catholics. When we explained that he'd had a cold (it was Boston in winter), the priest said sententiously, "All the more reason," as though the child had been at death's door.

All this, combined with a number of suspicious sidelong glances at Ned and a great huffing and puffing over the spelling of the exotic name "Rosenbaum," left us feeling that there was more going on than a simple misunderstanding over godparental requirements. Ned later said he'd felt like Judas, standing there being glared at.

NED
When you go to one of your spouse's religious services, you never know what sort of embarrassment or insult you may be subjected to. What do you do then? In this case, I was only upset that a priest with no talent for improvising had made a group of people acutely uncomfortable. I thought of asking Mary to leave or just leaving myself, but in the end I did neither.

We have learned since our early years to defend each other against our own coreligionists' intolerance, which is much preferable to having to stand out in an alien situation. In similar situations, one of you should take a stand, especially where children are involved, or risk repressed anger and resentment.

By the time our third child came along, our social situation had reversed itself. The friend who'd been godmother to our first two was no longer a practicing Catholic.

But we had acquired a male Catholic friend who provided us with a perspective you might find useful as well. He was a young German we'd met in Israel, where he was studying rabbinical literature. Of all of them, he was our only godparent who took the spiritual responsibilities of the position literally. Felix wrote that he'd considered very carefully before concluding it would be a "great honor and great pleasure." He would never try to interfere with our raising of the child, "But if, at the age of eighteen or so, he finds himself in spiritual difficulties, and if at that time he should come to me for advice, you must know, Mary, that I will say to him, 'Your first responsibility is to be a Jew; after that you can be a Christian.'"

MARY HELÉNE

I was delighted at Felix's attitude. It coincides with my own—which often surprises people, but which I think is one of the reasons our interfaith marriage is a success. Of course most Christians are aware that their religion is based on and comes out of Judaism. But one with a Jewish spouse is in a position to internalize that knowledge. When Sarah underwent formal conversion to Judaism (see the next chapter), I felt no sense of loss or separation from her. She believes nothing that I disbelieve. In this regard, I have it easier than Ned will if one or both of the boys espouses Christianity; he would not be able to help feeling that they were, literally, making a mistake—embracing a belief that he thinks is, on the most elementary factual level, wrong.

There is also the socio-historical factor. Any individual with a Jewish parent is going to be considered Jewish by some people for some purposes no matter what beliefs that individual adheres to. Our children will need to deal with that, and I think that a sort of

basic "Jewish consciousness" underlying their intellectual attitudes will help them to do so.

If you agree that it's appropriate for your child to have a basis in Jewish identity before or beneath any Christian affiliation, you may or may not conclude that baptism is an appropriate way of embarking your children on this course. Or you may disagree, thinking that Jewish elements in a child's background need not have any important long-term repercussions; in that case, you probably will decide in favor of baptism.

If you do choose to have your child baptized, warn Jewish family members that there will be prayers and liturgical responses they probably won't want to join, and that there's literally no way to conduct a baptism without the officiant's referring to Jesus as God. Make a special effort to have an individual ceremony, instead of the assembly line approach. Jewish relatives will feel even more conspicuous and left out if there's a large group of Christians all happily intoning together. If they're from traditional backgrounds, though, they'll probably be quite comfortable with the symbolism of water as a sign of regeneration; after all, the Christians got it from the Jews.

If your thinking leads you to the opposite conclusion—that baptism is inappropriate for your child, and a Jewish rite-of-passage is indicated—you will find that Judaism brings still another element, that of heredity, into the question of birth rituals.

THE COVENANT OF THE FLESH: CIRCUMCISION

Jesus was circumcised, but St. Paul made a point of baptising the uncircumcised Titus, even though he had both circumcised and baptised his own disciple Timothy. The Council of Jerusalem in 51 CE* declared circumcision unnecessary for Christians. Twelve centuries later St. Thomas Aquinas declared it equivalent to baptism in its power to remit sins, but obviously by that time he was thinking of something much different from the Jewish idea of the purpose of circumcision.

If you have boys, the subject of circumcision will probably arise. If the Jewish partner is the father, one decision will have been made for you: you cannot have a *brit milah,** a religious circumcision, since according to Jewish law the child of a gentile woman is not Jewish (no matter what they did on *thirtysomething*). Such a child would have to be circumcised at eighteen if he chose to convert formally to a traditional form of Judaism. (An Orthodox ritual circumciser to whom we once said, "But that's quite a problem," sagely stroked his beard and replied, *"Kol hayyim bayot,"* "all of life is problems.") Or if your son had a non-religious circumcision in infancy, he would have to have a token drop of blood drawn, like any other male traditional convert.

Remember, too, that finding a cooperative rabbi will be difficult, although we have a few suggestions. There has been a course established in Los Angeles for Reform rabbis to learn to perform circumcisions, but this is still a medical procedure rather than one that fulfills the religious requirements of Jewish covenant. On the other side of the country, Rabbi Benjamin Rudavsky of Hingham, Massachusetts will circumcise the child of a mixed marriage, but there must be no Christian terms involved and the ceremony must take place on neutral ground. Or you could contact the Rabbinic Center for Research and Counseling in Westfield, New Jersey—they keep a resource list. If you live in the heartland, try Rabbi Dena Feingold of Kenosha, Wisconsin, but you should know that her practice has been banned in Wisconsin by the Council of Rabbis.

In addition to religious reasons, there have also been medical and social justifications for circumcision. The surgical procedure per se can be done by a doctor during the first few days of the baby's life. It was almost universally performed on American boys for a generation or so, a practice first justified on the grounds of personal hygiene, then later reinforced by evidence that wives of circumcised men suffered less from cervical cancer than wives of uncircumcised ones. The hygienic argument has been discredited, however, and the data on cervical cancer called into question, so the medical tide has turned against automatically circumcising. But a recent study suggests that circumcised males are less likely to contract AIDS from diseased partners.

Oi. Discuss it with your doctor.

If there is no medical reason and no religious one to circumcise a child, you may still, as we did, choose to have it done so that a boy who is growing up with—as the news commentators carefully put it—"a Jewish-sounding name" will not be subjected to embarrassing questions in locker rooms. And he will be able to espouse Judaism later in life without undergoing what would then be a much more painful and tricky procedure. This may strike you as a flimsy basis on which to do such a thing.

MARY HELÉNE

I'll tell you a secret: it now strikes me the same way. With our first boy, the emotional backlash when kindly Doctor Blumenthal removed the tiny foreskin on the third or fourth day of his life surprised me. Looking at that hitherto perfect, unblemished body, I felt like Moses' wife on a similar occasion: "A bridegroom of blood you are to me."

When the nurse disappointedly said, "Isn't there going to be a party or anything? I thought Jewish people made a big deal out

of this," my sense of futility was complete. If it wasn't the sort of "big deal" she was talking about, what was it? We knew the simple surgical procedure didn't constitute a covenantal bond, and we had serious questions about the medical justification, so why do it at all? That's a question you'll have to answer for yourself.

As for our second boy, we encountered legal difficulties getting him medically circumcised in Israel that probably won't be relevant to your situation. Suffice it to say that we recommend a Jewish father/non-Jewish mother planning to have a boy circumcised time the pregnancy so that the birth takes place in this country. (And don't believe Israelis who assure you there'll be no problem—they're just trying to be helpful, but they don't really know.) In some countries—England, for example—you may have difficulty getting a religious circumcision even if the mother is a convert to Judaism.

Then consider the case of Nelly Ballonoff, a California rabbi's wife who sought a legal judgment against the ritual circumciser of her son, contending that it is illegal for parents to have this act performed on an individual incompetent to consent to it. (She later dropped the suit, "because it created such a fuss.") Trudie London, a gentile married to a Jew, similarly sued hospital and doctor for battery and false imprisonment via circumcision.

An oddity evidently based on emotional rather than strictly religious grounds is that almost no Jewish circumcisions are being done with the benefit of local anesthesia, which is permissible according to Jewish law. Lisa Braver Moss, in a *Tikkun* article on the subject, speculated that "if we acknowledge infants' pain and discuss anesthesia, we may call the entire ritual into question." We open the subject of pain associated with circumcision because the non-Jewish spouse is almost certain to, especially if uncircumcised him (or, God forbid, her) self, and the Jew shouldn't feel too confident about glib assumptions that "newborns can't feel much."

If you are a non-Jewish father and the mother is Jewish (so that a religious circumcision is permissible), you may have this problem. No matter which of you is Jewish, though, the issue can be compounded by the sometimes passionate desire on the part of a Jewish parent to have a child ritually circumcised. Emotions may be involved which you will have trouble understanding.

A friend of ours, a gentile woman, was romantically involved with two men of Jewish background in succession. The first was an anti-religious Reichian, dead-set against traumatizing an infant with any barbaric practice like circumcision. This jibed with our friend's attitude and, she assumed, with that of all humane, non-religious people. She was aghast to learn, then, that the second man—with whom she was by then discussing marriage—felt very differently about circumcision. He was not a religious Jew, but for him circumcision was a basic factor of Jewish identity, and he couldn't imagine having a son, even one technically not Jewish because of a gentile mother, without having it done. Our friend and he were unable to resolve the dispute. And indeed, there may not be an answer when two such strong emotions oppose. As she says now, "I would have felt terrible no matter which way it went, if it had gotten that far."

If you do decide on—and can arrange—a circumcision, there will also be the question of parental roles in a circumcision ritual. Just as Ned felt uncomfortable at our childrens' baptisms, a Christian parent may feel out of place or excluded at a *bris.* If the mother is a gentile who has managed to find a *mohel* to circumcise her non-Jewish (according to Jewish law) child, she may be insulted to discover that the mother is neither expected nor encouraged to take part in the action— traditionally, she waits in another room. If it's the father who's not Jewish, he may be equally dismayed to learn that he is center-stage, technically required to perform the act. Not to worry, the *mohel* is a legitimate stand-in (who, by the way, will expect something in the neighborhood of $150 for his services; they require more expertise than baptism, so it's unfair to expect him to let you decide on amount of the "donation," as most priests will).

As for other relatives, the non-Jewish ones will have to be informed that, barring medical emergency, the child is circumcised on the eighth day of his life no matter what—the date can't be altered to suit travel or other social requirements. And if the *mohel* is of the old fashioned European tradition, you would be well advised to prepare non-Jews for the shock of not being counted among the required ten legitimate witnesses, and the women for being generally accorded secondary status.

Again, as with baptism, we raise the question: If you don't believe God has a unique covenantal relationship with the Jewish people which mandates this permanent fleshly sign (historically a marker for persecutors to identify victims by), and if you aren't comfortable with the traditional social trappings surrounding *brit milah,* and you don't think circumcision is medically called for, why do it?

Do discuss these matters carefully, in advance—if possible before you marry. Don't leave them to "work themselves out"; they won't.

Another practice which a Jewish mother may want to follow involves the symbolic redemption of a boy from Temple dedication as "first–fruits" if he has, in the quaint phrase, "opened the womb," i.e., is the first born and not delivered by caesarean section. Following the prescription in Numbers 18:15-16, a firstborn son is redeemed from the theoretical duty of Temple service (theoretical since there is no place of Jewish ritual sacrifice since the fall of the Second Temple in Jerusalem in 70 CE) by his father. On the thirty-first day of the baby's life, the father offers money—usually five silver dollars or five special Israeli shekels—to a *kohen,* or descendent of the ancient priestly caste. The *kohen* takes it with ritual blessings and gestures, indicating that the child is now free of the obligation. Typically, the ceremony is followed by a celebratory meal, after which the *kohen* often gifts the child with the money. Called *pidyon ha-ben* ("ransom of the son"), this colorful rite is another occasion for rejoicing that, not-so-coincidentally, calls into sharper focus the heightened response in traditional Judaism to the advent of a male child. A female corrolary called, logically enough, *pidyon ha-bat* ("ransom of the daughter") has been introduced in some feminist Orthodox circles but has yet to gain legitimacy in the larger community. Anyone non-religious enough to marry a gentile is probably not going to lose any sleep over missing this ritual. We recommend that mixed couples skip it.

But here you are with the most wonderful baby ever born. You want to shout it to the skies, announce it to the community, and even put in a word about it in heaven. Well, you can still do all that without having to meet the standards of established religions, you know. Remember when we said you could break a glass at your wedding even without a rabbi? Similarly, you can invite friends over for a fancy brunch, put the baby in the gown great-grandma embroidered, hand out yarmulkes* and/or rosaries and say a prayer together, ending with, "This baby's name is. . . ."

NAMING

Aha. Did you think the ending of the sentence "This baby's name is . . ." was going to be left up to you, without our putting our two cents in? Think again. Even if you decide to go with a nondenominational, nonsexist naming ceremony, you still might want to consider some religious strictures on the choice of that name.

First of all, some traditional Jews won't want to pick a name before the birth of the baby, or tell anybody what it is till the official naming. There's also a folk superstition against making any prior preparations, including having a baby shower or furnishing the nursery, before the child is safely born; check out the practice in your Jewish partner's family before you plan any surprise parties.

Among Christians, naming restrictions used to center on the actual name chosen. Though official attitudes have relaxed in this area as in so many others, you will still find priests and some Protestant ministers who expect a "Christian" name to be just that, a recogniz-able part of Christian tradition. While if you're not having the baby baptized you don't have to worry about actually choosing the name of a saint (supposed to serve as example and special patron to the child), you should be aware that names can have religious or philosophical implications. Our son-in-law, on converting to Judaism, dropped his middle name of Paul because it evoked too strongly the Christian saint who started as a Jew named Saul.

Or look at the monikers celebrities saddled their kids with in the wave of the 60s counterculture. Just remember, the son of David Carradine and Barbara Seagull née (and again) Hershey, whom they named Free, now calls himself Tom.

By the same token, you don't want to name a child with a Jewish parent something like Christian, or its variants Christopher and Christine. Unless you're Hispanic, you won't even have considered Jesus; in any case, don't—and leave Jude/Judas alone, too. (And you weren't really planning on Yehudi anyway, were you?) Nor will Conservative rabbis perform a *bris,* even when the parents have determined to raise the child Jewish, if the name chosen is an obtrusively Christian one. You might consider giving the family name of the Christian partner as a second name.

MARY HELÉNE
When our daughter was born, my sister told her boyfriend we were naming the baby Sarah Catherine . . . "with a 'C,'" she amplified.

"Are they trying to make her sound Catholic?" he asked.

"What do you mean"

"Well, it's some kind of saint or something, isn't it? And besides, won't that be awfully long—'Sarah Catherine-of-the-Sea Rosenbaum'?"

Maybe this misunderstanding had some bearing on the decision of my sister and her husband to name their own girls Tracy and Carrie, names absolutely without religious implications and nearly gender-neutral as well.

We chose the name Sarah Catherine simply because we liked it. William David's middle name is after a close friend who killed himself just before our son was born. His first name is also a memorial.

NED
For centuries, Jews did not name children after living relatives, partly out of courtesy and partly out of superstition. But since Napoleon's time, this practice has become acceptable in Reform circles.

My father named his first two sons with his own two names. On my mother's side, there'd been a William since . . . William the

Conqueror? Well, maybe not that far back. My older brother, my mother, and her father were William, Wilma, and William, all alive at the same time, and brother Bill has also named his first son William.

Luckily for us, both my mother Wilma and my mother-in-law Olga said, "For heaven's sake, don't name a baby girl after me!"

A Jewish partner's feelings on naming a child for a relative still living will usually depend on whether the family background is Ashkenazi*—north/eastern European—or Sephardi*—Mediterranean. Most American Jews are of Ashkenazi extraction. Ashkenazim with traditional opinions on the subject will want a) not to name baby after someone alive, even your favorite sibling, and b) to name baby after some deceased dear one. But if Grandpa's name was Otto and you really can't see yourself dandling a Little Baby Otto, don't panic. On the grounds that English names are merely approximations of true Hebrew names, American Jews frequently opt for one that has the same initial as that of the relative being honored. (Oscar? Octavian? Orville? Quick, what was Grandpa's middle name?)

Religious Jews have standards regarding the provenance of names as much as Christians do. When we lived in Israel, our William, then two years old, was often taken for a girl in our Orthodox neighborhood because he wore no sidelocks or yarmulke and his name was heard as "Miriam" with the Middle Eastern liquid "r." We asked a non-Orthodox Israeli friend what his Hebrew name would be. "Well, William in Yiddish would be Velvel, which means wolf, which in Hebrew is Ze'ev." So we had a pudgy pink wolf in the family while we were in Israel. We were satisfied, but an Hasidic acquaintance once reproached us for calling our child such a meaningless, secular thing; he ought to have a biblical Hebrew name.

Our second son, Ephraim Samuel, was born in Israel. Our Orthodox neighbors there were impressed by our choosing such a distinguished name. Our American relatives were not. His Jewish grandmother wailed to an uncle, "They named the baby Ezekiel!" and avoided, criticized, and altered the pronunciation of the name ever after. We poor innocents recognized, of course, its biblical character, but thought it had a sort of colonial American ring as well, to go with Sarah and Will—remember Revolutionary War General Ephraim Blaine? No, of course you don't, and neither does anyone else, we have found.

Our son himself, after years of battling with a name no one could pronounce or even understand when spelled out on a piece of paper, took the opportunity of a year on Sabbatical in Chicago to call himself Danny. (Ironically, his best friend that year was named Sheenu.) It is interesting that he chose to revert to his childhood nickname "Rafi" on returning home, even though we told him we would support a name change if he wanted one. Since college, he has at last grown into Ephraim.

Yet we have Jewish American friends with sons named Yaniv, Ilan, and Moshe. When asked whether they would rather have had more conventional names, the boys were blankly uncomprehending. "Like if we had called Ilan 'Alan,'" their mother explained. "Ick," shuddered the twelve-year-old in question. The difference seems to be that they live in a city, we in a small town . . . yet another consideration in naming a child.

If your background is WASP and your family expects your son to be, say, Brooke Walker Lowell III, you could be in trouble whether you're marrying a Catholic or a Jew, unless you were smart enough to buy this book. If you're baptising the baby, you'll have to stick a saint's name in there as well; the upper crust relatives may be pacified by the parallel to multi-monickered royalty. If the ceremony in question is a *bris,* choose a Hebrew name with the same initial as the hoity-toity family one. This Hebrew name will be used publicly at the child's bar/bat mitzvah, and afterwards whenever s/he's called to the Torah, and if your Uptown relatives are mellow enough to attend those events, they probably won't get bent out of shape by that—they might not even notice it, amidst all the other Hebrew.

Do you notice how our sub-topics—parents, children, family, culture, religion, ritual—keep spiraling back on each other? You'll find they do this in your life, too. So, curving right along. . . .

Chapter 8
Building a Family

Okay. The child is born, named or otherwise launched, and gurgling in the crib. Your next major problem now is choosing a college . . . or might be if you didn't have an interfaith marriage. Since you do, you now face choosing what sort of religious identification and upbringing your children will have.

WHAT ABOUT THE CHILDREN? MAKING A DECISION

Ann Landers reports on a Catholic mother/Jewish father couple who decided they would "let the children choose for themselves," presumably on reaching adulthood. Unfortunately, when it came time to make the choice, neither parent was keen on seeing their offspring choose the other's religion. Ann's conclusion, a simplistic but common one, is: "Bummer. Someone always ends up mad" in the children's-choice option.

We don't mean to make light of the problem; the passions that can be produced by these situations make *Family Feud* look like more than a TV show. For example, several years ago a Hungarian Catholic man who married a French Protestant was in the news—his relatives stabbed her in the hospital where she'd just given birth, they were so disapproving of the prospect that the child would have a religious choice.

Less spectacularly, Samuel Silver, whom you may remember from Chapter 2 as one of the few rabbis who'll perform a marriage between Jew and gentile, tells of one couple who broke up over this question, though they were "desperately in love." We're sure this situation is more common. Contrast this with Silver's observation that he'd never known a case of a couple breaking up over their parents.

We were once approached for counseling by a mixed-faith couple who had been engaged for nine years and married for two, and had never discussed whether they wanted children, much less what religion they would be raised in. (What did they talk about for eleven years?)

Rabbi Steven Carr Reuben notes that many children of interfaith marriage complain that they don't know much about either religion. We think this happens most often when the parents don't know and haven't bothered to educate themselves—or sometimes even to think through what they're doing.

That couple who came to see us had avoided the subject of children because, as it turned out, the Jewish male partner had his own agenda. While the Catholic woman said she would consent to her children having a religious choice, the man insisted that either his children would be raised as Jews or else he would not have children.

Our reluctant friends—and you, too—would do well to look beyond the religion of your children to the religion of their children.

According to Dr. Matti Gershenfeld, one in five American Jewish couples will have no children; the Catholic proportion may be lower. But once you've decided, if you want to raise them as Jews, be aware that, of children of intermarried couples polled in 1983, only 18 percent expect to marry a Jew; 19 percent a non-Jew; 73 percent don't expect a spouse's religion to make a difference. (Some of them must have answered twice.) Don't be too sanguine about your children carrying on a Jewish tradition they may see you as not having valued.

Here's another thing to consider: if you plan to let your children decide what religion/s they will be, if any, be sure you're not using the phrase as a cover for a copout. Indifference is not the same thing as tolerance. Do you really not care what faith they espouse? Then you may not, at bottom, be so hot on your own. In that case, say so—to yourself and to your children. Maintaining a facade of religious identification with nothing behind it will result, at best, in a crew of cheerful agnostics who won't bother with the charade when it comes to raising your grandchildren. At worst, you may so confuse and/or alienate them by the mixed signals you give that they go off in search of religious exotica and fall off the deep end into cultism.

As you cuddle your first baby, you probably won't think that in fifteen years a child of yours could be selling flowers on some urban street corner for a self-styled messiah. But it happens, often to adolescents who feel their parents—whether mixed faith or not— weren't straight with them about their real priorities. If you're a secularist, be one vigorously. Tell your children you think religion is a load of codswallop, then let them choose for themselves.

Their choices may surprise you—as yours may have surprised your parents. C. S. Lewis, the popular Christian writer and theologian, late in life married—as fans of *Shadowlands* will know—a Jewish convert to Christianity. His wife, Joy Davidman Gresham, wrote a terribly biased account of Judaism based on her own childhood experience, in a book that was meant as a paean to Christianity and its freeing her from the narrow restrictions of Jewish Orthodoxy. Her two sons grew up in Lewis' household through her long illness and death. One of those sons is now married to a Roman Catholic and has (according to his own autobiography) an oddly hostile attitude towards the agreement he made on marrying that the children should be raised Catholic. The other son moved to Israel and joined an extremely religious Jewish community that specializes in people rediscovering the joys of strict traditionalism.

Another fairly common pattern of religious rebellion and reintegration: Michael Lerner (not the editor of *Tikkun*, though people often confuse the two writers) is the son of a Jew and an Episcopalian. He now practices yoga, meditating before an altar with the likenesses of the Buddha and of Jesus along with a Star of David and a candle symbolizing "the light of truth in all spiritual traditions." A 1988 *New York Times* article quotes him as saying, "Yoga is a practice that is fundamentally ecumenical in that it does not involve any rejection of one's spiritual traditions. I can comfortably say I am both Jew and Christian." However, there was a "terrific feeling of loss in not being part of the unbroken linkages of familial religious traditions. I feel that loss very acutely." Lerner is a brilliant, well–integrated individual; not all the products of secular intermarriage end up with such a balance.

If one of you has stronger religious convictions than the other, or belongs to a more intransigent religious institution, you may feel it makes sense for the children to be raised in that parent's religion. This is not without its problems too, however. At the very least it will produce what we call "odd–person–out syndrome." That's when one parent and the children are of a different faith than the other parent.

Mary Hoffman, a columnist on "Jews by Choice," is the only (converted) Jew in a Christian family. She says the minority–religion person feels "conspicuous" at holidays. This is an important point, but not the most vital one. If one of you is a Catholic, your choice may have even more constraints put upon it.

MARY HELÉNE

When we were married in 1963, the Catholic Church demanded that, in order for me to remain in good standing in the church, I had, first of all, to be married by a priest without any question of there being participation by non-Catholic clergy. That has changed, so that now your problem, as we detailed in Chapter 3, is more likely to be difficulty in finding a rabbi who will agree to participate in a mixed marriage. Also, I had to sign The Papers along with Ned. We've already discussed the provision about birth control. Another, as we mentioned in the last chapter, was a promise to raise the children as Catholics.

"How is that defined in Canon Law*?" I asked the priest. "What exactly am I promising to do?"

"The exact components of a Catholic upbringing are not explicitly defined," he answered.

We explained that we planned to have the children baptized, then educate them in both religions while withholding later sacraments unless they, at maturity, chose to receive them.

He told us children were like little plants in a garden, who

needed to be weeded and tended and watered and guided to grow in the right direction. We were very young and didn't know much, but we knew that children were not espaliered peach trees. We'd heard the fathers' rueful song in the show *The Fantastiks*: "Plant a carrot, get a carrot, not a brussels sprout/ That's why I like vegetables, you know what you're about." Carrots yes, children no, we insisted.

My sister was raised with exactly the same mixture of traditional Catholicism, cosmopolitan experience, and healthy criticism that I was. I remain an actively practicing Catholic; she rejects religion in general and the Catholic Church in particular.

Ned, on the other hand, was raised almost entirely without religious indoctrination, as were his brothers. They remain lukewarm toward formal religion at best, while he has become a more traditionally observant Jew than has been seen in his family in four generations.

This sort of observation helped convince me that Ned's desire to raise our children without religious identities previously determined by us might not be as irresponsible as it seemed when he first broached it to me. I was nervous about it, but I felt I had to put my money where my mouth was—if religion is so great, precept and example should lead kids to it, without the need to push them.

Over the years, I've become more convinced that this is the wisest, though possibly most difficult, approach to the problem. Ned, although he agrees it's worked out well in our case, has shifted in the other direction in general and is now more conservative than I. (We've done quite a lot of that in thirty years of convincing each other in our arguments—in astronomy, when two planets seem to change places it's called "precessing.")

Father Shea, a generous-spirited man, said he thought what we wanted to do was a perfectly terrible idea, but if our sincere conviction was that this was the best way to assist our children into religious life, we could sign the document in good faith. Remember Eileen Ogintz from Chapter 1? Her husband Andy Yemma's priest threw them out of his office over the same issue. They started out with the "choice" option, but with one partner disaffected from his religion found that amounted to "nothing," and ended up choosing Judaism for their children. You'll have to check with your local diocese to see what your bishop requires.

NED
In the archdiocese of Chicago as recently as 1975, when my 62-year-old mother married a Catholic, she still had to sign such a

promise. I asked, "Mom, did you find out whether it's retroactive?"

We found the whole question of the religion of her future children hilarious in light of the hysterectomy she'd had twenty-eight years before. After all, if she could conceive in that condition we might have started our own religion.

Ceding the children to the more assertive religious side can produce a stable atmosphere of near-unanimity similar to that in an unmixed marriage. The problems arise if the excluded partner secretly (or not so secretly) feels ill-done-by or bullied, or if the children themselves question the decision. Also, be ready for the following litany of questions from your children:

"Mommy, why doesn't Daddy go to church with us ?. . ."

"Does that mean Daddy will go to hell? . . . "

"Then why do I have to go to church?"

If you're raising them in both religions, at least you can fall back on "Daddy has his own 'church,' that you go to on Fridays, remember?" Your answer to "Will Daddy/Mommy go to hell?" we presume, if you're marrying a non-Christian, will be a resounding "No, and don't let anyone tell you differently." If you're a Jew marrying a Christian, even if you believe in hell you weren't taught every non-Jew goes there—lucky you.

The trouble here from the Christian perspective is that if you teach your children salvation doesn't depend on faith in Christ, you'll undercut a major emotional underpinning of church membership. We taught our kids that "outside the Church there is no salvation" means that good deeds by good people make up part of what Christians call the Body of Christ, whether the people involved are aware of it or not. This interpretation may make Jews uneasy; perhaps they'd feel better thinking about it in light of the Jewish precept that "the righteous of all nations (i.e. religions) have a place in the World to Come." Just remember, at this writing, none of our kids is Christian.

There are no pat answers—don't be afraid to tell that to your children. And if they don't ask, raise the subject yourself: children have greater fears and doubts about these things than they often let on to.

And ask yourself whether you have thought about your feelings on the subject in the years to come. If you are a Jew, do you really face with equanimity the prospect that your grandchildren will be Christians? If you are a Christian, will you worry about the fate of your children's souls—or of your own, for allowing them to be raised as non-Christians? We find these questions having more meaning for us as our children mature than they did in the first flush of romance.

NED
Even so, I had reservations I didn't share. In 1962 I wrote, but never sent, a letter to Mary that we came across a few years ago. It said:

"You and I are close in ethics and morals as well as love. If my children were guaranteed to be Christians like you, I couldn't mind. (I hope the reverse is true.) But I'm not assured of this, and the thought that they should become 'ordinary' Christians is frightening; I'd much rather they were ordinary Jews.

I could take the gamble if I had some way of knowing what my relationship will be to them as adults, but I cannot get around the conclusion that they'll hold me in contempt for what I will have done with them. . . . I get the hideous feeling I'll be an outcast in my own home.

I love you Mary, and I'll marry you come Hell or high water, but it may be very tough on me. I'm chicken. I want to spread the guilt feelings, I guess.

Anyway, here are my devil-inspired inducements not to have to sign:
1. No birth control until it is absolutely necessary.
2. Free practice of religion by the two of us.
3. Exposure to both religions for children.
4. Marriage in the Church after the children are grown (or is that dishonest, or illegal or something?)
5. Whatever else we mutually agree on.
Mary, do you really want me to sign that damnable agreement? Is a 'scrap of paper' all that separates us? Aargh! "
What can I say? I was twenty-three and very much in love.
Talking to Father Shea, as we explained above, allayed my fears to the extent of putting this letter aside without showing it to her . . . but I do still have it after all these years. And I still blush to read it.

For clarification of some questions, and ammunition against some misconceptions, your kids may come up with, see Chapter 11, with its accompanying discussion lists.

CULTURE AGAIN: STICKING TO IT

As with the relationship between you as a couple, your relationship with your kids will also be affected by ethnic and cultural assumptions underlying the more cerebral religious decisions. From specifics like how you'll explain to a small circumcised boy why his uncircumcised father looks different to generalities like how you expect to pass on the values you have decided to transmit, raising children is fraught with pitfalls for the Jewish-Christian couple.

Is your culture a "guilt" one or a "shame" one, for instance? That is, do you tend to see rules as enforced by the outside society (common for Protestants) or internalized (more usual, though in subtly different ways, for Jews and Catholics)?

Joel Crohn has a lot to say on this issue, too. After reiterating the common (correct) perception that Jewish parents tend to be more protective of their children where Catholic ones are more directive and WASP ones tend to let them go their own way to a greater extent, he looks at some other insights from his study.

WASPs and Irish Catholics considered meals a matter of survival—they eat to live, and valued not wasting food, good manners, and quietness at the table. Jews and Italians worried that their children weren't eating enough; their meals, the sociologist says, are lively whether from warmth or anger. WASPs and Irish were also similar, he found, in worrying that their children are too dependent, where Jews and Italians worry that they'll be independent too soon. There was an interesting rift in this WASP-Irish set of parallels, though: while both had clear rules governing behavior, with little open conflict, the Irish parents tended to enforce rules in a more authoritarian way and saw their strictness as necessary not, as with the WASPs, so that the children would achieve higher goals, but simply to enforce standards of behavior—to make them "be good."

If you do make family unanimity your number one priority at the expense of your own faith, don't think your concession gives you a bargaining counter. When you two are deciding whether to take the job closer to your parents or your partner's parents, you can't say, "I gave in about religion, you owe me a big one."

It also doesn't necessarily solve all problems. Sharon Griest Ballen ran into a conflict with her Jewish husband Ed even though they'd agreed to raise their children as Jews. She took their three-year-old up to Communion with her at her Lutheran Church to be blessed. She saw this as a nice gesture; Ed saw it as a threatening one.

MARY HELÉNE
One of the things I admired most about my father, who was raised Lutheran, is the fact that when we were growing up he never made difficulties about the imbalance that the demands of the Catholic Church created. Having decided with my mother that a household with only one religion being practiced was the best sort for children, he stuck to it—through insensitive remarks from nuns, insults from priests, and generally being made to feel odd-man-out. Only he knew what sort of havoc this created in his own religious life (it wasn't the sort of thing he talked about), but he always encouraged my mother to remain active in hers, even at times when she felt the institutional church's treatment of them as a mixed couple was alienating.

The recessive-religion option in an interfaith marriage isn't as easy to carry off as it might seem at first glance; if it attracts you, remember my father biting his tongue and smiling politely all those years.

Another possibility is to find some scheme by which offspring may be divided up. One such Solomonic solution is actually practiced by no less a figure than Jewish Baron Guy de Rothschild and his Christian wife (whose name happens to be Marie Hélène!). In that family, the two daughters are Christians and the son is a Jew. This might be "fair" in the sense that each parent can now pass on a personal religious tradition, but it seems to us to have the potential of turning the family into an armed camp. Jesus' remark about a "house divided against itself" seems appropriate.

Baron de Rothschild is, by his own account, not a very religious Jew. Had he been so, he would have asked for the daughters for his "side," so that the legally Jewish line would continue. Obviously, there were other priorities at work here.

The Rothschild dynasty is probably not an apt example for those of us in less affluent circumstances—most of us don't have centuries'-old family reputations to worry about. But as Tevye says, "When you're rich, they think you really know."

Our own approach (it's not exactly a solution) has been for both parents to raise all children in both faiths, a variation on the "let them choose" option, but the difference is vital. This option—Rothschild please take note—begins to pay dividends right away. The first thing it does is require you to learn about your partner's religion, and maybe even your own, in a way you never dreamt of before.

NED

In a way, our trajectories were set on this path before our courses ever joined. Mary had begun a private study of Hebrew when she was in high school. I had no Jewish training and, consequently, she knew more about my religion than I did: for example, that Hebrew was classically written without vowels, or that some Jews believe in an afterlife featuring reward and punishment very much like the Christian one.

At the time, I was a graduate student in American History at the University of Chicago. Thanks largely to the interest sparked by my discussions with her, I switched to the Divinity School and began to pursue religion as a career. Thirteen short years and a lot of sweat later, I received the Ph.D. in Near Eastern and Judaic Studies from Brandeis.

MARY HELÉNE

I had been studying Hebrew with a friend in high school because I naively thought that after a year or so I would be able to read Scripture in the original.

By the time I met Ned, I had begun to realize it wouldn't be so simple. But I have kept my conviction that the only acceptable religious stance for an intelligent person is one that involves constant seeking and learning.

Eventually, I learned to speak and read Hebrew, and graduated from college with a major in Religion and a minor in Greek.

Ned tells me my only career option with that training is to stand on street corners and give good advice. Or write. . . .

EDUCATION: TENDING THE CROP

While you may not wish to carry your lust for religious knowledge to the extreme of getting a Ph.D. in it, it is important that you be able to answer your children's questions about both faiths. You can't fob them off with, "Oh, that's Mommy's religion," or "Go ask your father, I don't know anything about what they do." Doing this would help set up two conflicting authority points, and your child won't take too long to figure out that if there is a difference here, there may be differences elsewhere. And from there it's a short step to exploiting those differences, the more so if either parent has any sort of hidden agenda to win the children over. For instance, a counter-productive response to a child's request such as, "I don't mind, but you know your father would have a fit," is bad enough without building it on a base of "I don't believe it, but you know how gullible your father is."

When our Sarah was three she came home from Brandeis nursery school and asked, "Am I Jewish?" We answered, "Your father is a Jew, your mother is a Catholic; you are a little girl." That satisfied Sarah (though not for very long) and made us chuckle. But we still think it was a good answer. We were saying, in effect, that choosing a religion is something you ought to be grown up for.

We have since found that one of the advantages for children in a mixed marriage is that they begin to think about making a serious religious commitment at the age when most of their friends are finishing, with relief, their formal religious training. Whatever religious identity they develop is likely to be more mature and thought-through than one that's merely the continuation of a set of habits inculcated in childhood. Meanwhile, you can expect them to be more inquisitive than "normal" children.

MARY HELÉNE

When Sarah was four, I took her to see Maundy Thursday celebrations at the Holy Sepulchre in Jerusalem. The patriarch came out dressed in his high, pointed gold miter, and elaborate cope to wash the feet of some carefully selected beggars while tourists shoved and flashbulbs popped. I left, disgusted and thinking the jaunt had been a waste of time. But Sarah had picked something up from the experience after all.

"Who was the king?" she asked.

"The king?"

"That man in the crown."

"Oh. That wasn't a crown, it was a special kind of hat that bishops wear; the man was a bishop."

"What's a bishop?"

"A bishop is a particular kind of priest, and you know priests are people who are trying to serve Jesus in a special way."

"But I thought Jesus said we weren't supposed to worry about fancy clothes and things like that. Would Jesus like it if he saw that man wearing a gold hat?"

"Actually, I don't think He would."

"Well, why don't you tell the bishop so?"

"Uh . . . I will, if he ever asks for my opinion." (Sarah wasn't old enough yet to detect adult waffling.)

When Sarah was seven she said she wanted to be "a Jew like Daddy." Even if you're not a convinced Freudian, you'll notice that there is a period during which the child identifies fiercely with the parent of the opposite sex. During this phase, remarks like the above should be taken as signs of affection, not religious insight. Of a slightly different quality was her next religious "choice." A year or so later, she still identified with Daddy and so was worried that he'd be hurt when he found out she couldn't be Jewish—"because the Jews killed Jesus." This gem came to us courtesy of a neighboring optometrist's child.

MARY HELÉNE

I had the dubious pleasure of dealing with this one. Since Sarah was an unusually articulate (not to come right out and unblushingly say brilliant) child, I felt she could absorb a pretty heavy dose of combined history, theology, and sociology. I tried to give her a picture of how this pernicious distortion arose, became popular, and has been perpetuated in much of Western society.

She absorbed it all, and seemed not only relieved but interested. The point here is that I think the explanation would not have had the same weight coming from Ned—as the one whose co-religionists were the accused—as it did from me as a member of the group that has been accusers.

Similarly, Ned has been known to defend Catholic beliefs and practices in the sense of ridding the children of misconceptions and oversimplifications about, say, the purposes and practices of the Inquisition or the doctrine of papal infallibility.

Incidentally, I was rather relieved to find that my seven–year–old daughter had not, in fact, completely grasped the larger picture of civilizations and their interactions over the centuries. That night at bedtime she asked, "Why didn't Moses help Jesus get away from Hitler?"

For better or worse, you will not be the only educating influence on your child, in religion as in any other area. What they hear from the neighbors and on TV will enter into their perceptions, and you will have to deal with that positive or negative input. In addition, there are religious schools. Most Christian and some Jewish ones will accept anyone who wants to come, but you cannot abdicate your own responsibility. If you feel unable to educate your child, you'll just have to educate yourself first.

NED
As an adolescent, I attended Presbyterian Sunday school for six years, basically out of curiosity. We were not members of any synagogue, so none would accept me into an education program. (My father rejected the idea of formal membership, and the local Reform congregation would not allow my mother to join alone—which she wanted to do precisely so my brothers and I could get some religious training.)

I had friends who went to the Presbyterian classes, and the layman who ran it was, and remains, a role model for me. Only when the rest of the class began to train for confirmation did I start to feel uncomfortable—I was after knowledge, not religious commitment. After six years I began to seek a Jewish milieu.

Some Reform Jewish congregations will now take children of mixed marriages, even where it is the father who is the Jew rather than the mother (i.e. the children are not considered "born" Jewish by traditional standards), if there is already a commitment to raise those children as Jews. This newly formulated principle—patrilineal descent*—has aroused bitter controversy within the Jewish community, of which the outcome is not yet clear.

We didn't feel that we could require our children to go to either Catholic or Jewish religious school and still maintain our ideal of religious equality within the family. Sending them to both seemed to us—and, emphatically, to them—an unfair burden to saddle them with. So we encouraged them to join either, both, or some other at any time and insisted only that a year-long commitment had to be made;

they were not allowed to go to the first two sessions and then drop out. This policy engendered inevitable arguments, but we stuck to our guns and each of our kids has had time in each, sometimes going to both in the same year. The youngest even enrolled in two nonsectarian Protestant Bible study groups to which a girlfriend belonged.

We parents attend each others' services on important religious holidays, important dates in our own lives (such as our anniversary) and when there's a special speaker or interesting liturgy. The children were expected to go along on these occasions, but they were not required to attend ordinary weekly services. At certain periods, they went with one or other of us because they were feeling closer to that parent, or because they were drawn by that religious atmosphere. As they grew older, they would sometimes voluntarily attend just out of a feeling that it had been a long time since they'd done it, and they ought to. We don't present this as an ideal situation: it completely skirts the issue of a moral obligation to attend regular worship; it tends to result in neglect of community-oriented prayer as opposed to private petitions; and it fails to instill the simple habit of attendance that often keeps people connected to religion even during spiritually arid periods. If we had it to do over again, we might impose more structure on their experience.

The only real religious requirement we put on the children was that they celebrate religious holidays only if they celebrated them religiously. That is, we would have a tree and presents along with Christmas mass, not without it. Similarly, they could stay home from school on Rosh Hashanah so long as they went to services. Of course, we encouraged them to attend worship at other times, and they did, and do, as the spirit moves them.

We had an odd advantage in living in a town lacking a large, formally constituted Jewish population. Our eclectic little Jewish community created no obstacles to our sending our kids to Hebrew school. Your community may not offer such an option, especially if you're not willing to make Jewish education the sole commitment for them.

Even if you are willing to make that choice, emotional backlash may be just around the corner: will a non-Jewish parent be allowed to sit on the *bimah,* the raised platform at the front of the synagogue, the way other parents do at their child's bar/bat mitzvah? You might want to check this out before joining.

You will also need to coach non-Jewish relatives on correct behavior. At Geraldo Rivera's bar mitzvah, the men on the Puerto Rican side of his family, in a touching desire to show respect at a solemn moment, took their yarmulkes off and clapped them to their hearts when the Torah was brought out!

The converse, of course, is true of Christian affiliation. If the congregation is very large, the fact that your children don't, or don't always, attend with you may not attract much attention—but you may have trouble with Sunday School teachers not attuned to your special needs. If the church is small, you may or may not find sympathetic ministers, teachers, or fellow congregants. And will the non-Christian parent be made to feel left out if your child becomes a communicant or confirmand? In some parishes, for instance, First Communion is not the old-style group event but one involving only the parents and new communicant going up to the altar alone, before the rest of the congregation, to receive the Eucharist. This is a great improvement over the former impersonal ceremony—unless one of the parents is left sitting in the pew, uncomfortably conspicuous.

We were lucky enough to have a pastor willing to attend our daughter's bat mitzvah himself; we hope you encounter such tolerance in your clergy.

Let's not pretend there are no problems as long as everyone's tolerant, though. Our kids never felt completely part of either religious group. We've said we don't believe unthinking group identity is the best way to cultivate a religious life, but there's no question that being one of the group is more comfortable than being an oddball. Perhaps it's only because we're inveterate oddballs in other ways that we continue to feel the advantages to them of broad exposure and freedom of choice outweigh the disadvantages. And we may have made a virtue of necessity: children have an unerring knack for picking out the misfits, even when the parents have tried to camouflage them by deciding on an identity for them; at least our approach didn't force our children to try to conceal their differences from the others, since that would have been impossible.

REAPING THE FRUITS

More important than outside institutional religion in our family has been what we do at home. And of the things we do at home, one practice in particular has shaped our lives as a family and brought us tremendous emotional and spiritual rewards.

The breakthrough for us occurred one Friday in November of 1966.

NED
It was dark when I came home from Brandeis and as I drove past our apartment I glanced up and saw there were two lighted candles in the living room window. I pulled the car into the garage and bounded up to the second floor.

Accosting Mary, I inquired, "What are the candles for?" She replied, "I thought it was about time we started [celebrating Sabbath]."

Tears came to my eyes then and they still do—every time I remember that day. I didn't know what prayers to say; I had to ask a classmate to write out the simplest blessings for wine and bread. Now, twenty-five years later, our Sabbath observance has grown a lot.

For one thing, I make the bread—hallah, the special Sabbath bread made with honey and eggs. Mary taught me how to make it following a recipe from a local Temple sisterhood cookbook.

The prayers have grown, too. Mary recites the blessing on the candles separating light from darkness and the Sabbath from the six days of work. After the wine and bread are blessed I say the blessings for our children, whether they're present or not, and "The Lord bless you and keep you . . ." for any guest at the table. We conclude with Proverbs 31:10-21, the "woman of valor," a paean of praise to the wife for her domestic AND outside-the-home enterprises.

We find it convenient to follow the Orthodox practice of delaying dinner until after Friday night services. That way whoever is going— Ned and whichever of the kids wants to—isn't rushed.

After dinner we retire to the living room where if it's cool Ned lights a fire (a very UNorthodox practice, to be sure) and we read aloud. For the past twenty–plus years we've read the same book every Friday. It's J. R. R. Tolkien's *Lord of the Rings,* and its three volumes take us from September 22, when we start, to some time in March or April, about the time when it gets too warm to want a fire.

Tolkien was a Roman Catholic and his book is a deeply religious work, despite the fact that God is not directly mentioned once in it. As we stare into the fire we meditate on its timeless themes: duty, friendship, regard for Nature. As it happens, our "woman of valor" also possesses a first-class reading voice, so it's a pleasure to listen to her as well.

The point is this: we've found a family Sabbath activity that all of us enjoy and urge everyone, but especially mixed couples, to do the same. It doesn't have to be reading aloud; a family board game, card game (if your traditions countenance it), sing-along, or charades would do just as well. And before you dismiss the idea as hopelessly outdated let us tell you that it comes with an added bonus.

In 1976 when we were living in a cramped, friction-producing apartment in Jerusalem, Mary had each of us write down what five things we liked best and what five things we liked least about our life as a family. What we all decided we didn't like amounted to a varied selection of household chores, but each of us put Sabbath as we observe it Number One on our "like" list. At the time Sarah was twelve, Will ten, and Ephraim seven. Until the three of them grew up and went to college they kept this enthusiasm and in fact still look forward to it when they come home as adults. Often enough our kids would decline to go out with friends on Friday so that they could stay home for the reading. Their friends, as well as ours, came to listen so that most Fridays we had a living room full of people.

In an age where everyone laments the breakdown of "values," we cannot emphasize enough how important this activity has been for the creation of close family ties amongst us.

It's important, of course, for families to do something together on a regular basis, but even more than bowling, picnics, or going to the movies, an activity that has a religious content is likely to produce less sweat but more warmth. Having a religious mandate also helps maintain the practice against conflicting claims on your time. We do not go anywhere that requires driving nor attend secular activities on Friday night—period. Our friends are not offended by our refusal of invitations (though our families are sometimes exasperated, a different set of problems) because it's a religious practice; it would be harder to turn them down without offense if it were simply "something we do."

You may have noticed that ours is a Friday night activity. If you think this is unfair, that it's subtly prejudicial in favor of Judaism, you may wish to plan yours for Saturday or Sunday. We also have a custom of Ned's making pancakes on Sunday morning for returning church-goers, for example.

An activity that wasn't tied to religion in our case but could be adapted to be: we frequently had Saturday night "sing-alongs" with friends—people would drop by with guitars and mandolins or whatever and we'd all, including the kids and regardless of talent, suggest and join in songs.

At first we would spend most of the night on 60s-style protest songs (though toward midnight, after a few beers or glasses of hard cider, Mary Heléne would get into Johnny Mathis oldies, to the jeers of the others). Then the little ones started chiming in with Pete Seeger children's favorites, or songs they'd learned in school. In their teens, they enjoyed leaving us gaping with such contemporary classics as "Whip It," but we soon learned to counter with our own classics— "Bee-Bop-a-Loo-La (She's My Baby)" for instance. Eventually we found common ground in James Taylor and Stan Rogers. Now that we have a son-in-law who's an accomplished musician, those evenings are more fun than ever, though less frequent than when we all lived under the same roof.

The important thing is to dedicate a time whenever the family can agree to put aside the other activities that members would otherwise engage in. If the two of you can do this before you have children, the kids will find it only natural to do it with you. And with any luck they'll

120

continue to do it throughout their high school years. (By the way, you may well feel you can't spare the two full days and three evenings— sunset Friday through midnight Sunday—for sabbath pursuits, however pleasant. We try to reserve the time from Friday evening till Sunday afternoon, which at least gives us an evening to get weekend chores done. Of course, if your day off is a weekday, take a tip from the Mormons and make that "family" day.)

We've also tried to concretize religion in other areas of family life. During Advent and Lent we had grab-bags each morning; slips of paper with extra activities each of us (including Ned) would undertake that day toward acknowledging the season, such as buying a toy for a poor child, going on a jaunt with another family member, whatever. This helped keep the upcoming holiday, whether Christmas or Easter, in perspective as part of a year-round religious cycle rather than a sudden blow-out.

This heterogeneous approach has had varying results.

By the time Sarah was thirteen she'd changed flags again (at least once), partly as a result of her noticing that the Creed said at mass characterizes Jesus as having "died for us men." "Didn't he die for me, too?" she asked the priest (not our current one). "Well, 'men' includes women," was the feeble response. She also began to notice that she often heard her father's religion criticised in her mother's church; she never heard the reverse. Finally, in addition to disaffection with the institutional church, she felt she simply didn't believe in the divinity of Jesus.

In short, she wanted to be a Jew. She asked to have a Bat Mitzvah and we refused. We thought she was too young to make such a grave decision. Finally she said, "Okay, it doesn't matter whether you let me have a Bat Mitzvah or not; I consider myself a Jewish person and intend to live as one." At that point we knew she was ready.

SARAH
They're so proud of that story. It's not that it isn't true, it is, and I meant it—but I also knew that's what they wanted to hear. They were concerned that my enthusiasm might stem from less than honorable desires: the excitement of a big party in my honor, the happiness of pleasing Daddy, or the burning quest for adult status. No doubt I felt all these things, but my declaration of faith convinced them of the very real inner conviction which was the heart of my decision.

She had made the important point. Still, we asked her to go to one more year of high school CCD to find out what the Catholic kids her age were learning and we required her to write several papers for us on religious subjects like the nature of Islam, the philosophical differences between Christianity and Judaism, and the causes and results of the Reformation.

Finally we began to feel we were being excessively rationalistic. There often is a flush of religious enthusiasm in early adolescence, and it seemed coldhearted and unnecessary to act as though faith were only a matter of intellectual assent without any emotional content.

So at the age of fourteen Sarah became Bat Mitzvah. Her calling to the Torah for the first time was the first such ceremony for a girl in the history of our town. It was a great social success and seems to have launched her very satisfactorily into Judaism.

After that she started going into nearby Harrisburg to study with a rabbi there preparatory to formal conversion. Many readers will recognize that this progression is the reverse of the usual. But the rabbi had said, "If she feels the desire to make the public commitment now, before the private one, let her do it. Everything else in your family is mixed up, this might as well be, too."

As Freud pointed out, no two children are born into the same family. The advent of each changes the dynamic that existed before. Our boys are both much older now than Sarah was when she converted and neither has declared any sort of formal affiliation. Perhaps Big Sister's enthusiasm influenced them not to follow her path. But they haven't been opposed to religious investigations either.

We described in Chapter 1 our older son's brief romance with Unitarianism. After that he lay doggo for several years and then surprised us by asking for a Star of David to wear around his neck when he went off to college. That seemed to mean more that he embraces a cultural and ethnic Jewish identity than that he'd made a religious statement. But let him put his position in his own words.

WILL

As I sat down to describe my religious and cultural standpoint, I realized that, now that I'm out on my own, I am no longer as actively involved in my parents' religious practices as I was as a child . . . What do I celebrate? The best I could come up with was the winter solstice and Franz Kafka's birthday.

I think that, being raised by devout mixed-faith parents, the foundation of my religious education was the observation that my two pillars of reference supported different temples. This has undermined any sense of urgency I might have had about my own choice of faith and its validity.

Although I'm far from through with religion on an academic and intellectual level, I don't foresee any organized commitment for myself in the near future.

Since our younger boy was born in Israel, he is an Israeli citizen, though not legally a Jew. This perhaps reflects the mixture of identities and interests he has developed since. He was taken aback, for instance, to realize that he couldn't take an aliyah (Torah reading) at the service the day of his sister's wedding, while his completely secular but nominally Jewish uncles could. But he, too, can speak for himself.

EPHRAIM
I am, at the moment, a confirmed agnostic. I have a close friend who is a devout Fundamentalist Christian, which has led to many an interesting discussion, both with her and her parents. I am interested in religion, but depressed by the seemingly endless competition for souls and the ever-present attitude that "We see the True Universe as it Actually Is." I, personally, do see some "organized commitment" in the future; religion is too important to go about having half-clear notions of a "could be" God, but for now I don't have any idea as to which one.

It is not pleasant for committed parents to watch their children playing religious roulette. We hope they will make serious, informed choices, and we're pretty sure we'll be able to respect and accept those choices, even should we not be thrilled with them. There are dangers and pitfalls in the path we have chosen for them, not least of which is that they might react from overexposure and withdraw from the whole question.

Still and all, the one disaster everyone warned us of at the beginning has not happened. They do not seem to be confused, rootless, insecure, or lacking in a sense of identity. Our conclusion is that those all-important qualities of self-esteem, security, and stability do not necessarily flow from having a built-in, unquestioned religious identity. And we are glad that we didn't settle for a contentless aesthetic experience for them, simply picking the most "beautiful" aspects of either religion and ignoring anything controversial or uncomfortable. We retain our original conviction that each individual has a soul to "make," and must make it, ultimately, alone.

Raising these children has been a constant series of extra challenges because of our shared and unshared religious ideals. The result seems to be well worth the effort. We hope and trust God is as pleased with them as we are.

TIES THAT UNBIND

This section will contain more questions than answers because it concerns subjects we haven't directly experienced. However, it seems useful, even necessary, to discuss these painful matters by sharing experiences recorded by others and our own theoretical approach; forewarned is forearmed. Besides, divorce and death in mixed marriages may leave complicated, ugly situations you simply have to know about. If you still think interfaith marriage is for you, we expect these considerations won't deter you. And working out compromises between the two of you won't guarantee that the rest of your families will be happy. But to avoid considering them at all because you hope they are only dim, distant, or distasteful possibilities would be shortsighted.

Even if you are determinedly non–religious and think death just means going to the great recycling plant in the ground, don't feel you can skip this chapter. Your feelings toward death will probably change as you age, bury your parents, and watch the obituary pages claim childhood friends.

Death, of course, doesn't always wait for old age and infirmity; divorce almost never does. And, as we're sure you've already been told, it happens more frequently in mixed marriages than in unmixed ones.

Chapter 9
Divorce: Severing the Cord

We've seen studies of divorce rates among interfaith couples that purport to show they are twice as high as those in the general population. We have seen others claiming there is no difference in frequency at all. (The discrepancy is partly due to differences in tabulating second or subsequent marriages—some count them into the same pot, others treat them as a separate category.) Since we are not statisticians, we'll set that question aside. Suffice it to say that divorce is common in our society, and religious differences are often a contributing factor.

CHANGING THE PATTERN: YOUR RELATIONSHIP

Do you and your partner have the same ideas about divorce?

Jewish tradition, though often limited by sexism in practice, in theory has held quite liberal guidelines for divorce from ancient times. The American Jewish Congress (Conservative) has recently reiterated, for instance, that incompatibility can be sufficient grounds. The Reform divorce rate is twice that of the Orthodox, while the Conservative rate is relative to the level of religious observance and commitment to Jewish identity of the individual—the more traditional, the less likely the person is to divorce. Presuming that people who intermarry are less bound by traditional strictures, this may mean that Conservatives who do intermarry are more likely to divorce than Conservatives who do not. Some commentators have speculated that the Jewish extended family system acts as a deterrent to divorce. On the down side, it might in fact encourage divorce in intermarriage, as a way of expelling the "foreign body."

In contrast, the Roman Catholic, Anglican, and some Protestant churches either do not allow divorce at all in the sense of the individuals then being free to remarry, or restrict it to extreme situations. (Or, in Europe, turn a blind eye if it involves royalty.)

For Roman Catholics, annulment is more likely than it once was, because of its greater availability since Vatican II. This situation is not without its own anomalies, however.

For one thing, an annulment—whether because the couple had no intention of procreating, or were too young to be responsible, or were under pressure from parents, or for any of the reasons the church will now contemplate declaring one—means that the marriage never in fact took place, was invalid. Such a declaration can make children of the marriage angry, hurt, and resentful; they're being told, after all, that they were born out of wedlock, "illegitimate" in the church's eyes.

For another thing, since annulment has to do with the nature of the administration of the sacrament of marriage rather than with the individuals involved, it can be done without the consent of one party. How does that grab you, Jewish partner?

If you're planning to marry under any sort of Catholic auspices, you will have to attend a series of premarital counseling sessions; use one of them to discuss the ramifications of annulment with the priest and your prospective spouse.

Some Protestant communities are experimenting with divorce rituals, religious ceremonies that mark the end of a relationship "in the sight of God and of this company," as the beginning of it was marked by the marriage ceremony. The United Church of Christ is the only one that actually has such a service in its prayer book, though the Evangelical Lutheran Church in America, the United Methodist Church, and the Presbyterian Church of the USA have used such services. These controversial programs are in their infancy, and will undoubtedly evolve in the next few years, but it's hard to imagine there being a theological bar to including mixed couples in them. The problem is more likely to be emotional, and mirror those surrounding the wedding: will you resent being sundered under someone else's religious auspices?

Yet it's possible the alienation you might then feel could be just the emotional tie-breaker you need to feel the relationship is over. How about co-officiating clergy, with the minister on one side and the rabbi on the other, each welcoming back the wanderers to their separate folds? Well, maybe not.

From the Jewish side, there is the complication that a religious divorce is a separate process from the civil variety—rather like the Catholic Church's annulment procedures. It's conceivable that a Jewish woman divorced from a non-Jew, and therefore not in possession of a Jewish religious divorce—a *gett**—would have difficulty getting remarried to an observant Jew. And a Jewish woman abandoned by her husband (an *aguna*) may not ever be considered free to remarry in Jewish law. Lest you think this archaic holdover has no repercussions today, there were an estimated 15,000 such women in New York State in 1987.

There were also ten times that number whose Jewish ex-husbands were refusing them religious divorces. An attempt by the New York legislature to require a Jewish husband to provide a *gett* in order to obtain a civil divorce, and a similar New Jersey statute, have been challenged by the ACLU as a violation of separation of church and state. An example: Myron Margulies was taken to court by his former wife, Selma, because he refused her a religious divorce even after he had remarried and had new children. The Conservative Jewish Theological Seminary maintained that the marriage was automatically annulled because he refused to appear before the appeals board . . . what a mess.

The ceremony of presenting the *gett* can be an emotionally satisfying rite of passage. However, the practice is rife with abuses and endemically sexist: a man whose wife has refused to accept a *gett* is free to go on and contract a valid Jewish marriage, while a woman similarly placed is not. Still, the New York Board of Rabbis (which includes Reform) in 1987 urged divorcing Jews to obtain a *gett* to avoid future complications.

If you're one of those rare gentile women who's married an Orthodox Jew without converting, you will have particularly serious problems in a divorce; religious courts may fight your getting custody of children or being paid alimony, and you may even have to pay a cash settlement to get disentangled. Even if your husband is non-observant but from an Orthodox background, he may still be influenced by this sort of bias.

In America, courts established by religious groups to deal with internal matters have no official legal status, but the decisions of secular courts are often influenced by them as determiners of "community standards." In 1991 the New Jersey Supreme Court upheld a decision made by a Jewish religious court over the synagogue's attempt at appeal.

In Israel, where religious and secular courts are more entangled, Jewish men have been known to go to jail rather than give up these traditional "rights"; in the case of Susan and Boaz Avitzur, for instance, his lawyer argued that he was justified in refusing a *gett* to his former wife because he "doesn't want his son calling another man 'Daddy'." A ray of hope can be seen in a recent Israeli decision: a religious court removed the children of a man living with a non-Jew, but the high court reversed the decision, saying religion was not a sufficient reason. Thanks a lot, guys.

This may all seem very distant to you, but remember, it can also affect you if you're marrying a Jew who was in a previous Jewish marriage. This is a common situation—maybe more common than the interfaith first marriage. As Susan Weidman Schneider puts it, "divorce leads to intermarriage" even more than the converse.

If you're getting married in a Jewish ceremony, you have a tool for dealing with possible future problems.

One of the ways in which traditional Judaism shows a pragmatic approach to life's entanglements is in the institution of the *ketuba,* a document signed and witnessed before marriage in which both parties agree to property settlements in case of divorce. But in a recent Canadian case, a rabbinical court determined that the gentile ex-wife of a ritual slaughterer was not entitled to continued support as provided for in their *ketuba,* since his income derived exclusively from the Jewish community—he was told to settle a lump sum on her instead.

Many rabbinical organizations are looking at the *ketuba* as a device for making the possible *gett* more equitable; Rabbi Louis M. Tuchman of Peoria makes this part of his marriage counseling. And this practice can ease dealings with remarriage and the blended family. Though the traditional *ketuba* stipulates only financial obligations, a mixed couple could enlarge its scope to encompass how children of either or both will be raised, especially if a first marriage involved two people of the same faith.

The only comparable practice in gentile society used to be in the case of the very rich, who needed prenuptial agreements to protect great fortunes from dissolution. Today, some sort of contract or blueprint for administration of material goods has become more common. You should be able to discuss these questions without becoming defensive or disillusioned. A prenuptial agreement will at least lead you to talk about raising your kids.

One thing you can be pretty sure of is that in the event of divorce the difference between your two backgrounds, even if one of you has converted, will loom much larger than it does now.

After all we've just said, you probably feel like Jordan's King Hussein during the Gulf War: caught between Iraq and a hard place. Or you may feel that the best approach is to shun religion altogether. In our view, this cure is worse than the disease, as the problems won't go away and you'll be losing something you may later miss.

MY PLACE, YOUR PLACE . . . THEIR PLACE?

Remember the decisions you made, or avoided making, about children's religious identity? Now comes the rub. If you signed a paper promising to raise your children Catholic, for instance, there are courts that will favor the Catholic spouse when it comes to determining custody. Even if you as a non-Catholic are granted custody, you may be required to honor the childraising agreement.

The converse situation has been in the news lately, too. In the Simms-Boeke case, the Catholic mother was given custody of the couple's two daughters, but the Jewish father was given "spiritual custody." The mother had converted to Judaism during the marriage, and the couple had agreed to raise the children as Jews. After the divorce, she reverted to her original religion and married a Catholic. The court's decision means, in practice, that the girls' Catholic mother was compelled to raise them as Jews and might not, by Court order, take them to church with her except at Christmas and Easter. (She had begun taking them every morning.) It is worth noting here that the judge's decision was based partly on the testimony of sociologist Egon Mayer that raising children in two religions is harmful to their emotional and psychological development, a consideration that evidently outweighed the mother's claim that the father was not in fact particularly religious and was using the issue as a power play.

It is interesting to us that on a televised talk show, Boeke (the mother) spoke of "lifestyle" and Simms (the father) of "confusion," while the lawyers focused on "the role of the court." No one mentioned particular religious values, Jewish law, or Christian belief. Perhaps symbolic of this distancing is the fact that the legal issue being argued is the mother's constitutional right to free association, surely something of a stretch in a situation that more directly would seem to relate to freedom of religion. (She did speak of her religious convictions in a September 1989 *Redbook* piece—this seems to have been another "timebomb" case, where neither parent was conscious of any attachment to their cradle religions, but rediscovered these bonds later in adulthood.)

But suppose you have an amicable divorce, and wish to hold by the terms you settled on at the beginning of the marriage. If you have agreed to raise your children as Jews, could you as the non-Jewish partner provide your children the support they would need to continue as they'd begun? If your children are of the same gender as you, you may not even know what their ritual requirements are, since you would presumably have only the example of your spouse to go by. But even if you have learned them, will you feel up to carrying them out?

And the situation can be just as tricky if you've agreed to raise them as Christians though you're not one. Could you teach them things you simply don't believe? Could you participate with other parents in religious-school events, holiday pageants, conferring of the sacraments and so forth, to say nothing of shlepping in the Christmas tree? What about where denomination and morality meet, as when you are called on to answer questions about birth control or abortion?

And, once again, you'll run into the family/culture questions. What will the children's relationship be to the grandparents in whose religion they are not being raised? Can the tendency of family members to blame an interfaith couple's problems on their religious difference turn vitriolic when the love connection is severed?

It probably won't help much for us to remind you that the ones who really suffer in these situations are the children, but we'll say it anyway. Try to focus on what's best for them, rather than on whose religion "wins."

There can be few less edifying models for children than the sight of parents using religion as a weapon to bludgeon each other. A child who's made to feel that attendance at church or synagogue represents another blow in the divorce war is liable to invoke a plague on both your houses, with good reason. These days, neither Judaism nor Christianity goes in for conversions by physical force; conversions by emotional bullying aren't any more valuable.

Consider which of you the children will spend most of their time with, and which tradition they have been most involved with, and don't forget to talk to them about it—not to make them take sides, but to get an idea of their own feelings on the matter. If it's not your religion they end up with, feel free to share your beliefs with them if you can do it with the same dispassion that you would with, say, a neighbor's child. But don't use spiritual blackmail ("If you're not a Christian you'll go to hell") or emotional usury ("If you're not a Jew you'll break my heart"). Remember, you and your ex-spouse got them into this mess; don't make it any harder on them than necessary.

Chapter 10
Death: The Third Strand of the Cord

DYING : UNRAVELING THE SKEIN

Here's another scenario.

What if you're a Jew married to a Catholic and you have small children whom you have agreed to raise as Catholics . . . and your spouse dies? A recent decision by the Michigan Supreme Court declared such contracts were not legally binding so, in Michigan anyway, you don't have to stick to the bargain. But what if you want to? Either way, the problems would be enormous.

If you choose not to continue the agreement, you would probably damage relations with your Catholic in-laws, your children's relationship with one set of grandparents. You might also have a hard time explaining to a child who is old enough to notice why it was no longer necessary (or possible) to be a Catholic. And if the child is old enough to disagree?

But what if you did want to continue the child's raising as a Catholic? Can you really do a convincing, good-faith job of educating someone in beliefs you don't share? What sort of role model will you be?

If the question is whether you, now a single parent, raise the children as Protestants or Jews, you won't have the technical burden of having made the formal vow many diocese still demand, but you may well feel a moral commitment. And the children will be just as confused.

You can see that, in an interfaith marriage there are more questions than answers even when the marriage ends at the hand of nature rather than the state. Many of them go to the heart of your relationship with each other.

These days, the process of dying involves at least as many ethical and religious considerations as any other aspect of living: decisions have to be made about what treatments can be suspended, when to suspend them, and what to do next.

Generally, Jewish teaching allows the removal of a life-support system, but not out-and-out euthanasia—involving for instance the injection of a poison. Traditional Judaism holds that action to hasten death is against the law, but decrees no penalty for it. Here, for once, Judaism and Catholicism are more or less agreed. Protestant thinking runs the usual gamut from conservative to liberal, but the Episcopalians at least have been experimenting with a religious ceremony in which patient (if possible) and family mark the decision to terminate "heroic" medical measures—"turning off the machines." This is great . . . if everyone involved is Episcopalian, or whatever.

The increasingly popular practice of signing a "living will" stipulating that you don't want heroic measures used to keep you breathing under any circumstances, is a sound one even where it isn't legally binding. But if your spouse has religious objections to your position on this question, you both have some talking to do—before either one of you is in that condition.

Or you may want to retrieve some benefit from your loved one's death by agreeing to organ transplants. But Rabbi David Feldman says an observant Jew is limited to the donation of one organ; a Jewish body may not be dismantled for spare parts. Presuming that your Jewish partner is incapable of participating in the decision, how will you make it?

Catholic teaching approves organ donation as long as the donor is not deprived of life by the removal of the organ(s).

These are practical matters. There is also the spiritual dimension of death and dying to be considered.

A Catholic who is dying will probably want to receive the sacrament now known as Anointing of the Sick (formerly Extreme Unction). This involves a ritual of symbolic cleansing along with Reconciliation (Confession) if the sufferer can participate or even can be supposed to participate on some level (in a coma, for instance). For non-Catholic family gathered at the bedside, this can be a very alien and distancing procedure.

For Jews, the custom of the "ethical will" is very ancient—it's mentioned in connection with Joseph in the Bible. It means the practice of gathering loved ones and passing on to them injunctions and advice based on a lifetime's experience tempered by the wisdom rendered by the imminence of death. In one particularly famous ethical will, the dying patriarch urged his son to take better care of his personal library! Christians shouldn't have any problem with this; it might be a good practice to emulate.

What if it's your child who's dying? How could your interfaith marriage divide you then?

The Rabbinical Council of America takes the stand that terminating the lives of brain-dead infants for the purpose of using their organs should be barred by law, but such use is permissible if the infant dies without medical intervention. The Catholic position is similar, with the extra sensitivity that the prohibition of abortion brings to questions of "harvesting" fetal tissue.

At the time of death itself, there are immediate decisions to be made that can have religious components, particularly in the questions of autopsy or embalming. Orthodox Jews don't allow either—the body is to be buried as quickly and as simply as possible, ideally in just a shroud, without even a coffin. You won't be able to do that in most states, but New York and Illinois have braved the funeral industry's lobbies to uphold the right of observant Jews to prompt burials, although that may mean cemetery work on Sunday. Would any of that disturb you, Christian partner?

Naturally, if the deceased isn't embalmed, there can't be a wake. (As Curly sings to Judd Frye in *Oklahoma*, ". . . it's summer and we're running out of ice"). Many Jews, in any case, find the practice of displaying the corpse disrespectful to the deceased and a bit revolting. There is no Christian mandate for such practices as the open-casket wake or the elaborate burial vault, but they are widespread customs. The wake, of course, was designed to insure that the person was really dead and would not be buried alive—as Poe feared he would be, and as the Blessed Thomas á Kempis evidently was. Today, with modern far-flung families, it also serves as something to do while waiting for out-of-towners to make their travel arrangements and arrive in time for the funeral.

The "viewing," where family and friends gather around the displayed corpse and engage in sharing and mourning rituals that can range from drinking and telling fond or raucous anecdotes about the deceased to saying a group rosary, is familiar in many Catholic circles. Even Protestant funerals, though often more restrained as a matter of cultural style, frequently have the option of a visitation period, when mourners are comforted by a last sight of the dead person looking peaceful and at rest. How will you, Jewish partner, react to all this?

Closed-coffin wakes have become more the norm in modern times; a problem here can be the increased focus on the receptacle itself.

In our society the highly burnished coffin made of fine wood or metal, the vault of concrete lining in the grave, or the impressive mausoleum setting, can owe more to the practices of undertakers in presenting these options than to any decision either the deceased or the survivors might have made in tranquil reflection. However, Christians—lacking Judaism's demand for strict simplicity—can undoubtedly find comfort in feeling that they have "done their best," that the funeral appointments were "beautiful" and an expression of love. But will you, Jewish partner, feel resentful at possibly being pressed by Christian relatives to an expense you consider both unnecessary and unseemly?

NED

Shopping for a coffin for my mother, z"l,* I saw one model for $27,000, a copper creation made without welds—completely sealable. Mom would have been outraged had we bought it. She only agreed to be buried, not cremated, at the insistence of my older brother. (She didn't have the common Jewish antipathy toward cremation—more on that below.)

I also saw the coffin I want for myself: a plain, poplar box with a raised Magen David* on the lid: $750. Not only am I unwilling to pour money into a hole, so to speak, but I have come greatly to respect the Jewish idea that my body should become one with the earth from which God formed it as quickly as possible.

MARY HELÉNE

Some Franciscans in Washington, D.C. offer a plain pine coffin (for $130 last time I looked) that is fitted out for temporary use as either a wine cabinet or a coffee table. I keep saying that's the one for me (the wine cabinet style; the coffee table does seem a bit macabre).

Naturally, neither one of us has done a thing about arranging these sensible choices. Do as we say, not as we do.

Then there is the burial service. Will you feel cut off sitting in a church next to your spouse's coffin covered with a pall that has a cross embroidered on it? Or listening to the priest or minister quote Jesus: "I am the Resurrection and the Life; whosoever believeth in Me will live and not die"?

Protestant services usually include such New Testament readings, along with prayers, a sermon, and psalms—all likely to be heavily Christian in content or intention. Catholic funerals follow fairly formal guidelines, and may or may not include a mass. Will these things make you feel left out, Jewish partner?

On the other hand, how will you, Christian partner, feel at a Jewish service that may be conducted partly or wholly in Hebrew? Will you understand what's being said? Will you feel shunted aside when some other family member says *kaddish,** because Jewish law forbids your saying it? (*Kaddish* is the mourning prayer a Jew says at the death of a parent, a child, a sibling, or a spouse.) Most American Jews don't believe in an afterlife—will this upset you? Will you be able to explain it to your children?

Jewish funeral services are short compared to Christian ones— usually about twenty minutes long. But the post-funeral mourning rites are much longer and more structured than modern non-Jewish practice, as we'll explain in the following section.

133

DEATH AND BURIAL: MY PLACE OR YOURS ... AGAIN

Burial in general is of central importance to the Jewish community. Burial societies are referred to in the Bible, and down to modern times the first responsibility a congregation has is to procure a cemetery. For Catholics, too, an identifiably Catholic burial ground has historically been a major priority.

Nancy Kleiman is a former Roman Catholic nun who married a Jew and converted to Judaism. Anticipating the inevitable, relatives on both sides got together and bought a joint plot in a secular cemetery so that no one would be excluded. An equitable solution, but one that implicitly denies the importance of being buried in ground consecrated to a particular faith. It used to be that Catholics and Jews who were buried in ground not consecrated by their respective religious authorities felt convinced—whatever the theology involved—that they would not go to Heaven.

Some Reform or Jewish-burial-society cemeteries allow the burial of a non-Jew, but not the use of Christian symbols on the grave. It is also more common now for Christian cemeteries to allow the burial of a Jew. Catholic ecclesiastical practice in this matter falls under the heading "pastoral care"—if the priest feels (as these days he nearly always does) that it's important for the survivors that a Catholic and a non-Catholic be buried in the same place, whether under Catholic auspices or some other religion's, he may allow it. But check it out with your particular clergy to make sure they're willing to accommodate your wishes. Don't leave it till you (and your in-laws) are in the throes of grief.

The questions are: will you both be comfortable in a secular or other-faith cemetery? More to the point, will your relatives be comfortable with you there, separated from the family plot? Do you care? Does your spouse? Will your family? Your in-laws? What about your children? If you don't examine these questions now, you'll inevitably leave messy situations later for your families to fight about.

It is always wise for people to make arrangements for their own deaths in advance, or at least to make their wishes known. In the case of an interfaith marriage, it is vital. If nothing else, you will protect your spouse from inevitable criticism or smoldering resentment from your side of the family if you make these decisions yourselves and before the fact.

Aside from the location, there is the manner of burial to be considered.

Before burial, Jewish parents, siblings, spouse, and children of the deceased are considered *onen,* exempt from any religious obligation except the burial of the loved one. Will this cause complications for the non-Jewish family? Samantha Lindblad, a convert to Judaism and columnist for the Jewish press, commented that when her Mormon father died, she was struck by how many decisions had to be made by the family. If Lindblad's father had been Jewish the family would have been able to concentrate on their principal function as mourners—getting on with the grieving process—rather than wrestling with practical issues about funeral arrangements, which are largely dictated by Jewish law. The Jewish rituals are simpler, since there are fewer options. This established structure will be an alien concept to the non-Jew, accustomed to choosing among a range of possibilities suited to personal taste.

At the grave site, religious Jewish mourners will resist the sanitized modern practice of leaving the grave before the coffin is lowered. Tradition requires (and psychology may encourage) the emotional finality of hearing and seeing the earth enclose the deceased. For the Orthodox, the obligation of burying the dead is not completed until the grave is filled. You will need to discuss this with your funeral director—and with each other.

Let's return to the religious and practical aspects of cremation. There are sections of Judaism and of Christianity that forbid or discourage it. Among Jews, only the Reform and Reconstructionist allow it as an automatic option; other Jewish traditions only approve it in times of disaster, such as war or plague. But you may be surprised when your liberal Jewish spouse opposes cremation, as many Jews do, because burning was the Nazis' preferred method of disposing of Jewish corpses.

The Catholic Church doesn't forbid the practice any more—the guidelines for approval in most diocese are so flexible as to be only symbolic and boil down to the caveat "unless it is chosen for reasons which are contrary to Christian teaching"—but many Catholics still don't like the idea. Other people just don't like the idea of being buried and left to decay in a cold, damp hole: something else to discuss.

There are also emotional components to these decisions. If one of you wants to be cremated and the other breaks out in hives at the notion, try to empathize—how would you feel if your spouse belonged to a Native American religion that favored exposing the dead to the wind and the birds? This may seem a farfetched analogy . . . if you've never argued with someone who feels strongly either way about cremation.

If we could tell you how to solve every problem and soothe every grief associated with death, we'd have solved the problem of suffering itself.

Then we might know what to say to people who lose a child.

What if, God forbid, your child dies? Whose methods will you choose for discharging your last parental responsibility? Will you be able to find ways to mourn together, or will you be sundered in this most poignant of losses? If a child and a parent die together, some Reform communities allow them to be buried in the same grave. Does your religious group? Do you want that? Does your spouse?

What about mourning rituals?

Observant Jews may not wear black, nor even black armbands, as a sign of mourning (although many, particularly the men, don black garments for everyday wear). Many Jews "sit *shiva*,"* spend the seven days following a death with slit lapel ribbons symbolic of torn garments, non-leather shoes, shrouded mirrors, low backless stools. No parties are attended (or, of course, given) for at least thirty days. In the most traditional households, it is incorrect for visitors to proffer such ordinary greetings as "How are you?" or to bring food. In such Orthodox settings, guests will not speak to the mourner until spoken to. A ceremonial meal of hard-boiled eggs will be provided for the family by friends following the burial, but condolence callers will not be fed or otherwise entertained. Even if your spouse does not expect or want this atmosphere, will your Jewish in-laws? In the words of Rabbi Felix Carlebach, "If the *shiva* is treated as a social occasion by visitors, it can be a terrible irritant to those who are sitting on low chairs."

And if it's the Christian who has died, Jewish partner, will you feel able to cope with the converse? Will you view with equanimity the Knights of Columbus* saying the rosary in your living room, or be up to explaining to your next door neighbor that even under these circumstances you don't want a seafood casserole in your kitchen?

Will you, in short, be able to carry out the wishes of a deceased spouse even if they contradict your own beliefs? And if you do, will you feel estranged at the very end of your lives together?

Irving A. Weingart, Rabbi Emeritus of Chicago's Central Synagogue, as chaplain of the local American Legion post once conducted the funeral of a fellow Legionnaire . . . who had been Roman Catholic. The deceased had no family of his own, and his former comrades had made the decision. Rabbi Weingart based his action on the Talmudic dictum, "It is incumbent upon us as Jews to bury the dead of non-Jews along with the Jewish dead for the sake of goodwill and peace." The Catholic Church prefers to have its deceased members buried according to Catholic rites, though there would be no church objection to supplementing them with a non-Catholic Legion chaplain's offices. Still, there is no Catholic dogma indicating that the dead person's soul is in any way imperilled by not having a Catholic funeral; Catholic burial is a preference, not a commandment.

136

Had the dead man left family behind, things might not have gone so smoothly.

Sometimes the death of a parent can trigger intermarriage "time bombs." Eileen Ogintz started on the path that culminated in the decision to raise her children as Jews when her father died, and the historical burden he had felt for carrying on the tradition seemed transferred to her shoulders.

Or, sometimes a parent's death can bring a mixed family closer together. According to an article in the March 1990 *U. S. Catholic* by Robert Reilly, Catholic Ruth Mendelson "sat *shiva* for [her Jewish mother-in-law] for three *[sic]* days." Her husband's eldest brother asked her why. "'Because I love your father,'" was her perceptive answer. Biblical Ruth hardly put it any better.

In other ways, a parent's death can serve as a sort of trial run for the problems you'll face when it's one of the two of you.

NED

We buried Mary Heléne's father in Arlington National Cemetery on December 15. The ceremony was most impressive; sixty Navy personnel participated. I hadn't seen a cortege like that since JFK was buried. I joked to my mother-in-law, "If I'd known Ralph was so important, I'd have been more respectful." I think she knows me well enough to understand that I meant the remark as a compliment.

On the 16th we drove to Massachusetts to do an intermarriage workshop at a Jewish convention. Mary's mother came with us. We— in consultation with the widow—had considered canceling out of respect to the dead, but decided it would be better to distract her with the change of scene. Now, you already know I'm from a family that hasn't "sat shiva" since we came to America, but many of the observant havurah (fellowship) members were taken aback by our presence the day after a family burial.

MARY HELÉNE

For my part, I only began to think in a personal way about the possibility that Ned or I might feel left out of things when the other dies at my father's funeral, even though that wasn't the first death we had to deal with.

When Ned's mother died, the ceremony was—fully in accord with her wishes—so secular in tone that we both felt religiously distanced. We were separated from her, but not from each other.

We felt more comfortable at the memorial service that preceded my father's burial. Though it didn't take place in a church, a local priest said a few words. (My father, you'll remember, was a Lutheran; the priest was there for my mother's sake.)

My nonreligious sister, however, was alienated by the theistic elements in the priest's comments and in the prayers that were said. From her point of view, such secular elements as Ned's salutes to Dad's military record and a friend's reminiscences of his social good works were meaningful whereas use of, as she sardonically put it, "The 'G' word" was not. In this, she (a non-religious gentile) and her non-religious husband (whose family background is Jewish) are at one. Their troubles in this situation are likely to come from relatives' wishes or practical complications rather than from their own feelings.

For Ned and me, it won't be so simple. Since we're probably not going to spend the rest of our lives where we're living now, it seems premature actually to make funeral arrangements. I'm tempted to let it ride and hope we manage to die together (I hope that anyway). Of course, that's not fair to our kids.

The choice seems to be either a secular cemetery or one of us being buried under the auspices of the other's religion, and we don't want either. Could we find adjoining Catholic and Jewish cemeteries with adjacent empty plots? It would probably be easier to start our own ecumenical cemetery.

Fortunately, we've bought a farm in Kentucky, where family burial plots on private property are still legal. We expect to retire there, and our children hope to live on the place as well. There's a sugar maple on a ridge—we've told the kids that when we feel our last weakness coming on, we'll crawl to the foot of that tree and expire, and they can just dig a pit and tip us in. Our daughter, who has inherited our habit of joking about even the most serious things, riposted, "Why don't you crawl up there <u>before</u> your last weakness and dig the pit yourself?"

This is all fun, but if our decease doesn't follow the neat plan we've laid out, the underlying problem will remain.

We think in principle that the wishes of the deceased should be paramount. In practice, however, if a survivor is going to be unbearably distressed by that decision, an accommodation may have to be made. On the other hand, this may cause resentment among other family members who feel things should have been done as the departed wanted—especially if the objecting survivor is of a different religion from the rest of the family.

We really have no solutions to suggest. Please try to be sensitive to each others' pain, and recognize that unreasonable anger or excessive anxiety over details can be symptoms of grief rather than attempts to sunder the family.

And if your partner's death rituals make you feel cut off and

138

alienated, remember that you can still seek solace in your own religion. However, take into account the following.

CARRYING ON ALONE: MENDING THE TEAR

What will your post-loss religious support be?

If you take comfort from the Jewish practice of saying the mourner's *kaddish* for the eleven months after a death, followed by the setting of the tombstone as a symbolic closure of the intense grieving period, will your sorrow be compounded by not being able to follow these procedures for a non-Jewish spouse? You could still follow the popular practice of financing a grove of trees in Israel as a memorial, or the personal one of lighting a *yahrzeit* (memorial) candle, but would these gestures have been meaningful to your loved one?

What if your way of dealing with death is having masses said for the soul of the departed? Although this can be done for a non-Catholic, what are the theological and emotional implications of your doing it for someone you loved who rejected this approach and denied its efficacy? And a mass for a non-Christian will not be publicly announced as such to the community of believers; will this leave you feeling like a second-class citizen in your own church?

Still, for some who feel cut off and alienated from their partner's death rituals, rites from their own religion, arranged quietly, may prove a solace. The best advice we can give you on all this is to remember Ruth Mendelson adapting her own traditions of mourning the dead to reflect her love for the living.

Another good example was presented by a cousin of Mary Heléne's who's a Jehovah's Witness. Her religion forbade her to attend her grandmother's funeral, but she did extra duty at the long and tiring wake/visitation, and later busied herself at the house getting things ready for the funeral-goers' return. She also—a very important point—wrote a letter afterwards to other family members, explaining why she'd felt unable to be at the church itself. This went far toward soothing ruffled feelings and clearing up misunderstandings.

At the funeral—it was our beloved "Nonni" who had died—Ned felt able to participate, even in a Catholic Church, to the extent of reading the "Woman of Valor" passage from Proverbs in her honor.

This doesn't answer all the questions, but we told you at the beginning we had more questions than answers.

Chapter 11
Spiritual Life and Intellectual Life

SPIRITUAL LIFE: WHAT'S IT ALL ABOUT?

If we haven't succeeded in causing you to reconsider, let's imagine you've actually done it. You've "married out." Both sets of parents have been successfully held at bay; you don't have children, or they're in bed, or grown up; your spouse is out bowling, there's nothing good on TV, your library card has expired, you're not sleepy and there ain't no place you're goin' to.

If you are at all religious, now is the hour when you might begin to reexamine the ultimate relationship, your spiritual state.

For the believer, the relationship to God never completely disappears, however strained it may become. Just as you can't put the final responsibility for your own happiness on your spouse, but must find it within yourself, so you can't dump the burden of your soul's salvation—to use a Christian term—on anyone else.

Stripped to its bare bones, this is where your mixed marriage will stand or fall. If you feel you can discharge your duties according to the dictates of your conscience and live the life you believe God intends for you without feeling your partner is an obstacle or a threat, you can have a successful marriage. If you can do those things while feeling your partner is an inspiration and a help, you can have a blessed marriage.

And it is possible. But it's going to be complicated.

MARY HELÉNE

The first time I saw *Fiddler on the Roof,* I cried continuously through the scenes where the youngest daughter, Chava, runs away to marry the Russian peasant, and her father, in agony, tells her she is no longer his child.

The gentile friend I was with patted my arm consolingly. "I know," she sympathized, "how can people reject each other like that?"

"No," I sobbed, "she shouldn't have done it . . . she betrayed her people!"

My friend was amused in a horrified sort of way. "Have you considered seeing a therapist?" she said. "I think you have some real contradictions stewing around in what passes for your brain."

How right she was. But they're my neuroses, and I'm sticking to 'em. And I still cry when Tevye sends Chava away; I tell myself

it's because I'm so sensitive to other people's points of view.

As William H. Willimon put it in the *Christian Century,* "Most people think that the toughest part of marriage is deciding whom we ought to marry, making the right choice. We say we are deciding whether or not we are in love with this person, whether we are emotionally attached. The church traditionally has cared less about our emotional attachments. The church cares about whether or not we are people who are capable of sustaining the kind of commitment that makes love possible. The pastor leading a marriage ceremony does not ask, 'John, do you love Susan?' The pastor asks, 'John, will you love Susan?'"

Today, Jewish concepts of marriage also assume a commitment to persevere in love.

But combining this mandate with differing religious duties is what this book has been all about. Just as marital life doesn't take place solely between two people in a bedroom, but develops in and through society, spiritual life isn't something that takes place only within the individual, in private. It depends on public, communal worship for sustenance. In an interfaith marriage both a Christian and a Jew trying to develop their inner spiritual lives can find themselves blocked or sidetracked by difficulties in expressing their religious convictions outwardly.

On the practical level, you'll have to decide whether you can or should join a synagogue or a church, separately or together. Most churches on the continuum between Fundamentalism and Orthodoxy/Catholicism will accept members whose spouses are of another denomination or faith. In Judaism (did you really have to ask?) the situation is more complicated.

According to a 1988 survey of 200 members of the Conservative Rabbinical Assembly: in 46 of the congregations, a non-Jewish partner would be allowed to lead an English reading, while in 22, the non-Jewish partner could open the ark. Intermarried couples could be affiliated in virtually all the synagogues of the respondents. One hundred three of the responding rabbis listed intermarried couples as singles on synagogue records; 76 recorded such membership as family membership. (Some listed them as singles unless or until they had children, then as families.) One hundred seventy–six of the 200 would permit a Jewish spouse to join the synagogue when the couple remains unresolved as to how to raise their children. One hundred fifty–one would cooperate with a family in which some, but not all, of the children will be raised Jewish. When the mother is not Jewish, 40 would permit a baby-naming ceremony prior to *mikvah* (conversion ritual). One hundred twenty–two would require the commitment of the non-Jewish parent to help raise a child Jewish prior to the rabbi's participating in a *brit* or a baby–naming.

The interfaith connection may also make the individuals feel more conscious of their backgrounds than they would have been if married to people like themselves. Ned's mother, after her first two Jewish husbands died, married a Catholic—and decided to have a Passover celebration for the first time in her life. We think that Ned's increasing religiosity was a factor. True to her classical Reform upbringing, however, she served bread and ham at the dinner. The only Jewish prayer she could remember was the *Sh'ma,* which in fact is not part of the Passover seder, but the point is that she felt some need to make a religious statement she had never experienced when married to Jews.

Joel Crohn found mixed couples who discussed religion formed stronger bonds than those who didn't, as long as they didn't start blaming all their differences on the religious one. He doesn't discuss what we have found, that such discussions and comparisons can help you sort out your own religious life and force you to face the question of what really matters to you. Rabbi Steven Carr Reuben finds this borne out in the couples he's counseled: there's tension where differences are denied, strength where they're discussed.

This is one of the reasons we think the exclusion of people who've married out is wrongheaded. Synagogues and churches who refuse to discuss intermarriage and make the intermarried into invisible people produce the very result they fear—they drive people away and eliminate the chance of rapprochement.

But even in cases where you are welcomed into a church or synagogue, how comfortable will the person whose faith it is not be?

The religious atmosphere in a traditional synagogue may be jarring to the Christian. The custom of praying at each individual's pace, with only occasional unison chanting, along with the practice of people taking "breaks" to chat with each other or wander outside, may seem irreverent to someone used to the American style of lockstep communal worship. Even back in Colonial times, Benjamin Rush of Philadelphia commented unfavorably on the fact that Jews he observed "freely conversed" during services. (Catholics raised in the European tradition will be less shocked.) Christians may miss the sense of solemnity and the attempt at mystical union they're used to in churches. There's a good reason for this—Jewish community worship emphasizes group affirmation of shared belief and focus on the Torah as the center of spiritual life. Even in the more "charismatic" Hasidic movement, the mystical state is arrived at through ecstatic dance and song; Pentacostalist Christians will relate more easily than "high" church members. They will also be more comfortable with the high degree of lay participation in the service; those used to having the priest or minister conduct almost everything will be less so.

NED

I've seldom felt more moved in a synagogue than I did in the one we went to in the Ghetto of Venice.

The Ghetto of Venice: it's a name to conjure by. The very word "ghetto" is thought to come from the name Geto Nuovo, "new iron foundry," the name of the moated area on which in 1515 the Republic of Venice enclosed the first Jewish community to be formally sequestered from their fellow citizens. Ghettos had a twofold purpose. They protected Jews—who were an important source of tax revenue for church and state—from unruly mobs at Easter, Christmas, or whenever else some rabble-rouser might choose to raise the cry of "Death to the Christ-killers." And they isolated the Jews from Christians, helping to protect the latter from the "insidious wiles" of the former. Except for prostitutes: these women were also directed to live in the Jewish ghetto, a fine insult to both parties.

We entered the Venice ghetto through its secondary entrance, almost a tunnel under the dilapidated seven- and eight-storey buildings that ring the central square. Adding to the sense of enclosure was the fact that all five of the synagogues inside, including the two still in use, are kept locked. When we were finally admitted for the Friday evening service, we found a man and a woman inside who collected all our gear and cameras before body-searching each one of us—with apologies on their side and understanding on ours for their need to prevent terrorist infiltration.

The sanctuary was on the second floor of the 16th century building. The interior was dark, richly polished wood, showing that the community at one time had been comparatively prosperous. The rabbi led opening prayers from a canopied reader's platform on the western wall, across from the family of a boy becoming Bar Mitzvah that Sabbath. The boy, in a Middle Eastern Hebrew accent purer than the Italianate inflections of his brother and father, read the passage that comes between mincha and ma'ariv with such feeling that I knew he understood it. I cried quietly and the others in the congregation politely refrained from coming to my aid. I'm sure the Italians had seen it before: an American Jew crying at services in the Ghetto of Venice.

Am Yisroel hai, the people of Israel live.

MARY HELÉNE

My mother and I, behind the partition separating the women from the men (and from the Ark, not so incidentally), were having a somewhat different experience.

The other women, in a practice I've seen often among females in Orthodox synagogues, were chatting, complimenting the Bar Mitzvah boy's mother on her dress, and occasionally peering through the wooden lattice screening our potentially lascivious selves from view to catch a glimpse of their menfolk. (The balcony we would traditionally have been relegated to is no longer structurally sound.) Mom and I struggled to find our places in the Hebrew-Italian prayer book, with limited success.

Not the most inspiring religious experience of my life, though I enjoyed the historical resonances.

The point to these differing experiences of the same event is that your own religious grounding will color your response to your partner's. Don't assume that you're both feeling the same thing at a service; it's a good idea always to talk about them afterwards. (Not in a spirit of recrimination! Remember the discussion technique where you always use "I" sentences rather than "you" ones: not "You have lousy religious services," but "I felt lousy during that service.")

The opposite is also true. A Jew accustomed to the relaxed atmosphere of an old-fashioned synagogue may feel ill at ease passively sitting in a church service conducted with an emphasis on unison prayer and song and American notions of decorum. But a Reform Jew will not have this problem; many Reform temples deliberately adapted to Protestant-American formats in their services as part of the principle of social assimilation where possible. But even the most Reform Jew is liable to be turned off by Christian kneeling— Jews just don't; the more traditional bend the knee and bow forward at certain moments during prayer (the most traditional do it constantly as they pray)—a movement called *davening* that has become synonymous with prayer itself. And the rabbi may prostrate him or herself flat on the floor before the Ark at one point in the Yom Kippur service. Kneeling is not in the Jewish style.

NED
But friendliness to strangers is. I've never had a grimmer religious experience than the time we, again with my mother-in-law, went to mass in the North German city of Bremen.

I wore a yarmulke—it was the only way I could bear going into a German church at all. But I don't think that explains the coldness we met: it seemed to flow naturally from the stones of the frigid architecture.

People wouldn't move aside to let us into pews; though there were no communal hymnals, none of them offered to share theirs with us; no one spoke to us or even made eye contact on the way out.

Ninety percent of the congregation were gray-haired women and

144

neither Mary Heléne nor I could keep from wondering what they had been doing in 1939.

Our South-German friend Felix says it wouldn't have been like that in his Bavaria. "We don't like them," he says of northerners. "Not nice people." I didn't feel I could remind him that the famous Passion play in the Bavarian town of Oberammergau had, and according to some Jewish observers still has, a decidedly antisemitic flavor.

But don't think you have to go to Europe to hear priests or ministers mouthing ignorant insults toward Jews; and if you intend to leave the building as a protest, warn your partner in advance.

MARY HELÉNE
When Ned asked whether I'd be uncomfortable if he wore a yarmulke to mass, I told him I'd be proud.

I was not proud of the atmosphere in that church; this was one case where we had the same reaction to a religious experience.

The fact remains that you're likely to have some unpleasant experiences in the services of another faith; be prepared for them, and be prepared to be supportive when your partner has them.

There is also a difference in style between traditional Catholic prayer and some charismatic, usually Protestant, spontaneous approaches to prayer. If one of you is a Conservative Jew and the other a traditional Catholic, you'll both be comfortable with formal, memorized or read prayer. If either of you is something else, you may feel peculiar.

MARY HELÉNE
Not that "feeling peculiar" can't be the introduction to a learning experience. When we lived in Israel, I went to the cathedral, St. Saviour's, in the Old City for mass. I knew it would be said in Arabic, but I wasn't prepared to hear the priest invoking "Allah." When I thought about it, I realized I'd been silly—of course he said the Arabic word for God, what else would he say? But I felt as though I'd stumbled into someone else's service.

That Christmas I brought a Jewish friend with me to his first mass—in a chapel in a hostel. There, I was prepared for the Arabic—but not for the fact that, because the Catholic priest was of the Melkite sect, the liturgy was Eastern Rite, and Greek to me. My friend kept whispering, "What's happening now?" and I kept hissing back, "I don't know!" much to his disillusionment.

For two years I attended a supposedly English mass at the

British scholarly institute called Terra Sancta. I say "supposedly" because the congregation typically consisted of ten French nuns, two Arab janitors, and me, together with visiting dignitaries such as African ambassadors in full regalia; the student-priests usually said the mass in Latin.

Eventually I discovered Isaiah House, of Project Hope, a movement led by Sister Marie Goldstein in which Catholics attempt to live like Israeli citizens, rather than as a foreign body uncomfortably lodged in the country's throat. That mass is in Hebrew; people *daven* in the Jewish style rather than kneeling. I've never felt more Christian.

All these experiences have helped me break free of social and cultural stereotypes when it comes to even my own faith.

Another major difference Jews and Christians have on the religious level is in the focus of worship and practice. Judaism in modern times (the two thousand or so years since the fall of the Temple and the end of ritual sacrifice) has used the synagogue as a tool for religious life, and an adjunct to learning; the core of Jewish life is found in the home. Christianity has tended to see the church as the primary spiritual focus, and home-based devotion as the supplement. As a mixed couple, you will be able to explore your partner's pattern of religious emphasis with an intimacy more difficult for people without an inside connection. This can enrich your own spiritual life immeasurably. If your prayer life, for instance, has been almost exclusively conducted in church or in private, you will find Jewish family prayer rituals open up a whole new world of experience for you. If your religious activity has been confined to—and maybe confined by—your family, you may find new freedom in strictly personal individual prayer or in univocal community worship.

And, in helping each other toward a fuller spiritual life, you never know when divine lightning is going to strike.

We both had a fine experience in, of all places, St. Mark's Basilica in Venice. We didn't expect it—our visit to the building as tourists had been marred not only by the usual gaping, flashbulb-popping throng but by the commercialism we saw in the fact that the fabled *Pala d'oro*, the incredible bejeweled and enameled gold altarpiece, was turned to face the wall and could only be seen after paying a fee. But St. Mark's was the only church in Venice with mass at a convenient time that Sunday, so we went through the unwontedly peaceful, early-morning piazza and followed a neatly dressed woman walking confidently to a side entrance.

Within, most of the forty or fifty worshippers had already gathered. We sidled into the narrow space between rows of folding chairs with lethally narrow wooden kneelers attached to their backs. A verger hurried down the aisle to hand us missalettes.

Music started—a "canned" pre-recorded hymn—but mercifully stopped. Coughs and rustles chased the dying notes around the vaults. Priest and attendants entered from the side without ceremony and approached the post-Vatican II altar table down by the chancel steps.

And then we saw it.

Behind the celebrant, the high altar was transformed. The *Pala d'oro* was turned around, facing, us, its radiance filling the church. Four feet high and six wide, its intricacies of color and form, its triumphant harmonies of skill and precious substance, stunned the eye. And for those who've come to San Marco to pray rather than to gawk, its magnificence is free to fill the heart with awe. In a moment we were swept back into the 16th century when the doges ruled the Republic and this church rivalled any in Christendom.

MARY HELÉNE

For Mom and me, the mass itself took on an added splendor, becoming the living focus of the spirit informing the works that generations of artisans made for the glorification of God. As mass ended the cathedral's own great organ thundered into life, and the transformation of tourist trap into sacred space was complete.

Five years before, Ned and I had been to mass in the cathedral at Chartres, in France. There at a fit-up altar on a plywood platform in a different part of the building from the magnificent baroque high altar, we felt like modern "British Druids"— interlopers trying rather pathetically to ally ourselves with ancient significance.

But in San Marco, I was at home. It was a vernacular Mass (though the Italian tended to rouse half-forgotten Latin on my fortysomething tongue), modern in form, low on pomp. But I didn't feel like a johnny-come-lately pretender; I felt like the latest link in a long, flexible chain. Along with the Eucharist I had taken in my own history.

NED

I probably go to four or five masses a year. I'm never completely comfortable in church, but at Saint Mark's I could feel what the centuries of faith and the decades of labor had wrought. I thought of all the anonymous people who had contributed to something that they knew was greater than they, to their community, to the ages. Christians, I thought, are a lot like Jews; their institutions can rise above themselves occasionally to produce monuments to the human spirit— whether in gold or in letters on parchment.

Making connections through experiencing each other's religions can enrich both of us. It's worth encountering some alienation once in a while to glean these nuggets.

Whether at home or in the community, though, a frequent occasion for tension—or opportunity for growth—is in how and why mixed couples celebrate their own and help each other celebrate religious holidays.

MARY HELÉNE

I was once part of a group planning a feminist ecumenical Passover seder. There was a snag when we came to the place in our source booklet where a list of role models or heroines was given. It included, along with Miriam, Sarah, and Huldah, such New Testament figures as Mary and Martha, Priscilla, and Phoebe.

The Jewish women protested. "I don't even know who these people are," one said. On their being identified, she was not mollified. "They're not my role models," she maintained, to vigorous nods from her coreligionists.

The Christians were bewildered, and a little put out. They felt they were doing their part by including Old Testament women; why couldn't the Jews "give" a little? The idea that many Jews see Christian use of the Old Testament (which Jews prefer to call Hebrew Scripture) as a co-opting, not a sharing, was alien to these Christians.

The solution we found was not a roster of heroines everyone could agree to, which would be at best bland and at worst exclusive; we decided to forego a joint list entirely. This meant that each of us in turn would name her own personal heroines, with a short explanation of their significance.

This could be a model for interfaith worship. Instead of struggling, with inevitably limited success, to reach common ground, let's each rejoice in our own and each other's positions— and hold hands across the gaps.

It's an attitude that can be useful in an interfaith marriage, too. If the Jew wants to say Grace, for instance, using the traditional Hebrew blessings, and the Christian wants to use the standard one ending "through Jesus Christ, Our Lord," you have several positive options.

One is to find a neutral compromise. The problem with that is, for most pre-composed prayers, the non-sectarian ones tend to be bland and/or childish: "God is great, God is good, so we thank him for this food" sort of thing. (Ned's irrepressibly secular brother once contributed, "God is good, God is free, we got it all at the A&P.") And many of us are not comfortable with spontaneous prayer, especially if we have to keep our minds on not saying anything offensive or exclusivist at the same time.

Another possibility is each to say your own silently, Quaker-style, perhaps while holding hands around the table—which of course you could do in any case. The glitch with the silent prayer option is that the Jewish spouse may be observant enough to feel bound by the injunction to say blessings aloud; the Christian partner may be uncomfortable at not feeling free to speak the name of Jesus: keeping him "in the closet."

A friend of our daughter's teased a guest by announcing, "In this family, while we say Grace we hold each others' ear lobes." The family went along with the joke, solemnly grasping each others' ears. We don't recommend this display of humor if your guest has never encountered your or your spouse's religion before—they might take it seriously! We go with the Hebrew blessing. We feel comfortable with it, since we both understand it (we translate when there are non-Hebrew speakers present) and its content doesn't exclude anyone as the denominational Catholic one does.

If none of the above appeals to you, try the pluralist approach that worked for the seder-planning group above. Each of you say your own Grace aloud, without feeling either abashed or contentious. Or assign each family member a day of the week to recite their favorite blessing—as long as it's a non-exclusionary one. You don't have to take the model of the melting pot; have your religions *en brochette,* setting them side by side, each maintaining its own character but adding its flavor to the other.

One of the obvious pluses of an interreligious marriage is that you learn first hand about a different religion. "In the beginning" we went to each other's services as well as our own. This soon palled, however, because it meant, ultimately, going Friday, Saturday, and Sunday. These days we content ourselves with going to each other's services on major holidays and suggest that, at least to start with, you do likewise.

If you are a Jew, being married to and exploring questions with a Christian can help illuminate for you aspects not only of Christianity as a religion but of Western "Christian" culture that may have been obscure to you. For instance, seeing Christmas celebrations from up close may give you a sense of the spiritual aspects as distinguished from the more obtrusive material ones.

If you are a Christian, you will find yourself in a perfect position to explore the Jewish roots of Christianity, making both religions more meaningful to you. Celebrating the birth of Jesus, for example, takes on a new resonance and clarity when you understand more about the history of Judea, letting you see Christmas as an event in the history of the Jewish community as well as in its more familiar aspects.

Just remember what we said back in Chapter 1 about not coopting Jewish practices and holidays into the service of Christian theology: there's a difference between drawing strength from the Jewish roots of Christianity and ripping them up to transplant them in alien soil.

SPIRITUALITY DISCUSSION POINTS

Things to Talk About with Your Partner and a Member of Your Partner's Religion's Clergy

(Ask each question of yourselves and of each other):

Do I/You . . .

Believe in God? What do we mean by "god"?

Ever pray privately? How—your own thoughts/traditional formulations? When? What for?

Ever pray communally? How often? In what sort of atmosphere—informal/formal? With/without lay participation?

Expect/want to say Grace at meals? Who says it? What prayer?

Expect/want family prayers? What kind? When? Led by whom?

Ordinarily pray in a language other than English?

Believe in an afterlife? What's it like? Who gets there? What about your partner?

Review the exploration of these questions in the first part of Chapter 11. Add those important to you. If you're uncomfortable talking on this subject, write your answers down beforehand and read them, or ask the clergyperson to read them and lead the discussion. Have at least two preliminary discussions, one with each of your clergy. Most important: get over the discomfort.

INTELLECTUAL LIFE: SOME COMMON MISCONCEPTIONS

A Jewish friend of ours was sharing a room in a labor ward with an expectant Catholic. Naturally, the talk turned to babies. The Jewish woman said, "If ours is a boy, we really don't know whether we should have a medical or a religious circumcision."

The Catholic was aghast. "You're not seriously considering a religious circumcision, are you?"

"Well, that's the problem. My husband doesn't want a religious ceremony, and I really do."

(Note that even in marriages between two Jews, religious differences can arise.)

The conversation between the two women continued at cross purposes, with the Catholic more and more dismayed and the Jew more and more bewildered.

Finally, the Catholic blurted, "I can't believe it. You mean you'd actually let a rabbi come and bite it off?"

This is a fairly extreme example of misunderstanding between faiths. For the record, Jewish ritual circumcisers are very well trained, know all about modern hygiene, and use the usual surgical tools to remove the baby boy's foreskin according to the Law of Moses.

Misunderstandings, even in this modern heterogeneous age of tolerance, crop up with surprising regularity between Christians and Jews—in fact, one small service a mixed couple can do for society is help to clear them up for each other's groups. But first they have to have the right information themselves.

At this point you should maybe go out and acquire a small theological library. (See our section on useful books, articles and magazines for our recommendations.) If you don't care to do that, let us give you a starter set of the most common misconceptions Christians and Jews have of each other's faith:

First, Christian misconceptions about Jews. We'll assume you don't believe Jews have horns (though you can still find Americans who think that's why they wear hats—to cover the horns). You know they don't use the blood of Christian children in their Passover rites (though as recently as 1928, when a child disappeared in a small New York town, the police chief questioned the local rabbi; this being America, not Russia, the rabbi raised a fuss and the chief had to apologize). If you're thinking of marrying a Jew, presumably you think they're decent human beings. But you should be aware that not everyone does.

MARY HELÉNE

When I was in high school, I worked in a Chinese restaurant that hired moonlighting GI's, mostly poor whites from Southern rural areas, as carry–out packers. I enjoyed chatting with them during slow periods and getting a different perspective from my middle class Northern one, while they took a fatherly interest in me.

One day I happened to mention that a friend was taking me to Rosh Hashanah services at one of the local synagogues the next day. The men grew very grave. "Don't do that," one said. "You shouldn't be going to a place like that."

"Why not?"

"They do real odd things at those meetings of theirs, things you shouldn't see."

"What are you talking about? What kinds of things?"

"Well, I wouldn't want to say in front of a nice young girl like you." The others nodded sagely.

"You know," I said, "you guys are wrong. I've been to Jewish services before, and they're just like anybody else's. They pray, they sing . . . nothing 'odd'."

"Is that a fact? Are you sure they didn't know you were coming and do something special?"

"Absolutely sure. There were hundreds of people there, and I decided to come at the last minute."

"And all they did was pray and sing?"

"That's all."

They shook their heads in wonder and some doubt. I only hope I convinced them.

A more common fallacy Christians hold about Jews involves their degree of patriotism. Most of the Jewish people we know have, at one time or another, been asked, "If there were a war between Israel and the United States, which side would you be for?" The question—in that innocent, open form—usually comes from fourth graders, but adults come up with more subtle forms of the same idea: Where is your first loyalty?

The problem is complex because Judaism is variously defined as a religion, a nationality, and a "people." In fact, American Jews have had an unusually fierce attachment to America.

Far fewer Jewish immigrants to the US returned to Europe between 1880 and 1924 than members of other ethnic groups. Europe was not a very hospitable place for Jews to return to. They had fewer romantic illusions about "the old country," and they appreciated that there had never needed to be a Jewish emancipation in America, as there had been everywhere in Europe including England. Jews in

America, though subject to prejudice from groups and individuals, never had a lower status than non–Jews in the eyes of the law. This may be partly why the number of American Jews emigrating to Israel, before or after 1948, has been significantly smaller than the number from other countries.

Jews have been involved with the life of America since the very beginning. Even if you don't think Columbus was a Jew (that's not a joke, but a serious scholarly theory), you should know that Luis de Torres, the interpreter-doctor who sailed with him was, and was the first member of the party actually to step on shore. (One can imagine a dialogue something like, "Eh, Capitano Colombo, who should we send out first?" "Might be quicksand—send the Jew.") Jews served in the Revolution, on both sides in the Civil War, and in all the wars we've had since.

Jews are under no more obligation to support the government of Israel than African-Americans are to serve any African nation. Jews, like African-Americans and others with strong ethnic identities, feel a kinship with their own everywhere. As for the state of Israel, it is a great comfort to many to know that if the old familiar disaster overtakes Jews even in free America, there exists a country that will take them in without question. During the Holocaust, there was no such place on the face of the globe—including America. So Jews may have a feeling for Israel that is more emotional than the nostalgia of the average immigrant for the Old Country.

But it is important to remember that here, as in so many areas, no sweeping statement can be made about the attitude of American Jews toward the only Jewish nation in the world. The most avid Zionists tend, of course, to transfer their allegiance formally and go there. At the other end, there are Jewish groups and individuals who hotly reject any special relationship with the modern state of Israel (some Orthodox Jews among them, as well as liberals from Reform communities). And there is a whole range of attitudes in between.

The question for the Christian marrying a Jew is, what is your partner's attitude toward Israel, and how is it likely to develop in the future? If he or she has thoughts of emigrating, you have some serious obstacles to navigate; mixed couples in Israel encounter substantial legal, social, and religious problems. You might also ask your prospective Jewish family whether any of them went or planned to go there to help on the domestic front during the Gulf War, as many Americans (not all of them Jews) did. Is that a trip you could have taken, or seen your spouse take with equanimity?

Then there is the question of the Jews as the Chosen People. Christians and even some Jews make the mistake of thinking this means Jews are superior. In fact, it is an expression of the belief that Jews have a mission in the world to be "a light unto the nations," bearing witness to the beauties of monotheism and ethical behavior. There is a *midrash* (rabbinic story) that God tried diligently to find other groups to carry out this task, but that the Jews were merely the first people to pay attention. There is no extraterrestrial reward for doing this, and certainly no terrestrial one.

Related to this is the notion that Jews are constantly conspiring to subvert and rule the world. This is not true; it's never been true. But there are always those who find comfort in blaming their failures or frustrations on some superior and sinister force and, for centuries, Jews have unwillingly played the part. As we were once told by a great aunt, Mary's distant cousin didn't get to college because "the Jews stole his scholarship."

It's harder to combat the misconception some Christians have that Jews think salvation is for sale. That's a crude way of saying that Jews consider "good works" sufficient, like piling up merit badges, without a place for the workings of divine grace and mercy. Not true. Jews don't expect to gain admittance to heaven (those who believe in heaven) by presenting the stubs of their checkbooks and UJA receipts. In fact, the widespread Jewish practice of making public charitable contributions relates more to the belief, typical in biblical times and among many Jews today, that there is no afterlife, and immortality is gained by leaving progeny and good works as a memorial—in effect, leaving the world a better place than you found it. But as far as the soul's standing with the Almighty is concerned, the Yom Kippur service each year has Jews reminding themselves "our deeds count for nothing."

The Royal Flush in anti-Jewish allegations, of course, is "the Jews killed Christ." This one is, unfortunately, still official teaching in some parts of the world and has been used over the centuries as a justification for persecution and hatred—a strange monument to someone who asked for forgiveness for the people actually pounding in the crucifixion spikes (who were, of course, Romans). Christian churches have begun to make public pronouncements exposing the historic falsity of this accusation and pointing out its theological inconsistency, but with so many centuries "momentum" behind it, don't expect people to give up the notion quickly or quietly.

MARY HELÉNE

I remember, at the age of seven, listening wide-eyed to an earnest nun who prepared my class for First Confession by explaining our personal responsibility for the Crucifixion.

"Jesus suffered and died for our sins. That means every time you disobey your mother, you press the crown of thorns deeper into His brow," she said. "If you tell a lie, it's like driving the spikes into His hands and feet yourself."

154

Now, this may be lousy child psychology, but it's impeccable theology. Whatever confusions I grew up with, the notion that the Jews killed Christ was not one of them.

The causes of antisemitism are complex and controversial, the subject of many books and much argument. But the fact remains that there are people who call themselves Christian who persist in hating Jews. If you're a Jew marrying a Christian, be prepared to have to deal with this phenomenon: know what Christian theology and Jewish history actually are, and brace yourself to witness to the truth. If you're a Christian you should be dealing with it already, in the same ways.

The misconceptions that Jews have about Christians fall into two categories.

The first one involves confusion over the doctrine of the Trinity. Some Jews take this to mean that Christians actually believe in more than one god. The practice among some Christian denominations of having statues and stained glass images in their churches as aids to faith can also lead Jews (and some Protestants) to thinking of them as idols: things being worshiped in themselves, rather than being reminders of what ought really to be worshiped.

Misunderstanding of this sort is perhaps most common among Jews who have had very little personal contact with Christians. The rabbinical establishment acknowledged that Christianity was not idolatry centuries ago, but we've run into more than one Orthodox Jew who remains skeptical.

The other major difficulty is over the relationship between grace and works. Just as some Christians think Jews try to buy salvation, some Jews have the idea that Christians believe they can do anything they please as long as they believe in Jesus. This misconception is not surprising in view of the way representatives of Christianity have behaved towards Jews while smugly proclaiming their own "saved" state. Nevertheless, the precise relationship between faith and works in the Christian scheme of salvation is very complicated (too much so to go into here) and differs among various brands of Christianity, especially between Catholics and Protestants. The one thing they would all agree on, though, is that neither can stand by itself.

Speaking of Catholic and Protestant differences, there are more weird ideas floating around about the Roman Catholic Church than about any other Christian group in this country (for historical, demographic, and theological reasons).

The first one we had to deal with as a couple was Ned's idea that "intelligent" and "Catholic" were mutually exclusive terms.

NED

When I was in high school I "knew" that the Catholic Church forbade its adherents from reading the Bible because it feared they would discover The Truth. They kept Catholics from attending other peoples' services for the same reason. Further, I thought, Catholics were required to accept any twitch or burp emanating from the Vatican as gospel.

Now, thirty years later and twenty-five years into my own serious study of religion, I realize how misled ANY untutored people can become who are let loose on Scripture without adequate training. Along the way I have also found out that Catholics (if my wife and most of our many Catholic friends and relations are any guide) can think as independently, and be at least as well informed, as anyone else.

You may never have thought any of these silly things, especially if you've grown up since the Second Vatican Council of the 60s. But older people—parents, for instance—may think them, and tell you about them in no uncertain terms.

The truth is that the Roman Catholic Church used to discourage lay people from going directly to Scripture without other guidance (it's one of the issues the Reformation was about). But it has swung very far the other way recently, with Bible study groups for children and adults alike proliferating.

The Catholic prohibition against participation in other Christian denominations' activities was based on a belief that the cause of Christian unity could only be served by Protestants "coming back into the fold." The aim of Christian unity is still the same, but the modern perception of how to achieve it recognizes that cooperative prayer and fellowship are more likely to work toward the goal. In effect, there are no longer any restrictions on a Catholic's attending other people's services, though the degree of participation, naturally, may be limited by Catholic belief. Also, there is a fluid situation regarding taking communion for Protestants in Catholic churches and vice versa. After Vatican II, restrictions were widely lifted or ignored, particularly between Roman Catholics and Eastern Orthodox, Anglican/Episcopalians, and Lutherans (since the apostolic succession had not been interrupted when those splits took place, so the sacrament has the same standards of validity for each group). In the drawing in that's taken place in the past fifteen years or so, Catholics have again been instructed not to receive communion under anyone else's auspices, nor to invite non-Catholics to do so under theirs. It remains to be seen whether this genie can be gotten back into the bottle; our experience is that even those Catholics aware of the recent tightening ignore it.

Now for the question of papal infallibility. Remember the scene in *Brideshead Revisited* when the priest asks the converting-for-convenience Rex Mottram what would happen if the pope said it was raining and it wasn't? "I suppose it would be sort of spiritually raining, only we were too sinful to see it," he obligingly guesses. Papal infallibility has many people, including cradle Catholics, confused.

The crux is to understand how limited a doctrine it is. It doesn't mean the pope is always right in his casual comments and opinions, or even in the serious and authoritative directions he gives the faithful in encyclicals or public letters. Only when he speaks officially as pope (the term is *ex cathedra,* or "from the chair") on a matter of faith and doctrine is he considered to be under the guidance of the Holy Spirit that will not allow the Church to give credence to an erroneous dogma. The original statement that the pope is infallible under these conditions was made in 1870.

The only *ex cathedra* statement that has been made since that time was in 1950, the Dogma of the Assumption of Mary. This is a rather mysterious pronouncement, based on theological reasoning and historical tradition, that when Mary died, she was immediately bodily resurrected, whatever that means, and entered completely into the eternality of heaven, wherever that is, and unlike the rest of us does not have to wait until the end of time, whenever that should be, to be resurrected. Whether you believe this, or even understand it, papal infallibility does not affect your right to exercise your intellect freely in day-to-day life.

As for Mary, you may like or dislike the idea that Catholics worship the mother of Jesus, but in either case you're wrong. Mary is venerated, honored, asked to use her influence with her Son, imitated, and loved—just like any other human saint or Jewish mother, only more so. Not worshiped.

By the way, contrary to what most people, including many Catholics, think, the doctrine of the Immaculate Conception has nothing to do with the Virgin Birth (or what came nine months before it). It refers to the belief that Mary was born without the stain of Original Sin that has been the universal lot of the rest of humanity since Adam and Eve. She was born in the usual, natural way (though her mother was old, like so many biblical mothers with a mission), but without the sort of starter-set sin the rest of us get. This should scotch any idea that the Catholic Church finds sex itself sinful, but probably won't. And even Mark Twain, who should have known better, couldn't keep the Immaculate Conception and the Virgin Birth clear in his mind. Now you can.

Confession. It never has been and never will be true that Catholics are allowed to lie to the priest, keep things back, and do what they please in between times in the carefree knowledge that all they have to do is mumble a magic formula, have one mumbled over them by the priest, and be free to go back to what they were doing before. The need for a true penitence and reconciliation with God for this sacrament to be effected is clearer now under the new, modern rite, but it's always been there, in spite of Catholics who've misused it.

What about the idea that only Catholics go to heaven? The doctrine that "outside the church there is no salvation" was first enunciated by Origen in the third Christian century, expressing an idea that was implicit in Jesus' teaching, "no one can come to the Father except through the Son," and the conviction that no one came to the Son except through the (Catholic) Church. However, there has been since earliest times a belief that virtuous people who were not Catholics, Christians, or even believers in God could also be saved by their sincerity in trying to be good—what St. Thomas Aquinas called "the baptism of desire." The Second Vatican Council explicitly joined these two elements in Catholic thought by stating the converse: anyone who is saved is by definition saved by the Catholic Church, even if they don't realize it. Now, you might not be thrilled with the idea of being sort of divinely kidnapped, but at least neither of you has to be afraid that the other is going directly to hell without passing GO or collecting $200.

Finally, you may find people who hold a negative attitude about the Americanism of Catholics similar to the one we discussed about Jews. During the presidential campaign of John F. Kennedy (as in that of Al Smith thirty-two years before), it was seriously suggested that a Catholic president would be under the thumb of the Vatican and forced to do its bidding. But no pope in modern history has had that sort of power (Henry VIII went ahead and started his own church, remember?). Nowadays popish plots to subvert governmental offices are the province of James Bond.

Still, don't be lulled into thinking that the church as an institution will never enter your lives in non-religious areas. What may become a question, especially in a mixed marriage, is the extent to which the Catholic as an individual is influenced by political attitudes taken by the church hierarchy. Abortion law (as distinguished from actual abortion practice) is an obvious case. The National Conference of Bishops has resorted to threats and calumny in its attempt to bring Catholics politically into line, with sanctions in the ecclesiastical sphere being used against positions in the civil sphere. Will it bother you if your partner feels bound by such magisterial teaching? Will you be able to be both sympathetic to the pain and supportive of the strength of a partner who feels conscience–bound to depart from it?

The American Catholic establishment is, remember, particularly conservative as national hierarchies go. Our German friend Felix is a very devout Catholic fastidiously conservative in his own religious practice, learned in traditional theology, and pious to the point of having considered entering a monastery. We were speaking once of the Dutch Catechism, a radical document of the 60s that had been approved by Catholic authorities in Holland but condemned as not a true expression of Catholic belief by the Vatican. We asked Felix what he thought about the incident.

"It doesn't matter," he shrugged, "Rome is wrong."

"What do you mean," we protested, "it doesn't matter? Rome makes the final decision."

"For Americans, maybe," he said. "In Germany, we don't pay that much attention to what they think in Italy."

Now, we don't present this as a model attitude for Catholics, but as an indication that the church is not the wall-to-wall carpet it sometimes appears to be. Many American Catholics, particularly women, virtually ignore church directives on birth control and abortion; in fact, there's evidence that more Catholics than Protestants get abortions—and have at least since the 1920s. Some of them may have less than well-thought-out reasons for departure from the official line. They may have abortions, for example, because the public evidence of mortal sin constituted by an out-of-wedlock pregnancy is more than they can bear. At the other end of the intellectual spectrum are those theologians, priests, and sisters who have publicly disputed the current papal interpretation of Divine Law, particularly in areas of sexual morality. The point is that not every Catholic behaves like every other Catholic, or believes exactly the same things.

We haven't said much about Protestant belief. One obvious reason for that is that there are so many denominations and attitudes, from high-church Anglicans almost indistinguishable from Roman Catholics to fundamentalists who call Catholicism a cult and who claim, as did one of their prominent ministers some years ago, "God doesn't hear Jewish prayer."

The main point to be made about your religious life and your partner's, no matter under what auspices, is that you each need to explore them both. If you marry within your faith, there's a lot that can be taken for granted, as when you marry someone of the same political party. If you're smart, even then you'll keep communicating about what's important to you. In interfaith cases it's vital: you have to be informed about each other's beliefs and practices even if you aren't particularly interested in religious discussions. If you're not willing to spend time and energy on this, you can almost expect to be unsuccessful. Think of it as like marrying a diabetic and not bothering to find out about your spouse's diet needs.

The bottom line in a Christian-Jewish marriage is: Jesus was a Jew, but Moses wasn't a Christian. That is, Christianity has its basis in Judaism and is influenced by its history, literature, thought, and beliefs. The influence of Christianity on Judaism has been historically late, largely superficial, and often negative.

Theologically, this means that the central truth of Christianity, the sacrifice and resurrection of the son of God, lies entirely outside the Jewish purview of salvation history.

In practice, this means among other things that a Christian can attend a Jewish service and feel comfortable saying "amen" to any prayer; there won't be anything said that a Christian doesn't believe, too.

MARY HELÉNE
I do keep quiet in Jewish services during the bits that speak of the nature and destiny of the Jews—"a holy priesthood, a consecrated nation" sort of thing. We say exactly the same of ourselves as Catholics during the mass, but I feel presumptuous saying it in a Jewish context.

Similarly, I close my mouth during prayers thanking God for saving "us" from oppressors. Remember the joke where Tonto says to the Lone Ranger, "What you mean 'we,' Paleface?"

NED
During Catholic mass I am as silent as Lot's wife, the one who turned into a pillar of salt. Some of what is said there, of course, comes straight from Hebrew Scripture (what Christians call the Old Testament), but I can't respond to that, either, because the whole service depends on that man up there on the crucifix and I don't pray through him. When the congregation kneels I sit up as straight as I can; I don't lounge, neither do I sit back against the hands of the person kneeling in the pew behind me. When they stand, I stand, but I'm not entirely comfortable even doing that. (We had a bitter argument about this one Christmas.)

I love the rousing old hymns that I learned as a kid going to Presbyterian Sunday school with my friends—but I would not sing the words in public, where it might be construed as agreement with their content.

Reading this book is not going to enable you to heal the rift between Christianity and Judaism, reconcile their theologies, and harmonize their histories. But we hope that it will help you keep in mind, when these painful issues come to the fore, that you shouldn't treat them as personal threats or affronts to yourself—and you should be sensitive to their seeming so to your partner. Both Christians and Jews would do well to remember Jesus' advice to get the plank out of your own eye before you start picking at the splinter in your partner's: be alert to the problems in your own religious institution; be relaxed

160

about those in the other's.

Remember, too, that elements of your religion that seem perfectly ordinary and benign to you can have quite different resonances for your partner. The crucifix is one example of this. Paul and Rachel Cowan found feelings about the cross cropping up again and again in their interviews of intermarried couples. And it can provide a nexus for feelings of guilt/anger/fear/anxiety on both sides. Some Christians were raised to think of Jews as having murdered Christ; it's a matter of history that Christians have murdered Jews with the cross as their emblem. House decoration will depend only partly on your aesthetic tastes—the way you respond to religious symbols will also play a part. Ned put up the crucifix in our little apartment in Boston because his sense of fair play outweighed his personal feelings about it. Don't count on your partner being so accommodating.

MARY HELÉNE

My mother was given a book as a confirmation gift called *The Catholic Girl's Guide* by a "Father LaSance," published in the early years of this century.

In the chapter on marriage, the author warns against marrying out (to a Protestant—the notion of a Catholic's marrying a non-Christian evidently never entered his darkest nightmare). As a horrible example, he cites a case where a young Catholic bride came home to find her husband had taken down and put in the attic all her crucifixes, holy water fonts*, holy pictures, sacred hearts, madonnas . . . the list went on. When I read this as a teenager, I could only sympathize with the poor husband. It seemed his wife had set up a bazaar atmosphere (pun intended) that could only make him feel surrounded by alien influences in his own home.

I have a crucifix and a small icon* collection in the corner of our bedroom where my dresser is, and a religious picture my grandmother loved in my study. Most of Ned's religious artifacts are in his office—he uses them as aids in teaching. But we do have a mezuzah* on the door and a menorah on the family–room mantel.

Use your head, and keep a lid on it.

Misunderstandings may crop up with parents in this regard. They may want or expect you to display various emblems of your/their faith, and be put off or threatened by those of your spouse. Conversely, they may also want you to keep a "low profile" in your intermarriage—and their reasons may have more to do with society than with belief.

They may simply be afraid you're letting yourself in for a lifetime of prejudice and discrimination, on behalf of someone else's religion.

MARY HELÉNE

When I told my Italian grandparents that Ned and I were engaged, Nonno (Grandpa) asked me, "Have you thought about how you'll feel someday when they say to your children, 'Jew?'" (This very acute question is broached in more detail in Chapter 4.)

"Yes," I answered, "I have. But you know, we'll be living and working on college campuses, and there usually isn't so much open bigotry there."

His shoulders relaxed and a beatific smile came over his face. "That's right," he breathed. "You'll be educated. When your Nonna and I were married, we used to fight about whether you put the fork here . . . or here." He mimed setting a table, then sat back triumphantly as he concluded, "But you won't have to fight. You'll be educated—you'll know!"

Education, unfortunately, is not an automatic cure for intolerance, among Jews or Christians—especially if you're related to them. In our case, Mary Heléne's encouragement of Ned's religious development was done in the teeth of objections from . . . his parents! They felt threatened by his going back to a tradition they had largely abandoned.

As we said earlier, indeed as the whole of this book is meant to say, the world needs as many good Christians and good Jews as it can get. Do not harbor thoughts that your partner will or might convert if only. . . . Instead, do what you can to strengthen your partner's commitment to his/her own faith. You'll find that your marriage benefits enormously as a result.

COMMON MISCONCEPTIONS ABOUT RELIGION
DISCUSSION LIST

Try doing this one with a group of friends, to keep from getting acrimonious. Think of it as religious (Not So) Trivial Pursuit™.

True or False:

Hardly anybody is seriously antisemitic these days.
Jews can't really be patriotic Americans because of their ties to Israel.
Jews think they're better than everybody else.
Jews run everything.
Jews think they can buy their way into heaven.
The Jews killed Christ.
Christians are idolaters, believe in more than one God and worship statues.
Protestants think they can do what they want, if they only believe in Jesus.
Protestants think they're better than everyone else.
Catholics aren't allowed to think for themselves.
Catholics think they're better than everyone else.
Catholics believe the pope can't make a mistake.
Catholics worship Mary.
The Immaculate Conception means Mary and Joseph didn't have sex.
Catholics think they can do what they want, as long as they go to confession.
Catholics think they're the only ones going to heaven.
Catholics can't be patriotic Americans because of their ties to the Vatican.
Jews/Protestants/Catholics are all alike.

The answer to all of these is, of course, False—but don't stop talking there. Explore what you think, what you used to think, how you feel about what you think, and where you learned those thoughts.

163

Chapter 12
The Seasons

SEASONS IN GENERAL

Intermarried couples we've talked to, and articles we've read, most often name the celebration of holidays—especially Christmas—as the major stumbling block in their marriage.

Following is a model approach to hammering out a workable family style.

We use Christmas for our model because, in America, it carries such emotional freight that its observance often becomes a major problem in an interreligious marriage. We don't need to take space here in exploring the historical, social, and political reasons for this fact. It will be more useful to give some suggestions for dealing with it that can then be applied to other practical, day-to-day situations.

Combining Christmas and Hanukkah is an increasingly popular approach. The *Wall St. Journal* of 12/10/90 reports on a company, Mixed-Blessing Inc., that specializes in Christmas/Hanukkah cards with graphics combining symbols—a tree transforming into a Star of David, Santa Claus playing dreidel or lighting a menorah. Wrapping paper, shopping bags, and a coloring book are to come. Hallmark also started a similar line.

Rabbi Aryeh Meir of the American Jewish Committee protests—"It's a travesty to both faiths." The National Council of Christians and Jews and the American Jewish Committee made a statement opposing such cards, which they say "diminish the sacred symbols of each faith and are an affront to Judaism, to Christianity, and to serious interfaith relations." They want a boycott of such products. We understand their point, but would like to maintain that neither the fir tree nor the six-pointed star is a "sacred" symbol; if the drawing were of a menorah sprouting a crucifix, we'd be more alarmed. The fact remains that, according to a Gallup poll, 10 million Americans kept a Hanukkah menorah beside a Christmas tree in 1989. Rabbi James Rudin of the AJC insists, "I find it offensive and it should be avoided. What I like to call 'The Season' overwhelms both of these holidays and weakens their significance" (*USA Today* 12/20/89). He's right, but we have some specific guidance to offer in finding a positive celebratory style that doesn't leave anyone out.

First of all, keep clear in your minds what is in fact a religious question and what isn't. The vexed problem of the tree, for instance, can be brought into perspective when you see it as a modern revival of a pagan Teutonic symbol of the promise of spring at the winter solstice—celebrated as the feast of Sol Invictus, the Unconquered Sun, by the Romans. Even hanging cookies on it in the shapes of humans and animals goes back to Druidic rites better not looked into too closely. So, Jewish partner, is it really so important? On the other hand, Christian partner, the elaborate celebration is barely over a hundred years old in our culture—is it really so important? We would say skip the tree and have a creche; go to church instead of wassailing; bake gingerbread stars but make 'em six pointed.

Sure, this is easy for us to say—we have a tree. In our case, Ned was raised with a secular Christmas, so that even though it's not something he would do now, left to his own devices, under the circumstances it doesn't make him unbearably uncomfortable.

In fact, ironically, of the two of us he has the longer Christmas tree tradition. His ancestors were Reform, in the classic 19th century manner. His mother reported having been taught in Sunday school that it was her duty as a Jew to assimilate (which would, they still thought in those innocent times, end antisemitism). She resented his higher degree of traditional observance as a rejection of her principles. Our friends who were rebelling against more observant parents were highly amused.

Mary Heléne's background is, on her mother's side, Italian. Her grandmother put a basket on the hearth for St. Lucia to fill on December 13. No tree. Her father's German-born mother did decorate a huge and elaborate tree, but it was kept carefully concealed in the closed-off front parlor till after midnight mass on Christmas Eve, when the double doors from the everyday sitting room were at last flung open to reveal the splendor her aunts had been working on for days.

What we don't do is have obtrusive decorations on the outside of the house that would seem to say, "This is a Christian home." We do put a simple wreath on the door, which seems to us to say "There is a Christian here," an entirely different statement, just as the Hanukkah menorah in our window signifies a Jewish presence.

Hanukkah can and should have meaning for the Christian, as well. As Rabbi Mark Greenspan of Harrisburg, Pennsylvania points out, if it weren't for the victory of the Maccabees over Hellenistic secularizers, Judaism would have vanished almost two centuries before the birth of Jesus. And for Catholics, at any rate, the books of Maccabees are part of Scripture.

Speaking of Hanukkah, we do not recommend "Hanukkah bushes" and other cutesy cooptings. The tree may not have been invented as a Christian symbol, but it has unmistakably become one, and equivocating over it brands you at least as insecure. When we were living in Israel in 1976 we found foil-covered chocolate Santa Clauses at our local grocery. Our Moroccan–Jewish neighborhood was not notable for its cross-cultural sophistication, so we were surprised—especially when we noticed the candy was made in the Israeli town of Rehovot. An Israeli friend explained, mockingly, "Those aren't Santa Clauses. They're Maccabees!" In Israel, that's funny. In America, it's pathetic. If you want to have a tree, have a tree and don't apologize.

The details of our style of observance are described in the holiday section below. Briefly, we have an Advent wreath, a door wreath, and a tree. Our actual celebration includes, in addition to the ubiquitous presents, the following—eating festive food, listening to the recording of Dylan Thomas reading his "Child's Christmas in Wales," church–going, and charitable projects. Other activities, such as carol singing, holiday baking, and gift shopping, are undertaken only by family members who are interested and feel comfortable doing them. When the children were young we used to sing "Happy Birthday" to Jesus because we wanted them to know what the holiday was all about. Don't press your Jewish partner on this.

We choose a greeting card with a nonsectarian religious (museum reproductions of Old Testament scenes often work) or family landmark (our daughter's wedding, our 25th anniversary) motif; we each are responsible for greeting our own particular friends on our own particular holidays, and Guess Who gets stuck with mutual friends who aren't particularly religious. The point is that there is a mix, a range of observances of varying religious and family significance, tailored to our needs and tastes as individuals and as a group. You will concoct your own mix.

We also don't recommend making Hanukkah a rival to Christmas. It's hard to avoid, but the effort is worth it in keeping a firm grasp of both Jewish and Christian identities. Hanukkah is a pleasant, minor, non-biblical holiday that happens to fall during what has become the annual Christmas madness. Its celebration should be pleasant and minor—including the token gifts given to children—and without heavy religious overtones.

If you want to give your kids a Jewish holiday to balance the weight of Christmas, look up "Sukkot" in the table below.

If you want to give them a Christian holiday that doesn't try to combine the effects of a Roman orgy with the last five minutes of the Indy 500 and a gathering of Potlatch Indians, see "Christmas" in the same place.

If our situation doesn't fit your needs, here are some common variations on the theme—and their problems:

1. The Christian is attached to the holiday emotionally, but has no great religious feeling about it. The Jew is comfortable with

Christmas as a secular holiday.

This is an easy one. All you have to do is define what is unacceptably religious to either of you. You probably won't display a creche. You may feel that elaborate outdoor decorations are out of place. If you play seasonal music, you'll stick to "Jingle Bells" and "White Christmas" while leaving "O Holy Night" alone. (You can dicker over old favorites like "Silent Night," which you may have heard so often your mind slips right over the religious grooves and just goes straight to a sort of diffused nostalgic warmth.)

2. The Christian has strong religious feelings about Christmas, while the Jew sees it as a pleasant nonreligious observance.

You'll have to tread a little lightly here. The Christian will have to remember that the essential religious experience of Christmas takes place in the heart, not in the decor or even in church. The Jew should be sensitive to the offensiveness of much modern secularization to the religious Christian and not blithely assume that an electrified Rudolph on the roof says it all.

3. The Christian, or rather gentile, is the secularist, while the Jew feels that any sort of celebration of the holiday is a religious statement he or she doesn't want to make.

Another tricky one. The Christian should keep in mind that even that patron saint of conspicuous consumption, Santa Claus, was originally a medieval bishop and saint, so that electric Rudolph is actually a sort of twice-removed reminder of religious content. The Jew must recognize that practices with their roots in memories of happy family occasions can be at least as deep-running as those with theological rationales. They can't be cavalierly dismissed without causing resentment.

Our advice, in either case 2 or case 3, is to follow half of the counsel of St. Paul to the early church—let the one without scruples (i.e., religious convictions) give way to the one with them. You may find that concentrating on creating that happy-family feeling without the assistance of the Chamber of Commerce is actually more rewarding.

4. Both Christian and Jew have strong religious commitments.

This, surprisingly, seems to us easier to deal with than the last two, perhaps because it is our own situation. What you do here is take all the above advice, combine it with a sense of humor and lots of good will, and work out the practical aspects step by step.

To run out all the combinations and permutations of every possible situation isn't possible here. Rather than attempt it, let us remind you that, in the case of mixed marriage, there's more likely to be a shift—call it growth, if you like—in one or both of your positions. So even if you arrive at a suitably uncomfortable compromise, there's no guarantee it won't come unstuck, especially after the children come.

Still, this should bring out another positive aspect to mixed marriage—in addition to finding out about someone else's religion, you're likely to spend a lot more time reexamining and learning about your own. With diligence, and a bit of luck, both of you will acquire real appreciation for both faiths.

You're necessarily making a bigger investment in developing a thoughtful religious life than those in same-religion marriages need to, and it's a commitment that can be frightening. You might compare it to prospecting for gold in a mine field. But as the late Paul Cowan said to us, "It's a complex but not untenable position."

THE SEASONS IN PARTICULAR

Spring/Summer

This is the oddest time for the Christian/Jewish household. High tide is Passover, preceded by Purim and followed by some religious ripples not so famous or so widely observed—counting the Omer through Lag b'Omer to Shavuot. Meanwhile, the Christian seasonal peak, Easter, has its wake before it in Lent and the mounting crescendo of Holy Week, and its backwash in Trinity and Pentecost.

Both sets of holidays are determined by the lunar calendar, but the Christian church made a deliberate and largely successful effort to sunder them by using a different system, so in a mixed marriage you'll never have the same spring schedule two years in a row.

All right. Ash Wednesday comes first (March 21 at the latest), ushered in by Shrove Tuesday (Mardi Gras or Carnival) if you're a traditionalist or from New Orleans. You make *fastnacht* or doughnuts and brush off your fish recipes. But then comes Purim. Have you the moral stamina to make *hamantaschen,* or even to live in a house where they're being made, without eating any? (Advice: don't give up sweets for Lent.) And the celebration itself—isn't it out of keeping with the spirit of the Christian season, even if you don't party and drink till you can't tell Haman from Mordechai but only dress in costumes and listen to the Megillah? On the other hand, aside from theological considerations, Purim is a nice holiday for kids, with its subtly subversive custom of sending costumed children out to bring sweets to the neighbors and the at-home intimacy of mild mayhem with noisemakers during the synagogue service.

You could simply unilaterally declare Purim an extra-Lenten holiday, like St. Patrick's Day. Or you could swap it for St. Pat's, especially if you're not Irish and could never see why nobody ever

168

painted a colored line down Fifth Avenue for the Feast of Santa Lucia. But this is all fairly minor, especially since the Catholic Church has relaxed the rigor of fasting requirements and allowed more space for personal adjustments. (There would seem to be no theological bar, for instance, to a Christian's reckoning days in the Jewish manner, sunset to sunset, and therefore being able to abstain from meat on "Friday" —i.e. from Thursday evening—and still have flanken for Shabbos dinner.)

The real complications set in later on. When Passover falls well before Easter, your only problem is to remember not to eat meat at the other two meals of the first two days so that you're free to partake of the seder. Unless, of course, one of those days falls on Thursday evening through Friday (make your decision about what time and day you're starting Friday disciplines beforehand; no fair switching in mid-Lent) or on Tuesday/Wednesday, if you're abstaining then too. Well, a perfectly lovely, if unconventional, seder can be made without meat; even without fish, if there's a vegan in the group, Friday or not.

If seder night falls on Holy Thursday, you're in luck, sort of. There is a certain piquancy in realizing that many Christian churches now encourage their faithful to celebrate some form of seder on the Thursday before Easter, as a recognition that what Christians call the Last Supper was evidently a Passover celebration at which Jesus presided and John, presumably, asked the Four Questions. (There is a scholarly hypothesis that there was still a division at the time, or at least in Jesus' Galilean group, between Passover proper and the Feast of Unleavened Bread, and that it was the latter they were celebrating. Let's not think about that.) You can find Christianized seder plates in liturgical catalogues, and reflect on the ironies of history as you participate in an activity that would have gotten a Christian or converted Jew burned at the stake as recently as 160 years ago. These same historical echoes—combining elements of the seder with a commemoration of the institution of the Eucharist—may make the Jewish partner uncomfortable. In fact, the whole idea of Easter, often associated with pogroms and slaughter in Europe, may make a Jewish partner edgy. You'll have to feel your way here.

When there's a seder designated for Good Friday, the situation is perhaps more emotionally sticky for the Christian partner. We've already settled the problem of meat—either end the day at sunset or have some nice salmon steaks—but a Christian may still feel uneasy about the celebratory atmosphere. It might be useful here to concentrate on the theologically positive aspects of the day for the Christian—that is, the reason it's called "good"—and recognize that there can be a close relationship between the holiday in which Jews celebrate their freeing from bondage in Egypt and one which Christians believe marks their freeing from the bondage of sin.

Easter can fall as early as March 22 or as late as April 25. The range for the first or second nights of Passover (seder nights) is March 25 to April 25. Easter and Passover coinciding represents no serious culinary problem. The two holidays have very similar spirits. You'll just have to save your yeast-laden *kuchen* and *kolacky* for years when the cycles of the moon have pulled Passover and Easter out of each other's orbit. (If you're an Orthodox Christian, you don't have to worry—your Easter is always after Passover.)

When they're riding in sync, have *matzo brei* with your colored eggs, enjoy the scrupulously clean house and the once-a-year dishes, put on your new clothes and go to church before the seder. At our church, where our whole family and all guests—Jewish or not—go to mass to show solidarity, the pastor tactfully passes by our section when sprinkling holy water on the congregation. We wish you clergy as considerate.

Fall/Winter

The Autumn holidays are much easier to schedule. There are no important Christian ones for the Jewish ones to conflict with, and the more–or–less secular ones can be combined with the religious ones at will. The danger you run is exhaustion. Labor Day picnic, Rosh Hashanah feast, Yom Kippur pre-fast and fast-breaking meals, building and decorating the *sukkah,* getting together the Halloween costumes and buying a supply of trick-proof treats . . . and if you wait till the Thanksgiving leftovers are gone before thinking about Christmas and Hanukkah, you've left it too late.

Actually, one advantage to the dual-faith household is that, if you're celebrating Christmas, you don't have to blow Hanukkah out of proportion to compete with it, but can celebrate it in the traditional, low-key, charming way that may even have the side-effect of draining off some of the hysteria that so often peaks on December 25.

A final suggestion: even if only one of you is responsible for the domestic side, cleaning and decorating the house; cooking and serving goodies; and shopping for and wrapping presents, to say nothing of inserting graphite rods in the children when they look like detonating; the other spouse should keep in mind that a double dose of holiday can bring on religious indigestion. She may resent buying presents for your holiday, or he may be irritated at having to learn complicated recipes that warm your heart but only burn his. Be flexible here. And remember, not every holiday has to be or can be a picture-perfect Saturday Evening Post combo of nostalgia, elegance and spiritual significance. Keep your eye on the main points and cut corners freely. Odds are that no one will notice but your mother-in-law, and she may be cordially invited to fill the gaps. She'll love it.

170

Harmonized Christian/Jewish/Secular Calendar

Jewish Holidays (Lunar Calendar)	Christian Holidays (Lunar and Solar Calendars)	Secular Holidays (Lunar, Solar, and Congressional)
	Jan. 1: Solemnity of Mary	Jan. 1: New Year's Day
	Jan. 6 (or nearest Sun.) Orthodox Christmas Epiphany (12th Night)	
10 Teveth: Jerusalem Seige Fast		Jan. 15/3d Mon. in Jan.: Martin Luther King Day
	Feb. 2: Candelmas	Feb. 2: Groundhog Day
15 Shevat: Tu b'Shevat		
	Feb. 14 <<<<<<<<<<<<<<<<<<<<<<<(St.) Valentine's	
		3d Mon. in February: Presidents Day
	Day before Ash Weds: Shrove Tuesday 40 days (excluding Suns) before Easter till Easter: Lent 1st day of Lent: Ash Wednesday	
14 Adar: Purim (There is also a leap-month, II Adar, every few years in a nineteen-year cycle; in such a year, Purim is celebrated in II Adar)	March 17 St. Patrick's Day >>>>>>>>>>>>>>>>>>>>>>>>>>>>>>>	
	Sun. before Easter: Palm Sunday	
15-22 Nisan Passover		
16 Nisan-6 Sivan Counting the Omer	**Holy Week:** Thurs. before Easter: Maundy Thursday Fri. before Easter: Good Friday Sat. before Easter: Holy Saturday First Sun. after first full moon after the vernal equinox: Easter Sunday (see below for date of Eastern Orthodox Easter)	
		27 Nisan: Holocaust Remembrance*
		5 Iyyar: Israel Independence*
18 Iyyar Lag b'Omer	Sun. after Easter: Trinity Sunday	

*Often observed by American Jews

JEWISH HOLIDAYS	CHRISTIAN HOLIDAYS	SECULAR HOLIDAYS
	40 days after Easter: Ascension Thursday >>>>>>>>>>>>>>>>>>>>>>	May 1 May Day, etc.
6-7 Sivan Shavuot		2d Sun. in May: Mother's Day
	50 days after Easter: Pentecost	
		May 31 or last Mon. in May: Memorial Day
		June 14: Flag Day
17 Tammuz: Fall of Jerusalem		3d Sun. in June: Father's Day
		July 4: American Independence
9 Av: Tishe b'Av	August 15: Assumption	August 26: Women's Equality Day
Elul—preparation for High Holydays— repentance		1st Mon. in September: Labor Day
1 Tishre-10 Tishre: **Days of Awe** 1-2 Tishre: Rosh Hashanah 10 Tishre: Yom Kippur		4th Fri. in September: American Indian Day October 12 or nearest Mon.: Columbus Day
15-22 Tishre Sukkoth 21 Tishre HaShana Rabba 22 Tishre: Shemini Atzeret 23 Tishre: Simkhat Torah	Last Sun. in Oct.: Reformation Day >>>>>>>>>>>>>>>>>> >> November 1: All Saints Day November 2: All Souls Day	October 31: Hallowe'en November 11: Veterans Day
<<<<<<<<<<<<<<<<<<<<<<<<<<<<<<<<<<<<<<<<<<<<<<<< Heshvan: no holidays		4th Thurs. in November: Thanksgiving Day
	4th Sun. before Dec. 25 till Dec 25: Advent	
25 Kislev-2 Tevet: Hannukah	December 8: Immaculate Conception December 25: Christmas >>>>>>>>>>>>>>>>>>>>>>>>>>>>>>>>>>>>	
First of each month: Rosh Hodesh		5:00 pm Fri.-9:00 am Mon.: Weekends
Sunset Fridays to full dark Saturdays: Sabbath	Midnight Saturdays to midnight Sundays: Lord's Day	

Chapter 13
The Holidays

HOLIDAYS NOT INCLUDED IN THE FOLLOWING:

If your tradition includes special remembrances for St. Nicholas or St. Lucy; if you're observant enough to celebrate Tu b'Av or Yom Kippur Katan; if your family history keeps you attuned to Pearl Harbor Day or Kwanzaa—don't be offended at their being left out. You already know more about them than we could include here, and if we tried to put them all in we'd be sure to miss a couple. This way we can pretend we left your favorite out on purpose. For our part, we like St. Swithin's Day—July 15—as honoring the most obscure saint in modern times who has his own holiday; if we feel like giving each other presents, we say it's for his feast. Since he's traditionally associated with rain, any drought is probably our fault.

TABLE OF HOLIDAYS AND THEIR CELEBRATIONS

Midnight Saturday to midnight Sunday
Lord's Day (often—inaccurately—called Sabbath)
                                     Christian   Major
Significance—Commemoration and, for sacramentalists, re-enactment of Christ's death and resurrection.
References—Acts 20:7-12 (which also contains a cautionary tale about keeping awake during sermons), I Cor. 16:2, Col. 2:16, Rev. 1:10.
Religious activities—Go to church at least once. (Some denominations have an evening service as well.) If you're Catholic, though, you can satisfy your obligation by going to mass on Saturday afternoon, which blurs the distinction between Lord's Day and the Jewish Sabbath—maybe just the ticket for a mixed-faith family, providing family members who won't ride on Shabbat can walk to the church. If you're a Seventh Day Adventist who keeps Saturday Sabbath rather than Lord's Day, you may have a problem with your morning services conflicting with morning Torah service; you'll probably have to make up your minds to worship separately on Saturday.
Food—The British traditionally went in for roast beef or mutton, Yorkshire pudding, and a heavy dessert pudding in the afternoon no matter what the temperature outside. Sunday night the servants had off—cold buffet supper for toffs Upstairs. The American remnant, the elaborate Sunday brunch, has adapted itself nicely to secular sleeping-in and mammoth Sunday newspapers.
Customs—Wear good clothes to church; rip them off immediately after and get into golfing, lounging, or lawn-mowing togs.
Requirements—Strict "sabbatarians" such as Puritans, Amish,

and a few other denominations forbid any sort of work. The Catholic Church used to forbid "unnecessary servile work," prompting endless discussions of definitions but establishing pretty certainly that the laundry should wait till Monday. In these days when people have to run faster and faster just to stay in the same place, you may not have the luxury of slacking off on Sunday; it may certainly be difficult for both of you to take off both Saturday and Sunday. We have chosen to celebrate a sort of Sabbath-and-a-half—Friday evening till Sunday noon.

Sunset Friday till full dark (three stars visible) Saturday
Sabbath (Seventh Day)

Jewish   Major

Significance—Commemoration of the seventh day of creation, on which God rested, and of the liberation from forced labor in Egypt.

References—Gen. 2:1-3, Ex. 20:8-11, 31:12-17, Deut. 5:12-15.

Religious activities—Home-centered prayers and ceremonies, synagogue services, Torah study.

Food—Hallah (a braided egg bread), wine (grape juice will do, or in emergencies kiddush can be said over the bread), and something delicious for Friday dinner. On Saturday, three meals should be eaten before sundown, often including chollent, a bean stew that can be kept warm for hours so no cooking is required on the day itself.

Customs—The observance of the sabbath is so important in Jewish life that it's hard to separate custom and law (and if you're very traditional you'll consider them identical). Some nice ones include— making the house beautiful beforehand; blessing the children; the husband's reading "The Woman of Valor" (Prov. 31:10-31) to the wife (if you can come up with an appropriate passage for the wife to read the husband, please let us know); enjoying marital sex.

Requirements—These will vary especially widely along the Reform/Orthodox continuum because the day is so central and recurs so frequently. A middle-of-the-road course might be: light the candles, attend evening services, bless the bread and wine at a festive meal, refrain from work*, study Torah, and finish off when three stars are visible in one area of the Saturday night sky with *Havdalah,* or "Separation" (of the sacred from the profane)—a special candle, wine, spices, songs—a lovely service and especially appealing to children.

*"Work" in Jewish ceremonial contexts is a technical term with many ramifications. In practice, it can range from simply staying home from the office and relaxing in any way that seems appropriate, to the elaborate structuring of the Orthodox that encompasses pre-Sabbath tearing of toilet paper and unscrewing the little light in the icebox. We suggest that Christians and nontraditional Jews for whom any curtailment of normal activity seems alien, repressive, or superstitious experiment before making judgments—find out how liberating it can be, for instance, to refrain from riding in or driving any vehicle on holidays and one day of the weekend; no malls, no beach-bound traffic jams, no distant social obligations, etc. Try it, you'll like it.

December 30-January 1
New Year's Eve   Secular   Major
Significance—The first day of the secular year since the establishment of the Julian calendar in 46 BCE.

Religious activities—None for New Year's per se.

Food—Elaborate buffet dishes with the emphasis on elegance; eggnog and other alcoholic beverages; "breakfast" or late supper after midnight. Greeks make a bread baked with a luck-bringing coin. Many people hold open house on the day. There are many ethnic food customs: blackeyed peas for Southerners; the French eat pancakes, Germans fish; Swiss whipped cream; Pennsylvania Dutch pork and sauerkraut. The idea is swelling, fecundity, abundance.

Customs—Making resolutions for the coming year, reviewing the one past; partying; kissing someone, making loud noises, and singing "Auld Lang Syne" at midnight.

Requirements—New Year's Day is a national holiday; no work except for service and support personnel.

January 1
Solemnity of Mary, Mother of God (formerly **Circumcision**)
                    Christian (Catholic)   Minor
St. Basil's Day (Eastern Orthodox)
Significance—Eighth day after the birth of Jesus, therefore the anniversary of his circumcision, this day's identity was shifted after Vatican II to commemorate a holiday already celebrated at various times in various cultures. If you're in a good mood, you can see this as a growing recognition of the importance of women in the church. If you're in a bad mood, chalk it up to progressive de-Judaizing.

References—Luke 2:21.

Religious Activities—In either case, a Catholic has to go to church—something that may have a salutary effect on the excesses encouraged by the secular January 1 celebration, especially since the disappearance of the notorious twenty-minute 6:00 a.m. New Year's Day mass (the priest could say it faster in Latin, since few understood it anyway).

January 6 or nearest Sunday
Epiphany (Twelfth Night)   Christian   Major
Significance—Commemoration of the arrival of the magi with gifts; major because it constitutes the first acknowledgement of Jesus's kingship by "the world."

References—Matt. 2:1-12.

Religious Activities—Go to church.

Food—The goodies off the Christmas tree; a cake with three beans

175

in it—the people who get the pieces with the beans reign for the night. Serbians make a walnut-filled yeast pastry called *kifle*.

Customs—Our son-in-law's mother made this a major event, with the children who'd gotten the three bean-pieces of cake donning paper crowns; their father then wrote blessings in chalk over each door lintel and they processed in and out of the house through each door carrying candles (flashlights for the little ones) and singing "We Three Kings."

Eastern Orthodox Christmas follows the Old Style Julian rather than the reformed Gregorian calendar. Therefore, Orthodox Epiphany takes place twelve days later, on Western January 18, and is celebrated with water rituals commemorating the Baptism of Christ.

10 Tevet*
Jerusalem Seige Fast   Jewish   Minor
Significance—The anniversary of the day the Babylonians beseiged Jerusalem—a seige that ended seven months later in the destruction of the First Temple.
References—II Kings 25:1, Jer. 39:1.
Religious activities—Special prayers in the daily liturgy.
Food—None during daylight hours.
Customs—Get up before dawn to eat. This is often a young person's first fast, since it's the shortest of the year.
Requirements—No washing or bathing except for necessary hygiene.

January 15 or 3d Monday in January
Martin Luther King Day   Secular   Major
Significance—Recognition of great civil rights leader.
Customs—Many communities hold candlelight processions ending in ecumenical, interracial religious services.
Requirements—Legal holiday in most states; no work for many.

February 2
Candelmas or **Lady Day** (British) Christian Varying
Groundhog Day   Secular   Minor
Significance—Both the post-childbirth ritual purification of Mary and the presentation of Jesus in the Temple (for *pidyon ha-ben*—see Chapter 8 if you don't remember what that is).
References—Lev. 12; Ex. 13:2-13, Lk. 2:22-39.
Religious activities—Procession with candles in church; blessing of candles to be used during the year.

*The meanings of Hebrew month-names are ancient, often obscure, and about as relevant as knowing our "May" comes from "Maia," the goddess of increase and growth, or that "August" refers to the Caesar of that appelation. Remembering them is hard enough—don't worry about understanding what they mean.

Customs—The coincidence of this religious feast with the secular Groundhog Day isn't such a coincidence after all—they both have roots in ancient rites calculated to bring on the warm weather for spring planting. If the groundhog (in Germany it was a badger) sees his shadow (i.e. it's a bright day) and is frightened back into his hole, no dice—spring will be delayed six more weeks.

February 3
St. Blaise's Day   Christian   Minor
Significance—Anniversary of a bishop-saint's beheading in 316.
Religious activities—Blaise is said to have miraculously cured a child's throat infection on his way to execution; Catholic churches still bless the throats of people who wish it on this day.
Customs—The blessing is done with crossed candles, which is why this otherwise obscure feast is associated with the more important one of Candlemas.
Requirements—None.

15th of Shevat
Tu b'Shevat (Short for the 15th of Shevat)
                              Jewish   Minor
Significance—New year of the trees, a legal standardization for commercial practices. You could combine it with Arbor Day or with Martin Luther King Day, which it often falls near.
References—Talmudic.
Religious activities—None out of the ordinary in the synagogue, except that penitential prayers are omitted.
Food—Carob, almonds, or anything that grows on trees native to Israel. Some people celebrate a sort of mini-seder, featuring coconuts or walnuts (which with their hard shells and soft insides symbolize Earth) and winter-white wine, soft pitted fruit like cherries (symbolizing Water) and spring-blush wine, fruits soft throughout such as grapes or strawberries (symbolizing Air) and summer-light red wine, and full red fall wine (symbolizing Fire) with no fruit—the wine is the essence.
Customs—Planting trees (start one in a pot, if you live in snowy climes) or sending money to Israel for tree-planting; exploring mystical symbolism regarding trees. Talk to the kids about conservation.
Requirements—None.

February 14
St. Valentine's/Valentine's Christian/secular   Minor
Significance—Pagan origins in the Roman fertility festival of Lupercalia became attached to a couple of 3d century Christian martyrs who supposedly sent messages from prison by carrier pigeon.

In the 16th century the upper classes started exchanging love messages as a custom that would set them apart from the despised, newly arising middle class. Of course, the middle class took the practice over and it's been going strong ever since.

Religious activities—None. However, some Jews object to the pagan associations as much as the attenuated Christian ones, and won't celebrate it.

Food—Sweets: coeurs de creme or anything heartshaped. We favor heart-shaped chocolate layer cake decorated with crushed candy canes leftover from the Christmas tree. Waste not, want not!

Customs—Sending greeting cards; exchanging candy, flowers, or personal gifts with a lover; proposing marriage.

Requirements—None. If you don't have kids who've been told to bring to school thirty comic cards plus one nice one for the teacher, and you feel you've had it with holidays for the time being, ignore it; you can enjoy feeling superior to mindless consumerism.

Third Monday in February
Presidents Day	Secular	Major
Lincoln's Birthday	Feb. 12	
Washington's Birthday	Feb. 18	

Significance—Congress has agreed to combine observance of the birthdays of these two presidents and stick the resulting diploid onto the most convenient possibility for a three-day weekend.

Food—People used to go in for cherry pie for Washington and they used to drink a toast for each state of the union ... when there were only thirteen states! Honest Abe doesn't seem to have an associated food. You do enough, forget it.

Customs—Retelling the quasi-mythical lore—here Lincoln comes to the fore: slip *Young Mr. Lincoln* or *Abe Lincoln in Illinois* on the VCR, put your feet up, and relax.

Requirements—A national holiday; no work except for service and support personnel.

Forty-one days (excluding Sundays) before Easter
Shrove (Confession) **Tuesday** or **Mardi Gras** (Fat Tuesday)	
Christian	Minor

Significance—The last day before the beginning of the Lenten season.

Religious activities—Going to confession, planning personal Lenten observances.

Food—Doughnuts or *fastnacht* (doughnut-like dough pillows), hot cross buns, anything fat or sweet, in addition to meat, all of which you will be doing without or cutting down on during Lent.

Customs—Carnival (*carne vale*, "farewell to meat"): dressing in costume, parading, partying.

Requirements—none.

Forty Days, excluding Sundays, before Easter

Ash Wednesday   Christian   Varying

Significance—The first day of Lent, the forty day (excluding Sundays) preparation for Easter commemorating Jesus's fast in the desert.

References—Gen. 3:19, Qo. 3:20, Matt. 4:1-11, Mk. 1:12-13, Lk. 4:1-13.

Religious activities—For Anglican/Episcopalians and other denominations with "high" liturgies, a special church service. For Roman Catholics, the priest smears a cross on your forehead with his thumb dipped in a mixture of ashes from last Palm Sunday's palms and holy oil, saying, "Remember man, dust thou art and to dust thou shalt return."

Food—No meat.

Customs—Giving up some lawful pleasure for the purpose of keeping the penitential spirit of the season present to your mind. That is, giving up an unlawful pleasure like shoplifting or giving up something for another reason such as refraining from dessert in the hopes that you'll be set up for bathing suit season might be laudable, and this might be a good time to undertake them, but they don't fill the bill for Lenten self-denial. A border–line practice like smoking, which is not unlawful for most Christians and which there are other good reasons for giving up, could serve—and the element of religious duty plus the promise to yourself that you can go back to it after Lent may make it easier for you to undertake a smoke-free period. After all, nobody will say, come Easter, that you must have a cigarette.

Another custom, which is getting more attention these days, is that of the positive Lenten practice. Instead of merely giving something up, vow to do something: give a sacrificial amount to charity, attend mass oftener than once a week, read a devotional or theological work, set aside time for meditation, etc.

Requirements—For "high church" Christian adults who are not infirm, elderly, pregnant, nursing, or required to do heavy labor, eating only one full meal a day (the other two together should not equal it), with meat only at that meal and none at all on Friday (some people also abstain from meat on Wednesday). Eastern Orthodox Christians traditionally abstain from fish, wine, oil, eggs, and dairy products as well. Their Lent is also often at a different time, since Orthodox Easter must, like the first one, fall after Passover. For Catholics, receiving the Eucharist some time between now and Trinity Sunday, the week after Easter. This usually also involves going to confession, and is known as "Easter duty." Please try to partake of the Sacrament of Reconciliation, as it's more properly called today, early in the season. Don't shortchange your own spiritual life or try your confessor's by waiting till Holy Week when the line stretches all around the narthex and the confessional screen is sliding back and forth so fast it's starting to smolder.

14th of Adar
Purim (Feast of Lots)   Jewish   Major

Significance—Commemoration of Queen Esther's foiling of the wicked vizier Haman in his plots against the Jews in Persia (legendary).

Reference—The Book of Esther.

Religious activities—Synagogue service at which the Book of Esther (*Megillah*) is read. Noisemakers (*graggers*) may be brought along and sounded whenever Haman's name is mentioned.

Food—Beans and peas, *kreplach*, turkey, *hamantaschen* (Haman's pockets, or in Hebrew, *oznei Haman*, Haman's ears)—tri-cornered pastry folded over poppy, prune, or other sweet filling.

Customs—Dressing in costume, sending children to neighbors with goodies, giving to charity, drinking alcohol "till you can't tell Mordechai from Haman" (the only Jewish holiday on which inebriation is ok).

Requirements—Hear the Megillah read, feast, and be friendly. (Work is permitted.) The observant fast the day before.

March 17
St. Patrick's Day   Christian/Secular   Varying

Significance—Feast of popular 5th century saint whose missionary work was carried on in Ireland.

Food—Irish (lamb) stew and soda bread or corned beef and cabbage; Irish coffee, green-tinted beer.

Customs—The shamrock, symbol of the Trinity, is displayed with abandon; there is a major parade in New York City, with the central line of Fifth Ave. painted green. If your background is Italian and you resent the dominance of the Irish in the American Catholic Church, focus on the Feast of St. Joseph two days later; for the Welsh, eat leeks on St. David's Day March 1.

Requirements—The Lenten fast and abstinence rules are suspended for American Catholics.

Sunday Before Easter
Palm Sunday   Christian   Varying

Significance—Commemoration of Jesus' triumphal entry into Jerusalem, when the people waved palm fronds and shouted hosannas in token of his kingship.

References—Matt. 21:4-9, Mk. 11:7-10, Lk. 19:35-38, Jn. 12:1-19.

Religious activities—Attending church, procuring a palm frond.

Customs—Processing around the church waving your palm leaf, placing the palm someplace prominent and/or devotional in your home—pinned behind the crucifix is a popular choice—or plaiting it into a cross or other meaningful shape to keep throughout the year. (Ashes for Ash Wednesday are obtained by burning the previous year's palms; you can throw yours away if burning it isn't convenient.) In the Philippines, they bless the coconut palms on this day.

15-22 Nisan
Passover (*Pesach*)   Jewish   Major

Significance—Re-enactment of liberation from Egyptian slavery under Moses. Celebration of spring in pastoral and agricultural feast (once possibly two separate ones). Probably the oldest extant religious holiday anywhere.

References—Exodus, Leviticus, Deuteronomy.

Religious activities—Ridding the house of *hametz* (see below). Partaking of the seder ceremonial meal on the first two nights of the week (or the first night only in Israel). You'll need at least one Haggadah: a book or pamphlet retelling the story, recounting the order, and listing the necessities for the meal. Counting the Omer from the second day.

Food (see also Requirements)—A traditional European seder includes, aside from the ritual foods required by the ceremony, hard boiled eggs dipped in salt water, gefilte fish (you can buy it in a jar), matzo balls in chicken soup, roast chicken or pot roast of beef, *tzimmes* (a carrot dish), *kugel* (potato pudding), fruit compote and sponge cake. This can be adapted to a meatless menu by serving the matzo balls in vegetable broth and substituting fish as the main course. To make a more strictly vegetarian meal, use balls of egg salad (or, following Sephardi custom, bean salad) for gefilte fish and have nut cutlets made with matzo meal or an eggplant casserole (soy patties are acceptable if you're Sephardi) for an entree. If you don't eat eggs either, and are determined to follow Ashkenazi tradition, I'm sure you've faced tougher problems than this—you're on your own. Italian Jews always eat artichokes on Pesach—*carciofi alla Giuda,* "Jewish-style artichokes," trimmed and double-fried whole, are labor-intensive but fabulous—as are matzo balls with ground chicken and its liver in them.

Customs—Giving the whole house a facelift along with ferocious cleaning, "finding" the last (previously planted) bits of *hametz* (leavened crumbs) with a lighted candle, brushing them up with a feather and burning them; wearing new clothes, eating matzo throughout the week (serve plenty of greenstuff, since a diet heavy in matzo can be binding), singing comic songs after the seder, inviting an outsider to share the seder.

Requirements—Removing from the house and refraining from consuming anything containing any sort of leavening and any wheat or grain product besides those specially prepared of matzo meal. Ashkenazi Jews refrain from beans, peas, peanuts, and rice as well—Sephardim do not. Religiously observant people use dishes and utensils set aside for use at this time only, to keep any trace of leavening from contaminating the food. Refrain from work on the first two and last two days. Blu Greenberg says she feels her experience "making Pesach" year after year ought to go on her resumé. If you've never done it before, don't expect to be perfect the first time.

Holy Week
Thursday Before Easter
Maundy (Mandated) **Thursday** or **Holy Thursday**
                                          Christian   Minor
Significance—Commemoration of the Last Supper partaken of by Jesus, especially the washing of the apostles' feet and the institution of the Eucharist. *Tenebrae* ("shadows") prayer services are often held in the evening; Protestants who don't celebrate the Lord's Supper or communion every week usually do so on this night.
References—Jn. 13: 1-17.
Food—Unleavened bread, wine, fish.
Religious activities—Attending church, partaking of a ceremonial re-enactment of the Last Supper at home or at church. Just remember what we quoted in Chapter 1 about not co-opting the seder to this without being sensitive to Jewish feelings.
Customs—Washing each others' feet.
Requirements—None.

Friday Before Easter
Good Friday   Christian   Varying
Significance—Commemoration of the crucifixion and death of Jesus.
References—Matt. 27:31-61, Mk. 15:21-47, Lk. 23:20-56, Jn. 19:17-42.
Religious activities—Attending church for a special service emphasizing prayers for the world and its peoples.
Food—No meat, spartan fare. Many Christians who otherwise don't engage in penitential practices fast on this day alone. Greeks eat lentil soup.
Customs—Refrain from all work between noon and 3:00 p.m. (the traditional time of Jesus' actual suffering on the cross); contribute to the upkeep of the Christian shrines at places associated with Jesus'

182

life; shroud all holy pictures or statues.

Requirements—Fast and abstinence (as for Ash Wednesday).

Saturday before Easter
Holy Saturday

Significance—A waiting time—the crucifixion has taken place, but the Resurrection is yet to come—Jesus is still in the tomb.

References—Matt. 27:62-66.

Religious activities—Easter vigil is held in the evening; the new fire, the paschal candle and holy water are blessed.

Requirements—Evening or midnight services fulfill the requirement to attend church on Easter.

27 Nisan
Holocaust Remembrance *(Yom ha-Shoah)*
                    Jewish Secular/Religious   Varying

Significance—Commemoration of the unspeakable horrors of the Nazi terror. The date is the result of compromise among various schools of thought; it comes, as Blu Greenberg puts it, "between Pesach and Shavuot, in the springtime of a Jew's heart."

Religious activities—This observance is still developing and does not have a formal liturgy as yet. Many communities, Jewish and Christian, gather for a mourning service, perhaps with reminiscences of survivors. If yours doesn't, maybe you should start one.

Food—Ned's college sometimes does a lunchtime remembrance at which the menu is a cup of potato soup, an unbuttered whole wheat roll, an apple, and a glass of water. This supposedly spartan fare is so luxurious in contrast to what concentration camp inmates were actually given to eat that it is food for thought indeed.

Customs—Again, these are developing. Refraining from jolly music, secular TV, and other distractions seems appropriate.

Requirements—Remember.

First Sunday following First Full Moon after Spring Equinox
(Eastern Orthodox—First Sunday after Passover)
Easter   Christian   Major

Significance—Commemoration of Jesus' Resurrection from the dead, proclaiming victory over sin and salvation for the world.

References—Matt. 28:1-10, Mk. 16:1-8, Lk. 24:1-12, Jn. 20:1-18.

Food—Lamb, as a symbol of Jesus as Paschal sacrifice, the Lamb of God (grisly notion, in a way, but there it is); the last winter ham or the first spring chicken, depending on your agricultural tradition (and how the Jewish partner feels about eating pork—ham originally became popular for this day as an expression of contempt for Jewish practices); egg and lemon soup or lamb-organ and rice soup *(mageritsa)*, spinach-cheese pastries *(spanakopeta)*, and a sweet round bread and a braided wreath-shaped one if you're Greek: all kinds of regional and ethnic fancy pastries (matzo-meal carrot cake or nut torte or flourless chocolate cake are good Passover choices); whatever you gave up for Lent.

Customs—Coloring eggs and hiding them, with candy, for the children to hunt (the Northern European fertility goddess whose name gives us the word "Easter" had the hare and the egg as her symbols—the Easter Bunny is a she); wearing new clothes; eating some newly ripe fruit or vegetable such as strawberries or asparagus for the first time of the season (the Jewish partner has a special blessing to say for this); greeting neighbors with joy.

Requirements—Attending church (sunrise outdoor services are wonderful), rejoicing.

5 Iyyar (or previous Thursday if the 5th is Shabbat)
Israel Independence Day (*Yom ha-Atzmaut*)
                    Jewish/Secular   Varying
Significance—Anniversary, in the lunar calendar, of the solar date May 14, 1948—the day the State of Israel was established.

Religious activities—Another still-evolving holiday. Special psalms of praise are sung at the evening and morning services, while penitential prayers are omitted. The shofar may be blown.

Food—Israeli: *hummous* (chickpea and sesame paste) or *felafel* (fried chickpea balls with pita bread and diced cucumbers and tomatoes; *baba ganoush* (eggplant salad—tastes better than it sounds); *tabouleh* (bulghur wheat salad); stuffed vegetables.

Customs—Naturally, they're more elaborate in Israel than here—speeches, parades, fireworks, etc. In America, Jewish community centers are often hung with Israeli flags and educational books or films about Israel are made available.

Requirements—None.

Sunday after Easter
Trinity Sunday   Christian (Catholic)/Secular Varying
Significance—A feast only formally made part of the liturgy in 1911; since Vatican II this day is simply "The Second Sunday of Easter," part of the series leading to Pentecost.

References—John 20: 19-31.

Customs—In England, this day has traditional implications for the legal divisions of the secular year.

Requirements—Demarcates the end of the period in which Catholics must "make their Easter duty"—i.e. receive the Eucharist (preceded by, if necessary, the Sacrament of Reconciliation) which began on Ash Wednesday.

April 30
Walpurgis Night
Significance—Ushers in May Day revelry; usual pagan origins appropiated to the 8th century German abbess St. Walburga.
Customs—Scandinavians and some British have dances and bonfires to scare witches away.

May 1
May Day (also **Feast of St. Joseph the Worker**, formerly **Feast of Our Lady**)   Christian/Secular   Minor
Significance—The Romans celebrated the feast of Flora, goddess of gardens; the Christian church expropriated this for their "Queen of the May," Mary. In this generation, evidently in response to the Communist world's socialist labor parades and demonstrations, the Roman church has transferred the focus to Jesus' foster father.
Religious activities—Since May is still Mary's month, her statue is often decked with flowers, but somehow it's not the same.
Customs—Leaving baskets of flowers on the doorknobs of your friends and lovers; dancing around a maypole (the Puritans forbade this as a popish, idolatrous practice, and many Protestants still don't care for it—the Jewish partner might not, either); gathering spring flowers and flowering branches in the woods. Visit Bryn Mawr College for an old-fashioned English-style May Day, complete with May Queen (the college president) on a white horse, and flower-bedecked oxen bringing in the maypole.

18 Iyyar
Lag b'Omer (Thirty-third Day of Sheaf Counting)
                            Jewish   Minor
Significance—Various historical, agricultural, symbolic, and mystical meanings are attached to this day between Passover and Shavuot, a period whose days are counted off from the second day of Passover by the pious.
References—Leviticus 23:9ff.
Religious activity—Counting the days of Omer, if you've been doing so all along.
Food—Wheat-based and first-fruit dishes.
Customs—The period of the Omer is one of mourning, which Lag b'Omer partially lifts. Therefore, this is a day for getting married, for getting a haircut, for listening to music and lighting bonfires (not necessarily in that order). Because of some unclear historical associations, it is customary for children to play with toy bows and arrows.
Requirements—Vary from community to community. If you're new at all this, don't worry about Lag b'Omer for now.

Fortieth Day After Easter
Ascension Thursday   Christian   Varying
Significance—Commemoration of Jesus' ascension into heaven.
References—Acts 1:6-11.
Religious activities—Blessing of bread, herbs, and new fruits.
Food—Tea made from at least seven herbs; fish (the symbol of
Christ—and just in time for shad or smelt season).
Customs—This is a major holiday for the Amish and Mennonite
communities; it used to be for all Christendom.
Requirements—Attending church for Catholics.

6-7 Sivan
Shavuot (Weeks) or **Pentecost** (50th Day)
                                 Jewish   Varying
Significance—A midsummer harvest-and-sowing festival, once
marked by a sacrifice of first-fruits at the Temple, later commemo-
rating the giving of the Torah to Moses by God, on Mt. Sinai.
References—Deut. 16:9-12, Lev. 23:15-21, Ex. 19-20.
Religious activities—Synagogue service featuring readings from
Ruth and Exodus and, in some circles, decorating the building with
greenery and flowers. Many Reform congregations hold confirma-
tions on this day.
Food—Dairy: blintzes and three-sided cheese *kreplach*; two
loaves of sweet, extra-long hallah.
Customs—Rejoicing, feasting, meditating on the Ten Commandments, introducing children to Torah study (with cakes and
honey to make the experience a sweet one), studying Torah all night.
Since the last of the Passover matzo should be gone by the end of
Shavuot, some Italian Jews ceremonially bring out the remnants to
the nearest water and feed them to the fish.
Requirements—Candlelighting and *kiddush* (wine-blessing
prayers).

Second Sunday in May
Mother's Day   Secular   Minor
Significance—Though there have been similar celebrations in
the past elsewhere, notably "Mothering Sunday" in England, the
American feast—adopted widely elsewhere—was established by
(childless) Anna Jarvis in Augusta, Georgia in 1907; it was formally
recognized by President Wilson in 1914.
Religious activities—Since it's always on Sunday, many churches
acknowledge the day in prayers or songs.
Food—Roast lamb or veal (seems a poor way to honor sheep and
cow mothers, doesn't it?); fruitcake, rice pudding or anything symbolizing fertility....Look, just take Mom out and let her pick her own
menu.

Customs—Wear a red carnation for a living mother or a white one for a deceased one; buy a corsage of her favorites for her; visit and bring and/or send cards, gifts, flowers.

Requirements—Be nice to your mother—and any other woman who's been a mentor to you or a force for good in the community.

Fiftieth Day After Easter
Pentecost (Fifty Days; English **Whitsun**)

Christian   Varying

Significance—Commemoration of the descent of the Holy Spirit (the Third Person of the Trinity in Christian belief, also called the Paraclete) on the disciples in the form of tongues of flame over their heads, whereupon they began to speak languages they had never learned. (This is not, evidently, the same phenomenon referred to elsewhere in the New Testament as "speaking in tongues" or *glossolalia,* still practiced by Pentecostal Christians as part of a religious ecstatic experience.)

References—Acts 2:1-13.

Religious activities—Special liturgy in church; some denominations do baptisms on this day.

Food—Roast veal, ale, baked custard, gooseberry pudding, cheesecake.

Customs—A priest we know wonders why Pentecost isn't celebrated as fully as Easter or Christmas; after all, this is the advent of the Third Person of the Trinity. Houses decorated with crepe paper tongues of flame and papier mache doves; trefoil cookies... you could think up your own, if you have the energy.

Requirements—Attending church.

May 31 (actual)   Last Monday in May (observed)
Memorial Day   Secular   Varying

Significance—With its roots in pagan observations celebrating the ordering of the world out of primal chaos (including the separation of the dead from the living—a state of things always iffy to the ancients), this day became a legal American holiday on May 5, 1866, as a remembrance of the Civil War dead. Since then, it has been formally expanded to include all deceased veterans.

Customs—Having a family reunion or barbeque; decorating and refurbishing the graves of one's family, especially the military.

June 14
Flag Day   American secular   Minor

Significance—On this day in 1777, George Washington presented the first official flag to the Continental Congress in Philadelphia, which resolved to adopt it. In 1949, President Truman declared this a national holiday.

Customs—Displaying the flag.

Requirements—Learn the flag code: don't display it at night unless it's spotlit, don't display it in bad weather unless it's a special kind, fold it right when you take it down. If we're going to have quasi-religious secular symbols (that is, if we can talk about "desecrating"—i.e. making "un-sacred"—a flag), let's keep the ritual straight.

17 Tammuz
Fall of Jerusalem   Jewish   Minor

Significance—Commemoration of breaching of the walls of Jerusalem by Babylonian troops, ushering in the Exilic period; and of the sacking of Jerusalem by Roman troops 500 years later, ushering in the period of the Diaspora.

References—II Kings 25:8-12, II Chron. 36:19, Jer. 39:8-10; 52:12-27.

Food—Fast during daylight.

Customs—Ushers in a period of mourning that climaxes at *Tishe b'Av*—no celebrating, haircuts, or weddings.

Requirements—Fasting and prayer for the observant.

Third Sunday in June
Father's Day   Secular   Minor

Significance—This is a 20th century American observance; no one else has found it necessary to set aside a particular day for fathers—either because they were thought not to need recognition, having most of the money and power already, or because their parenthood was considered the least important thing about them. Here's hoping both those considerations are incomprehensible to the next generation.

Customs—Same as for Mother's Day, except that unless Dad is the family cook he'd probably just as soon have his special dinner at home.

July 4
Independence Day   Secular   Major

Significance—Anniversary of the signing of the Declaration of Independence from England.

Historical references—Declaration of Independence.

Religious activities—Many churches have special services and, on the day or its nearest Sunday, sing "America the Beautiful" or "God Bless America" (written by the Jewish—and intermarried!—Irving Berlin).

Food—Native or particularly American dishes, especially corn on

188

the cob, hot dogs, hamburgers, and watermelon; something red, white, and blue for dessert—angel food cake with coconut icing served with strawberry and blueberry sauces is a good choice.

Customs—Picnicking; family reunions; municipal fireworks displays, parades, and patriotic speeches.

9 Av
Tishe b'Av (Ninth of ((the month of)) Av)
Jewish　　　　　　Varying
Significance—Anniversary of the destruction of the First Temple in 586 BCE and of the Second Temple in 70 CE, to which other historical disasters have traditionally been attached.

References—II Kings 25:1-7; Jer. 52:4-30.

Religious activities—Praying in a darkened, shrouded synagogue, reading from Lamentations, mourning as for a family member.

Food—None from sunset to sunset: a large meal in the middle of the preceding afternoon; bread and a hardboiled egg just before sunset (dip the bread in ashes to really get in the mood).

Customs—Sitting on the floor or a low stool, not wearing leather shoes, visiting the Western Wall in Jerusalem.

Requirements—Fasting, refraining from various sensory pleasures. Necessary work is permitted.

August 15
Feast of the Assumption
Christian (Catholic and Orthodox)　　　　Minor
Significance—Commemoration of the Virgin Mary's bodily assumption into heaven. This is the most recently promulgated (1950) of Roman Catholic dogmas and reflects a long-standing tradition that Mary has already experienced the bodily resurrection promised to all the saved (whatever "already" may mean in the context of eternity).

References—Gen. 5:21-24, II Kings 2:11-13, Rev. 9:1-17.

Religious activities—Blessing the summer harvest—the new grapes in Southern Europe; in Poland it's the onion festival—and the fleet, where there is one.

Food—Logically, whatever you just blessed (no, not the fleet, but what it brings in, silly).

Requirements—Mass, for American Catholics and some others.

August 26
Women's Equality Day　　　Secular　　　Minor (sigh)
Significance—Anniversary of the ratification of the 19th Amendment (Women's Suffrage) in 1920.

Religious activities—Re-read Sojourner Truth's remarks to the Seneca Falls Convention of 1848.

Customs—The League of Women Voters, direct descendent of the Suffrage movement (and open to men as well, incidentally), celebrates with speeches and articles.

Requirements—Take your civic responsibility seriously.

First Monday in September
Labor Day　　　　American secular　　　Major
Significance—Recognition of the role of labor and laborers in the building of the nation, first celebrated in 1882. The date was chosen because it's halfway between July 4 and Thanksgiving, but it's come to seem an appropriate closure to summer frolics.

Food—Fried chicken, spareribs (beef ribs barbecue fine if you're kosher), the last watermelon.

Customs—Having the last beach picnic of summer; getting organized for back-to-school.

Requirements—National holiday; no work except for service and support personnel.

Last Friday in September
American Indian Day　　　Secular　　　Minor
Significance—Acknowledgement of the First Americans originally celebrated in Rochester, New York in 1912 and since taken up by some (not enough, in our opinion) states.

Food—Succotash, hominy, squash.

Suggested activity—Look up the history of your particular community's interactions with Native Americans, and find out about them.

1-2 Tishre
Rosh Hashanah (Head of the year) or **New Year**
　　　　　　　　　　Jewish　　　　Major
Significance—The first of the High Holydays, ushering in the ten "Days of Awe," Rosh Hashanah commemorates the creation of the earth and is considered a day of judgment.

References—Gen. 1, Neh. 8:10.

Religious activities—Solemn synagogue services including the blowing of the *shofar* and the saying of prayers emphasizing judgment and the kingship of God.

Food—Festive, featuring a special fancy loaf of challah, often round, and honey into which challah and apple slices are dipped (for a "sweet year"). No nuts. (Don't worry about why, would we lie to you?)

Customs—Greeting one another with the wish (in Hebrew), "May you be inscribed (in the Book of Life) for a good year," or *"Shanah Tova,"* (Happy New Year—may be said in English), or (in English/

Yiddish), "Good *Yontif*," an all-purpose holiday greeting.

Modern—sending greeting cards. Ancient—going to running water—sea, lake, river, or in the last resort a well—and emptying your pockets into it (include a little small change) while reciting prayers that your sins should only do likewise. Attending synagogue. This last is included here as a custom since there are Rosh Hashanah Jews just as there are Easter Christians—people whose only formal religious community observance is this one (hence the invidious practice of charging for seats in the synagogue, so that regulars won't be crowded out). While this once-a-year practice is not encouraged, it is probably better than nothing. Something might Happen to you, watch out.

Requirements—Attending synagogue, hearing the *shofar,* beginning to set your spiritual house in order. Candlelighting and *kiddush.* No work.

October 12 (actual)   *Second Monday (observed)*
Columbus Day   Secular   Minor

Significance—Commemoration of European "discovery" of America.

Customs—New York City has had a parade since 1792; it's been a federal holiday since 1937. A good day to remember that 1492 was also the year of the expulsion of Jews from Spain, that Columbus' ship's doctor was a Jew, and that there is evidence indicating the possibility that the explorer himself was a secret Jew (don't tell your local Catholic Knights of Columbus chapter that, unless you're ready for some volatile discussion).

10 Tishre
Yom Kippur (Day of Atonement)   Jewish   Major

Significance—A day of penance and renewal.

References—Lev. 16:29-31, 23:27-32; Num. 29:7.

Religious activities—Ideally, the whole "day" (sunset to sunset) should be spent in prayer in the synagogue.

Food—None on the day itself, a light meal before the opening sunset (makes fasting easier than on a stuffed gut) and an easily digestible one—usually dairy—after the closing one.

Customs—Yom Kippur Eve—Giving to charity, settling all debts and asking forgiveness of anyone you may have injured, lighting ceremonial candles, blessing children. (A very old fashioned custom involved the sacrifice of a chicken. We don't recommend it.) Yom Kippur itself—Wearing white, not wearing leather shoes, not shaving nor washing beyond hygienic requirements, not indulging in gossip or any casual speech.

Requirements—Abstaining from all food and drink, even water (unless you are very old or young, ill, pregnant or nursing, or required to do physical labor) from sunset to sunset, repentance. No work.

Last Sunday in October
Reformation Sunday
    Christian (Protestant)   Varying
Significance—Commemoration of Martin Luther's launching the Reformation by nailing his list of Ninety–Five Theses to the cathedral door at Wittenberg on October 31, 1517.

Religious activities—Some congregations have a procession with the minister leading, carrying the Bible aloft (since the right of individuals to read and interpret Scripture for themselves was a major proposition of Luther's). Others think that smacks of popery and confine themselves to appropriate sermons.

15-22 Tishre
Sukkot (Booths or Tabernacles) Jewish   Major
Significance—A harvest festival in which the booths the Children of Israel used to dwell in the wilderness during the Exodus are commemorated. Also associated with renewal of the Covenant and with the onset of winter rains—Edna Servi Machlin says that, in her childhood Italian village, if the fall rains didn't come on time the gentiles blamed the Jews!

References—Deut. 16:13-15, Lev. 23:34-36, Ex. 23:16, Num. 29:12-38.

Religious activities—Building a *sukkah* or booth with temporary walls—at least two, plus some of a third—and with branches for roof. In the synagogue, there are processions with the Torah and with special symbolic greens and fruit (myrtle, willow, palm, and citron).

Food—At least one fruit not previously eaten that season, all sorts of sweets and goodies, and, the first night, a piece of bread at least the size of an olive (so you can say the important bread-blessing over it). You can eat the citron (*etrog*) after the holiday, but the ones grown for ceremonial use are non-hybridized; they don't taste like grandma's fruitcake. Stud it with cloves and use it for a pomander instead. (You'll want to do something with it, when you see how much they cost.)

Customs—Invite guests, especially the poor, to the *sukkah,* decorate it with fruits and pictures (particularly one of Abraham and Isaac on Mt. Moriah) as elaborately as you like—this is a good outlet for the cut-and-paste-and-hang-it-up urges of children that may be unsatisfied if you don't go in for Christmas decorations.

Requirements—To eat in the *sukkah,* sleep there if possible, wave the *lulav* and *etrog* (the ceremonial group of greens and fruit). No work on the first two and the eighth days. (The last day of Sukkot is called **Shemini Atzeret.** See **Simkhat Torah.**)

23 Tishre
Simkhat Torah (Rejoicing in the Teaching)
          Jewish   Varying
Significance—The end of Sukkot (observed in Reform communities and in Israel on Shemini Atzeret).
References—Deut 33-34.
Religious activities—Synagogue service, unusually raucous, in which the Torah readings for the year are completed and the scroll turned back to the beginning.
Food—Italian Jews drink sweet vermouth and eat the candy-coated almonds also seen at weddings.
Customs—Torah readings by as many people as possible, including a group one for children; procession of adults with Torah scrolls and children with toy scrolls, flags, and/or apples with lit candles inside them; dismantling the *sukkah*. This was a day of special remembrance for Soviet Jews; perhaps it will be used to commemorate another oppressed group.
Requirements—Hear the end and the beginning of the Torah, be happy. (If you get a chance, attend a Hasidic celebration and see what rejoicing in the Torah is all about.)

October 31
Hallowe'en (Holy Evening) or **All Hallow's Eve**
          Christian/secular   Minor
Significance—Derives from a combination of the Roman harvest feast of Pomona and the Celtic Samhain, on which the souls of the dead were thought to roam the earth, giving rise to various propitiatory and pious practices.
Religious activities—None.
Food—Harvest fruits (we like a pumpkin stuffed with meat and rice and baked whole), taffy apples, cakes decorated in orange and black.
Customs—Dressing in costume; playing pranks; giving out sweets to children who come to the door; telling fortunes and otherwise playing at occult practices and toying with their symbols. This is done, largely, by people for whom these practices and symbols—e.g. calling up spirits, pretending to be witches, or displaying black cats—represent exploded superstitions without reality and therefore without importance. If your spouse is a Fundamentalist Christian or observant Jew, you may be surprised to find that these things are still regarded with dread and deadly seriousness by some people.
Requirements—None.

November 1
All Saints Day   Christian   Minor
Significance—Since there is not room on the calendar for each saint to have a separate feast, and since the identities of all the saints, i.e. those in heaven, are not known to us, the Catholic Church recognizes them all on this day.
References—Rev. 7:2-4, 9-14.
Religious activities—Attending mass.
Requirements—Holy Day of Obligation for all Catholics.

November 2 (often observed on November 1)
All Souls Day   Christian   Varying
Significance—Following immediately on Halloween, this day is set aside to commemorate those who have died.
Religious activities—Praying for the dead, for those who believe in Purgatory and therefore that souls are not designated for heaven or hell immediately upon death, but may still be assisted in achieving salvation by the grace obtained through people still on earth.
Customs—Catholics often ask to have masses said for the repose of the souls of their deceased family members and loved ones.
Requirements—None.

November 11
Veterans Day (formerly **Armistice Day**)
                              Secular   Minor
Significance—The guns of World War I stopped firing at 11 a.m. on this date in 1911: the Armistice with the Central Powers.
Religious Activities—The nearest Sunday is World Peace Sunday.
Customs—Tend the graves of the war dead; make a donation to a Vets hospital.

Fourth Thursday in November
Thanksgiving   American civil religious   Major
Significance—Commemoration of the Pilgrims' feast in thanksgiving, with their Native American teachers, for having come safely through the year of 1621 with a bountiful harvest. Since 1863 it's been a national holiday, though the date didn't settle down till recently.
Religious activities—Many communities have an ecumenical service.
Food—The first Thanksgiving did not include turkey; the Puritans later encouraged people to have it, and mince pies, on that day instead of Christmas—which they disapproved of celebrating. So now many of us have it both times, with such Native American and harvest-oriented foods as corn (as a vegetable or in stuffing, cornbread, or

Indian pudding), sweet potatoes, pumpkin and pecan pies, etc. If you're trying to keep kosher but afraid you'll miss the traditional oyster stew, try homemade mushroom soup instead. And remember, you can use non-dairy ice cream on the pies.

Customs—Getting together with family and eating far too much; saying grace before the meal even if you usually don't; making donations to the local food bank or organization for the homeless.

Requirements—National holiday—no work except for service and support personnel.

Fourth Sunday before Christmas
Advent   Christian   Varying
Significance—Symbolic of the traditional 4,000 years between Adam and Christ; a penitential season of preparation for Christmas.

References—Gen. 3, Rom. 5:12-21.

Religious activities—Bible reading, meditating on the meaning of Christmas.

Food—No meat on Fridays. Eastern Orthodox also abstain from meat, butter, milk, and eggs throughout the season.

Customs—Gathering greens and making an Advent wreath: a horizontal arrangement of evergreens incorporating three purple candles and a pink one (one to be lit each Sunday, with the pastel second-to-last one signifying the imminent rejoicing) and sometimes a central white one to burn on Christmas Eve. Some people display an Advent Calendar, an elaborately detailed picture with flaps to open on successive days. Buying and wrapping Christmas gifts, sending greeting cards, giving to charity.

Our local religious council churches send roses to each other and to the Jewish congregation—also a member of the council—with messages of peace and good will. Our Jewish congregation reciprocates by bringing a similar message to the churches on Tu b'Shevat, along with flowering branches of something called lepko that the florist assures us looks like almond blossom, and a donation of trees to the community in honor of Martin Luther King.

December 8
Immaculate Conception
          Christian (Catholic and Orthodox)   Minor
Significance—Commemorates the dogma, originating in the Eastern Church and formally adumbrated by Rome in 1849, that Mary the Mother of Jesus was conceived without Original Sin tainting her soul as it marks those of all other human beings since the Fall. It has nothing to do with the Virgin Birth or with the sexual activities either of Mary's own parents or of Mary and Joseph. (Notice, it's nothing like nine months before Christmas—did you think the early church was

just too stupid to notice that?) Incidentally, in 1849 the American Catholic bishops declared Our Lady of the Immaculate Conception the patroness of the US.

References—Rom. 5:12-14.
Religious activities—Attending Mass.
Requirements—A Holy Day of Obligation for American and most other Catholics. (Not Australians. How should we know why?) It's also Ned's birthday, if you want to send a card.

25 Kislev
Hanukkah (Dedication) or **Feast of Lights**
Jewish   Minor

Significance—Commemorates Jewish zealots' battling the Syrian tyrant Antiochus Epiphanes in the 2d century BCE and the subsequent cleansing of the Great Temple in Jerusalem. The popular legend is that the heroic Jewish Maccabees found only enough oil to light the ceremonial menorah (candelabrum) for one day; miraculously, it continued to burn for eight days, till the new supply could be brought. This holiday, like Christmas, seems also to have a solstice referent.

References—I Macc. 4:36-59, II Macc. 10:1-8 (not in Jewish or Protestant Scriptural canon).

Religious activities—Lighting the *hanukkiyah* or Hanukkah menorah each evening, with appropriate blessings.

Food—Dairy, especially anything containing or fried in oil—therefore, potato pancakes (*latkes*) for Ashkenazim and jelly doughnuts (*souvganiot*) for Sephardim are popular; an Italian delicacy is a fritter filled with anise seeds and raisins; nuts; candies (especially the gilt foil-covered, coin-shaped chocolates called Hanukkah *gelt).*

Customs—Displaying the menorah where it can be seen from the street, playing dreidl with a special little top something like a die; singing holiday songs; giving children a small gift (traditionally a coin) each night. (As our kids got too old to be interested in dime store stuff, we started getting one single family present for Hanukkah, such as a jigsaw puzzle or board game, that we could enjoy together throughout the week).

Requirements—Lighting one more candle or oil wick each night till the total of eight plus the shamash or master candle are lit, while saying the prescribed blessings.

December 24
Christmas Eve   Christian   Major
Food—Catholics and Orthodox refrain from eating meat. Moravians make special cookies; Poles eat *pierogi, borscht,* and *babka;* many Eastern Europeans distribute white communion-like

196

wafers to the family at the supper table; Italians bake *biscotti*.

Customs—Light candles, go to midnight mass. Some traditions open gifts this night instead of in the morning; we followed Mary Heléne's family's custom of opening one apiece to siphon off some of the hysteria.

December 25
Christmas

Christian and American secular   Major major!

Significance—Commemoration of the birth of Jesus. The date reflects an ancient association with various pagan winter solstice/ rebirth festivals rather than anything known about the season of the actual historical event.

References—Luke 2:1-20.

Religious activities—Attending church; giving to the poor.

Food—Many ethnic variants: British influence on American culture has made roast goose and plum pudding popular in many circles, but the Christian partner in your marriage probably has ideas about "proper" Christmas fare that verge on the ideological.

Customs—Displaying a decorated evergreen tree; decking the house and grounds with seasonal ornaments and lights; burning a Yule log (though the practice was widespread in antiquity, the word derives from the Persian—that is, it's an Iranian custom!); exchanging gifts; caroling; visiting; reading aloud such family favorites as "'Twas the Night Before Christmas," "A Christmas Carol," or "A Child's Christmas in Wales."

Requirements—National holiday—no work except for service and support personnel; keeping your head (see general notes on Winter).

First of each (Jewish) month
Rosh Hodesh (Head of the Month)   Jewish   Varying
<u>Significance</u>—In a lunar year with ritual feasts, it's very important to keep track of what the moon is doing. This is a semi-holiday particularly sacred to women. Traditionally it's a reward to them for not having given their jewelry to make the golden calf in biblical times.

<u>References</u>—Num. 10:10, 28:11-15, I Sam. 20:18, Amos 8:5, II Kgs. 4:23 etc.

<u>Religious Activities</u>—Torah reading in synagogue; reciting special blessings there and at home.

<u>Food</u>—No fasting, even on the eve of a wedding; round food and new fruits.

<u>Customs</u>—Giving to charity, lighting candles, wearing new clothes, starting new projects. Some feminists have reclaimed this observance's importance; others scorn it as too little too late, and too associated with fertility.

<u>Requirements</u>—Refrain from work half the day, limit mourning, rejoice.

198

PRACTICAL POINTERS

Chapter 14: Food for the Body

We've previously discussed the many ethnic and cultural aspects of meals and their trappings, and we've touched on Jewish and Christian holiday traditions regarding food. Now we'd like to give you some specifics that encompass religious culinary requirements.

Unless you're Orthodox—either Christian or Jewish—you probably won't have strict parameters for what may be eaten and when. But even an attenuated religious background can leave an aftertaste that makes traditional food sweet to the palate and soothing to the spirit.

For Christians, food laws (as opposed to customs) tend to cluster around Lent and a few other days of fast and/or abstinence. Roman Catholics used to be well known for their abstaining from meat on Fridays; since Vatican II removed the moral necessity for doing so (though the faithful were still encouraged to follow the practice as a personal spiritual exercise) almost none of them have kept it up. We run into more Episcopalians who observe meatless Fridays than we do Catholics these days.

If one of you does, good for you. But if it causes a conflict, remember that one of the major departures of institutional Christianity from Judaism was when St. Peter had a revelation that all food was now "clean" or ritually acceptable (Acts 10:10-16). For Christians, considerations of charity, good will or harmony should outweigh strict adherence to rules about food.

Focus on making meals a channel for peaceful fellowship.

MARY HELÉNE
When I was a child, there was a family get-together for which my Italian grandmother prepared a lavish meal. I can still see it, laid out on trestle tables under the poplar trees in her huge back yard: lasagne with meat sauce, chicken cacciatore, sausage. . . .

As we hungrily gathered around the feast, a great-aunt officiously exclaimed "It's Friday!" We stood transfixed in horror, and wishing she'd held her tongue. There would have been no serious transgression in eating the meat if she hadn't spoken, since we'd all sincerely forgotten what day it was.

There was a moment's stunned silence, then my grandmother cheerily announced, "Never mind; I take all the sins on me!"

We feel sure that her overriding desire to provide nourishment and pleasure to her loved ones far outweighed any sin involved in the eyes of God.

Dietary requirements for Jews have more far-reaching implications. The observant believe that they are commanded by God explicitly—not, as for Christians, that they're a matter of institutional spiritual discipline. The rationales applied to specific cases also follow different lines of reasoning.

One of our favorite examples of historical lunacy is a medieval argument Jewish and Catholic scholars had over the barnacle goose. The discussion centered on its nature: was it a fish or a fruit? (No, that's not a misprint.) The waterbird's flesh evidently tastes like fish, and it roosts hanging from trees (or was thought to—we don't guarantee the zoological accuracy of this dispute) like a fruit. Starting from the same observations, the two groups came up with opposite conclusions. The Catholics said, "Whichever it is, it's not meat, and that's all we need to know—it's ok to eat it on Friday." The Jews said, "Whichever it is, it's weird, and it doesn't fit into the normal categories of food—don't eat it."

Jewish dietary laws stem from classifications of lawful and unlawful food in the Torah that seem to have a common thread linking them to a notion of cosmic order as opposed to chaos. Animals that eat other animals shouldn't be eaten by humans, for instance: nor should things that live in the water but don't have the characteristics of fish— fins and scales—such as shellfish. This isn't a neat or complete explanation; it doesn't cover such anomalies as why herbivores that don't have divided hooves or chew cud, such as horses, aren't kosher.

And nobody is sure why pork is forbidden. We personally don't buy the rationalist explanation, popular a generation ago, that Moses somehow understood more than anyone else in the ancient Middle East about trichinosis. Some scholars point to Canaanite boar worship as the source of the prohibition, but the pagans worshipped bulls, too, and beef is kosher. One notion that appeals to us is the observation that the pig is the only domestic animal that has to be killed to be used. It doesn't give milk or wool or eggs; in line with the overall sensitivity regarding cruelty to animals in the Torah, it seems likely that raising an animal solely for slaughter was distasteful.

But when it comes right down to it, attempts to find "reasons" for the laws of kashrut are irrelevant. A professor of Ned's at Brandeis, after discussing the possibility that the prohibition against mixing milk and meat—based on a text forbidding the cooking of a kid in its mother's milk—derives from a misreading, said, "But if an Angel of God came down right now and said, 'It is a misreading; the law really relates to cooking a kid in its mother's fat,' I would still not mix milk and meat. The Jewish people have kept the law this way for three millennia. I'm not going to break the tradition."

Many Jews, even ones without strong religious beliefs, hold similar attitudes about dietary laws. Even if you don't keep separate sets of dishes for milk and meat, or don't eat only meat that has had all possible blood leached out of it, you will still want to be responsive to the pull of ancient practices and ingrained tastes.

If you as the non-Jew are really dying for a cheeseburger or shrimp cocktail, remember that there's no moral imperative for gentiles to keep kosher, even if their kitchen is. Keep a supply of paper plates and plastic utensils and maybe even a cheap pot or two separate from your regular stuff (wash the pots separately too, with their own sponge or brush). And of course, out of sheer consideration, you won't cook pork and sauerkraut when your Jewish spouse is at home, or some redolent sauce during the Yom Kippur fast, any more than a Jewish cook should fix pot roast for Good Friday dinner.

If you'd rather not be bothered with all this, and don't have the money to eat out all the time, consider becoming vegetarian. We don't know of any vegetable or fruit (except the barnacle goose!) whose consumption is forbidden by either Christianity or Judaism. (The little "K" or circled "U" signifying kosher inspection that you see on some packages means, in the case of non-meat and non-milk products, that the jelly or whatever hasn't been in contact with unkosher food in its production and, for Jewish-owned businesses, that laws pertaining to tithing crops for the poor have been observed.)

If you do like to mess around in the kitchen, you're in luck. There's plenty to mess with when you're cooking for an interfaith household.

MENUS FOR CHRISTIAN HOLIDAYS WITH JEWS AND VICE VERSA

Meatless Kosher Christmas Eve
Brie cheese baked in puff pastry studded with almonds
Cream of mushroom soup
Noodles sauced with shredded smoked salmon, peas and
    cream
Dilled zucchini
Bûche de Noel

Non-dairy Christmas Dinner
Chopped liver pate on melba rounds
Beef and onion broth
Roast goose with chestnut stuffing
Red chard sauteed with sour apple slices
Orange–baked yams
Spinach salad
Pecan pie, pumpkin pie made with liquid non-dairy
    creamer
Tofutti

Good Friday Seder
Chopped egg and olive mold
Matzo balls in vegetable broth
Baked eggplant, tomato, and fresh tuna casserole
Carrot souffle
Stewed fruit compote
Crême caramel

Easter Morning Passover Brunch
Easter eggs
Matzo brei
Sour cream
Charoseth
Flavored neuchatel cheese

Recipes for these dishes can be found in most comprehensive
cookbooks. What's trickier is figuring out how to make traditional
dishes to kosher standards.

RECIPES FOR THE KOSHER/CHRISTIAN COOK

Sabra Mousse (Pareve, lo-cal, no gelatin*)
2 eggs, separated
8 T. sugar
pinch salt
2 T. frozen orange juice concentrate
4 T. unsweetened cocoa powder
Beat yolks with half the sugar, juice and cocoa over hot water till thickened. Whip salted egg whites stiff, add remaining sugar slowly while beating to glossy peaks. Fold into custard mixture, pour in greased mold, chill.

*Ordinary commercial gelatin is made from horse hooves—not kosher—or cow hooves—a meat product.

Kosher Dairy Lasagne alla Bolognese for Shavuot
1 lb. green* lasagna noodles, cooked, drained and rinsed
2 C. soy granules soaked in 4 c. hot water or pareve "beef" bouillon
6 C. tomato-based meatless spaghetti sauce
3 C. bechamel sauce
1 C. freshly grated parmesan cheese**
Spread thin coating of tomato sauce in bottom of 9" X 5" X 3" casserole. Layer remaining ingredients in this order—pasta, soy granules, tomato sauce, cheese, pasta, bechamel sauce, cheese, pasta; repeat till pan is 3/4 full, ending with tomato sauce and cheese. Bake uncovered at 400° for 1/2 hour or till browned and bubbly. Let rest 5 minutes before cutting. May be frozen after assembly; defrost in refrigerator or bake frozen at 325° for 2 hours.

*Make your own, using chopped defrosted frozen spinach instead of egg, or use commercial yellow egg noodles.
**If your partner's too kosher to eat hard cheese, that's the way the cookie crumbles. You tell us what you did about it.

Pareve White Gazpacho for Summer Shabbats
3 slices firm white bread (last week's hallah is perfect), de-crusted and torn, soaked in 1 C. cold water
6 oz. blanched almonds, ground
2 C. seedless white grapes
1/2 C. olive oil
2-3 T. white wine vinegar
3-4 C. ice water
Grind first four ingredients in blender or food processor. Add oil by droplets, stir in vinegar and water slowly. Chill and garnish with more grapes, halved. Nobody will guess what's in this; everybody will rave over it.

Mock Crab (dairy)
2 T. butter
1/2 lb. Swiss or neuchatel-style cheese
1 T. anchovy paste
2 egg yolks
1/2 C. cream or evaporated milk
salt, pepper, powdered mustard and cayenne to taste
Melt butter, stir in remaining ingredients over moderate heat,
serve on toast.

Milchig, Fleishig, or Pareve Breakfast Casserole
sliced dairy-free bread (Italian is good, hallah ok) to line
    13" X 9" pan
1/2 C. liquid non-dairy creamer
1/4 C. melted non-dairy margarine*
6 eggs
1 lb. smoked beef or turkey strips (optional)
or 1 C. shredded cheese (also optional—this casserole is
    ok without either one)
Beat liquids and eggs together, pour over bread in casserole, top
with meat strips or cheese if desired. (May be refrigerated overnight
at this point.) Bake at 325° for 1 hour until set.

*Will have a "P" for *Pareve* right next to the U or K.

Pareve Christmas Tree Cookies
1 C. poppy seeds
4 eggs, slightly beaten
1 C. cooking oil
1 C. sugar
2 tsp. baking powder
1 tsp. salt
4-5 C. unbleached white flour
Combine ingredients in order, chill. Roll out on heavily floured
board. Cut into shapes, sprinkle with colored spiced sugar. Bake on
oiled cookie sheet at 350° till golden (about 12 minutes). Pierce with
needle and heavy thread to hang; will stay good on tree for 2 weeks.

Pesadich Pareve Flourless Chocolate Cake
1 C. pareve unsalted margarine
7 oz. unsweetened baking chocolate
1 C. sugar
5 eggs
7 oz. ground almonds
Melt margarine and chocolate, beat in remaining ingredients.

204

Bake in greased egg-shaped pudding mold 40-45 min. at 325° (will still be soft). Unmold when cool, decorate with piped, colored, sweetened, whipped, non-dairy cream cheese ("Mr. Smoothie").

Ned's Hallah
4 eggs at room temperature (reserve a 5th for glaze)
1/4 C. honey
1 T. salt
1 oz. yeast
1/4 C. oil
2 lb. unbleached flour
1/2 C. lukewarm water
sesame and/or poppy seeds (optional)

"Prove" yeast in water and honey; beat in 4 eggs, salt, and oil; add flour till stiff but not dry dough forms. Knead for 15 minutes till elastic and not sticky, adding flour if necessary. Place in oiled bowl; oil top of dough; cover and let rise in warm, draftless place till doubled in bulk. Punch down and turn over. Let double again. Divide in half; divide each half in thirds; roll each piece into "snake"; braid dough to make two loaves. Let rise again, covered, on oiled baking sheets or loaf pans if desired. Glaze with beaten egg; bake at 375° till golden brown and loaves sound hollow when thumped. Cool before slicing, if you can stand to wait.

Some general hints

Non-dairy soy "cream" and beef or poultry smoked "ham" or "bacon" work quite well as substitutes in almost any dish. We haven't found any satisfactory cheese substitutes that are truly non-dairy; try replacing the meat element with textured soy products instead.

If none of the above satisifies your particular longing for beef stroganoff or pork egg foo yung or meat tacos with cheese, start browsing in bookstores and catalogues for kosher cookbooks adapted to various ethnic cuisines. If you can't find one for your cradle family's comfort food, consider writing one yourself! (And let us know so we can pick up a copy.)

Chapter 15: Food for the Mind

AD (Latin *Anno Domini*, "Year [of our] Lord": Calendar term dating from a 6th century monk's (inaccurate) calculation of the year of the birth of Jesus, which in this system is the year "1" (there is no "0"). Therefore, a Christian term. Similarly, BC ("Before Christ"). See BCE/CE.

Ashkenazi (adj.; pl. noun: Ashkenazim): Jew from Eastern and/or Northern European background—as distinguished from Sephardi.

Baptism: Christian practice of immersing or sprinkling adults or infants with water as a sign of spiritual regeneration.

BC: See AD

BCE/CE (Before [the] Common Era/Common Era): Calendar terms preferred by most Jewish and many non-Jewish scholars and others for dating years in relation to the birth of Jesus.

Bris: Yiddish form of Brit (Milah)

Brit Milah: Lit. "covenant of circumcision"; Jewish practice of ritual circumcision.

Canon Law: Codified Roman Catholic body of 1,752 laws. (Remember this next time you hear a priest homilizing on "legalistic" Judaism, which has a mere 613).

Catholic: Used in this book in the common sense of Roman Catholic. Anglican, Armenian, Byzantine, Coptic, Greek, Russian, and Syrian Catholics please don't be irritated; we thought constantly qualifying the term would irritate everyone else.

CE: See BCE/CE

Circumcision: Medical or ritual procedure of removing the foreskin from the male penis.

Consecration: For Catholics and those Protestants who believe the Eucharistic elements of bread and wine literally become the body and blood of Christ, the moment at which the celebrant speaks the words that enact this "transubstantiation."

Cross/crucifix: Properly speaking, the word "cross" refers to the asymmetric conjoining of horizontal and vertical bars representing the instrument of Jesus' execution. This is a powerful religious icon on its own. Recognizing this, the organization most of the West calls the Red Cross is the Red Star of David in Israel and the Red Crescent in Islamic countries. "Crucifix" is the term for a cross with a Corpus, or representation of the body of Jesus, more used by Catholic and Orthodox Christians—whose theology tends to emphasize the Crucifixion as the ransom of souls from sin by the death of the Son of God. Protestants, with a theology broadly centered more on the Resurrection as the symbol of the conquering of death, and with a greater historical aversion to the use of human images in worship, usually prefer the empty cross.

Gentiles: Lit. "peoples" or "nations"; term usually used to differentiate non-Jews from Jews (also non-Mormons from Mormons).

Gett: Jewish religious divorce

Goyim: Yiddish/Hebrew for "gentiles" (sing. goy), often but not necessarily derogatory.

Grace: Jewish and Christian concept of unmerited blessing; some Christian denominations have elaborate theologies of grace, its nature and conditions.

Hasidism: From hesed, Heb. "grace"; Jewish mystical/charismatic sect founded in the 18th century. Many people, some Jews among them, think of Hasidism as ultra-ultra-Orthodoxy. This is a misapprehension, indignantly denied by the traditional Orthodox (called Mitnagdim by Hasidim—no one else much uses the term).

High Holydays: The Jewish holidays of Yom Kippur and Rosh Hashanah; generally, the period they encompass.

Holy Water (font): Roman Catholic churches typically have receptacles near their entrances containing water which has been blessed by a priest with which people entering or leaving bless themselves by dipping in the fingers used for making the sign of the cross. Holy water is also used in the ritual of annointing the sick, blessing homes, and other Catholic rituals. Although the use of such aids to devotion (called "sacramentals") has fallen off in recent years, holy water fonts may still occasionally be seen in the homes of the pious.

Huppah: The canopy used in Jewish weddings, and the marriage element of cohabitation it represents. Traditionally, it consists of a prayer shawl affixed to decorated poles held aloft by members of the wedding party. In America today, it often is an elaborate arch of flowers held by a trellis. Many variations on either of these two options are acceptable.

Icon: Christian image of saint or divinity painted or carved on a flat surface; more typical of Eastern Orthodox piety than of Western churches.

Jewish: Used in this book to refer both to people and practices adherent to Judaism, and to people and practices identified with ethnic, non-religious Jewishness.

Judaism: We generally use this term to refer to the wide range of beliefs and practices embraced by the four major movements within it today.

The strictest and most bound both to ancient rabbinic practice and medieval European custom is the Orthodox segment—though "orthodox" means "right thought," and the group in fact is united more by uniformity of practice than by conformity of theology.

The Reform movement began in the 18th century as an attempt to bring Jews into the modern world of rationalist theology and of practices based on scientific and practical considerations (rather than on divine revelation). It was also thought that social assimilation would bring about an end to antisemitism.

As it became clear that this was not a likely outcome, and in response to a feeling that the baby had been thrown out with the bathwater in classic assimilationist Reform, the Conservative movement developed as a middle way, in both theology and practice.

Most recently, Reconstructionist Judaism has developed—a sort of Jewish Congregationalism, in which individual communities make their own decisions regarding their place on the traditional spectrum, but commonly combine a more liberal theology than Conservatism's with a more traditional practice than Reform's.

There are groups both farther right and farther left on this spectrum, but these four are those most representative of the vast majority of Jews.

Kaddish: Prayer used repeated in Jewish liturgy praising and glorifying *("kaddesh")* God; since it is said particularly by mourners, a folk usage has a man speaking of his son as "my kaddish," signifying that the boy will someday undertake this duty for his father.

Ketuba: Jewish nuptial contract, signed before, but very much as a part of, a traditional wedding. It stipulates the rights of the bride in case of divorce.

Kiddushin: Element of a traditional Jewish wedding involving the blessing *("kiddush")* and drinking of wine by bride and groom.

Kipa: Hebrew for yarmulke.

Knights of Columbus: American Roman Catholic fraternal and benevolent order founded in 1882; the Knights were instrumental in getting Columbus Day recognized as a holiday.

Kosher/Kashrut (adj./noun): Lit. "prepared"; usually refers to the body of Jewish dietary law, derived from Scripture and elaborated by tradition; notably, the eating of pork, shellfish, carrion birds, or mingled meat and dairy products is forbidden.

Lector: Lit. "reader"; in the Catholic Church, layperson authorized to read Scripture (excluding the Gospel, reserved for the ordained) during public services.

Magen David: Lit. "Shield of David," also called "Star of David"; six-pointed star used since the 19th century as emblem of Judaism and on the national flag of Israel.

Menorah: Lit. "Light-bearer"; candelabrum used in Jewish ritual. The traditional Sabbath menorah, like the huge one in the Great Temple of old, has seven arms or branches; the Hannukah menorah, more properly called a *Hannukiah,* has eight plus a "servant" from which the others are lit.

Mezuzah: Small receptacle, often elaborately ornamented, containing a scroll with the verses mandated in Deut. 6:9 and 11:20. Traditionally put on the doorposts of a house (the pious touch it and kiss their fingertips on entering or leaving) it is also widely used today as an amulet. A "kosher" or correct mezuzah must contain a ritually perfect scroll, which can be quite expensive.

Mikveh: Ritual bath, constructed according to strict liturgical standards and used by women after menstruation and childbirth, by men in ancient times after incurring ritual uncleanness disqualifying them otherwise from Temple service, by the observant today for spiritual cleansing especially before Sabbath, and by converts to traditional Judaism. Blu Greenberg gives a compelling account of the uses of mikveh and the laws of family purity in maintaining a high level of romantic commitment in marriage and a respectful familiarity with one's body for women.

Mitzvah (pl. Mitzvot): Technically the 613 commandments of traditional Judaism (hence the Bar/Bat Mitzvah, the Son/Daughter of the Commandment, now responsible for observing them); often used to mean any good deed.

Original Sin: Christian doctrine that the sin of disobedience committed by Adam and Eve in Eden (whether seen as literal historic fact or as metaphor for intellectual pride) continues to affect the human condition in the presence of death and suffering on earth and ineligibility for salvation in eternity. This sin was atoned for by the crucifixion of Jesus, but its stain remains on every soul (except, in the Catholic view, that of Mary) unless removed by baptism. It is also thought to account for the general human propensity for sin, in which it has a slight similarity to the Jewish notion of *yetzer ha-ra,* evil inclination (though Jewish tradition also posits a *yetzer-ha-tov,* an inclination for good, absent in standard Christian formulations).

Patrilineal descent: Controversial Reform innovation of considering a child born to a Jewish father and a non-Jewish mother Jewish without conversion, if Judaism is being practiced by the individual; opposed to traditional, scripturally mandated matrilineal descent, predicated on the confidence that a baby's mother is always identifiable.

Pharisees: Members of a rabbinic school emphasizing interpretation and modification of scripture, rather than "strict constructionism" (exemplified by the Sadduccees). Normative Judaism has followed pharisaic principles and traditions. Frequent disputes between Jesus and Jerusalem Pharisees as recounted by (often non-Jewish) evangelists have left most Christians with the image of Pharisees as hypocritical, legalistic, and superficial. Prof. David Flusser, among others, convincingly argues that philosophical differences with Jesus in the Gospels reflect a regional conflict; that Jesus was, in fact, a Galilean Pharisee. In any case, Christians—especially if married to Jews—should refrain from using the word generically to mean "bad guy." Catholics may be enlightened by comparing it to the non-Catholic use of "Jesuitical" to mean wicked, tricksy, and false.

Phylacteries: See Tefillin

Prayer shawl: See Tallis

Protestant: Lit. "for the text," i.e. Scripture; though we are aware that both on the right (Anglicans/Episcopalians) and the left (Unitarians etc.) there are non-Catholic and non-Orthodox Christians who object to the term, we have adopted the common usage to mean any Christian-derived denomination organized after Martin Luther said, "Here I stand; I can do no other" in 1521.

Rosary: A string of beads numbered and arranged in a particular order to aid Roman Catholics in keeping track of prayers in a devotional practice focused on Mary and used as a sort of mantra to give the forebrain something to do while the spirit's being refreshed. There are designated "mysteries" based on the lives of Mary and Jesus to be meditated on for various occasions. Rosaries have usually been blessed, often by a pope; may have been passed down in a family for generations; and are often a nexus of great pious sentiment, though actually "saying the rosary" or "telling one's beads" is not as popular a practice as it once was.

Sacrament: For Christians, practices modeled on those in the New Testament; the extent to which they are felt to have efficacy apart from the spiritual worthiness of administrator or recipient varies—this was a major dispute in the Reformation. Roman Catholics acknowledge seven sacraments: Baptism, Confession (Reconciliation), Communion (Eucharist), Confirmation, Holy Orders, Matrimony, and Anointing of the Sick (Extreme Unction). Other Christians, finding the biblical basis of some of these shaky, hold to fewer.

Seder: Lit."order"; the ritual of the Passover meal, therefore often used of the meal itself.

Sephardi (adj.; pl. noun: Sephardim): Jew of Mediterranean and/ or Middle Eastern background; in America, Sephardic Jews are most often of Spanish or Italian descent, while in Israel the term usually refers to those from Arab countries.

Shaygetz: Yiddish word referring to a male gentile; not as common as the feminine shiksah.

Shiksah: Yiddish for female non-Jew; traditionally a maidservant, often derogatory.

Shiva, Sitting: Jewish funereal practice of active ritual mourning for seven days after a death.

Shofar: Ram's horn sounded to call the faithful to repentance and renewal on the Jewish High Holydays.

Star of David: See Magen David

Tallis (Sephardic pronunciation Tallit): Prayer shawl worn by pious Jews; traditionally a male garment, but Jewish feminists have begun to wear them in public worship.

Talmud: Lit. "teaching"; ancient compilation of Jewish rabbinic law and commentary; the Orthodox believe it was given orally on Mt. Sinai and give it equal authority to Scripture.

Tefillin: Jewish prayer aids. Tiny scrolls with prayers (as in the mezuzah) are encased in small leather boxes attached to thongs which are then fastened to the main artery in the left arm and to the forehead (Deut. 6:8 and 11:18) during morning prayers by the observant. (This, combined with the practice of covering the head with tallis and/or yarmulke, may be the origin of the Jews-have-horns canard—or that may derive from the misunderstanding of Ex. 34:29, 30 and 35 immortalized by Michelangelo.) As with the tallis, some Orthodox Jewish feminist women have begun "laying tefillin" in the traditionally male practice.

WASP: Acronym for White Anglo Saxon Protestant; often but not necessarily derogatory.

Yarmulke: (Yiddish) Skull cap worn by Jews; the most traditional wear black silk ones at all times, the observant but less traditional wear crocheted or knitted ones most of the time, some people wear them only at prayer. Here again, a traditionally male accoutrement is being coopted by women—with more success and less acrimony than some of the other sartorial or ritual practices, since this mode of headcovering is not biblically ordained and since it's hard to maintain the attitude that a woman may cover her head only with a hat that's not small and round.

Yid: Lit. "Jew" in several Eastern European languages, but always derogatory in English.

Yiddish: Language spoken by European Jews; a combination of Hebrew and German, Russian, or whatever the vernacular of the gentile community of origin was. Not the language of Scripture (Hebrew); also not a derogatory term.

Z"l: Abbreviation for Heb. *Zichronoh/ah l'Bruchah*, "May his/her memory be for a blessing," pious Jewish ejaculation when speaking or writing of the dead.

212

BOOKS & ARTICLES:

Charlesworth, James H. (ed.), *Jews and Christians: Exploring the Past, Present and Future*; Crossroad, 1990; papers on various aspects of interreligious contact—with the discussion that followed each at the original symposium. Some of it's a little dry, but the determined reader will mine much of value in looking at religious, historical and scriptural insights.

Cowan, Paul and Rachel, *Mixed Blessings*; Doubleday 1987: written by a couple who began as agnostics and then both became practicing Jews—only their backgrounds were actually different. Their book consists primarily of interviews of people floundering with their problems—reading them together may spark some useful discussions between the two of you. We are featured in a twelve-page profile, if you want someone else's impression of us; Paul told us that, of 300 couples they interviewed, we were the only ones successfully managing a dual-faith approach.

Day, Thomas, *Why Catholics Can't Sing*; Crossroad, 1990; a humorous but well-founded treatment of Catholicism that uses church music as a jumping-off place but says much about influences of ethnicity, history, and sociology across the board.

Deedy, John, *The Catholic Fact Book;* Thomas More, 1986; a handy, compact reference including brief lives of major saints, glossary of terms, and a history of the church and its teachings.

Fridman, Edwin H., "The Myth of the Shiksa" in *Ethnicity and Family Therapy,* Monica McGoldrick (ed.); somewhat heavy going for the lay reader, but well worth searching out in its vivid anecdotes of conflicting stereotypes and ethnic assumptions, and its exploding of what everyone's parents are sure is "true" about people who marry out.

Goldberg, Michael, *Jews and Christians: Getting Our Stories Straight;* Abingdon, 1985; the author asks the question, "What if more fundamental than our quarrels over discrete religious doctrines were our disputes about overarching master stories, through which our various theological convictions gain their sense and from which they draw their power?" The answer—this book's exploration of "The Jewish Master Story" and "The Christian Master Story"—is a readable and thought-provoking approach to each group's basic assumptions.

Greenberg, Blu, *How to Run a Traditional Jewish Household;* Simon & Schuster, 1983; the title doesn't quite say it all—in addition to vital instructions and descriptions, the reader gets a charming glimpse into the Greenberg household, an inspiration for anyone trying to raise kids in a religious ambience these days.

Hardon, John A., S. J., *The Catholic Catechism;* Doubleday, 1975; a readable discussion of Catholic dogma and its post-Vatican II interpretations—will make a good reference for arguments with Catholic parents or in-laws.

Jegen, Sister Carol Frances, and Rabbi Byron L. Sherwin, *Thank God;* Liturgical Training Publications, 1989; a beautiful book, in format and content, containing prayers and liturgies Jews and Christians can use together. Highly recommended for the mixed-faith couple.

Mayer, Egon, *Marriage Between Jews & Christians;* Plenum Press, 1985; a sociological study replete with interesting, if discouraging, statistics.

Meier, Levi (ed.), *Jewish Values in Bioethics;* Human Sciences Press, Inc., 1986; a thorough treatment of problems from removing life support to *in vitro* fertilization by some stellar names in the field: Irving Greenberg (Blu's husband), David Feldman, Emmanuel Rackman, Fred Rosner, Immanuel Jakobovits, David Bleich, Viktor Frankl, to say nothing of Rabbi Meier himself; even Elie Wiesel has some relevant, if chilling, words to say.

Petsonk, Judy, and Jim Remsen, *The Intermarriage Handbook: A Guide for Jews and Christians;* Wm. Morrow, 1988, is by "an actively involved conservative Jew [who] is not intermarried but has dealt with a number of intermarriages in her family" and a "lapsed Methodist married to a Jewish woman [who] assists in the Jewish upbringing of their children." "Handbook" is the operative word for this book. It is a useful guide, in a workbook format, that relies on interviews (including many with converted couples, i.e. the no longer technically intermarried) and provides exercises derived from psycho-social analytic and negotiating techniques. We recommend it for these exercises and for its excellent brief history of antisemitism.

Sarosky, Marlene, *Year-Round Holiday Cookbook;* Harper &

Row, 1982; imaginative menus, inspiring pictures, mouth watering but not unrealistically elaborate recipes.

Schneider, Susan Weidman, *Intermarriage: The Challenge of Living with Differences;* Simon & Schuster, 1989. This is a well-written and useful sociological and psychological treatment, using selections from workshops and interviews. It contains some inaccuracies about Christian beliefs and practices, which is not surprising since conversion to Judaism is the only option it seriously considers as viable.

Schneider, Susan Weidman, *Jewish and Female: Choices and Changes in Our Lives Today;* Simon & Schuster, 1984; a useful and lively treatment of issues in modern Judaism of interest to any Jew or partner of one trying to design a lifestyle that incorporates Jewish values.

Shannon, Thomas A., and Charles N. Faso, O.F.M., *Let Them Go Free: A Family Prayer Service to Assist in the Withdrawal of Life Support Systems,* Sheed & Ward, 1991; the prayer service is distinctly Catholic, but could serve as a model for a more ecumenical version; it is prefaced by a simple, clear discussion of the options and implications of life support withdrawal that might well be more helpful to those in the midst of such a trauma than a fuller, more scholarly treatment would be.

MAGAZINES:

The Christian Century, a publication with Disciples of Christ roots that today addresses political and religious issues in a liberal light across a broad denominational spectrum.

Commonweal, a progressive political commentary with a Catholic perspective.

Daughters of Sarah, a Christian feminist publication geared to a different moral or social theme in each issue.

Lilith, a Jewish feminist publication edited by Susan Weidman Schneider.

Tikkun, a non-doctrinaire, intellectually sophisticated exploration of political, sociological, psychological, and ethical questions from a Jewish perspective.

CONCLUSION

Writing this book has been like a refresher course in weaving for us. We've gone over the tapestry of the lives we've woven together, enjoying some of the brightest spots of color and best executed designs from our past, seeing where in other places we've muddied the colors and muddled the patterns, and doing some repairing of snagged or broken threads and refurbishing of threadbare patches. We've also become more aware of the holder of that third cord in the strand, the Master Weaver who keeps us from getting too far off track and who sees what the finished product will be. Of course, the whole thing is still on the loom, and the complete design won't be clear to us till we're finished and ready to lie down on it.

We hope our tapestry has given you some help in fashioning your own.

216

INDEX

Abby Van Buren   52, 130
abortion   72-74, 158
Abraham   75
AD (definition)   205
Adam   156, 194, 209
Advent   120–122, 171, 194
aguna   125
Ahab   78
AIDS   71, 98
alcoholism   35
All Hallow's Eve. See Hallowe'en
All Saints Day   171, 193
All Souls Day   171, 193
American Indian Day   171, 189
American Jewish Committee   123
American Jewish Congress   123
Amish   172, 185
Ann Landers   105
annulment   124, 125
Anointing of the Sick   130, 210
anti-Zionism   82
antisemitism   57, 59-61, 150-151, 153, 213
Arbor Day   176
Armistice Day. See Veterans Day
Artificial insemination   75
Ascension Thursday   171, 185
Ash Wednesday   167, 170, 178, 180, 183
Ashkenazi (definition)   205
Assumption of Mary, Dogma of the   171
Assumption, Feast of   188
Athaliah   78
autopsy   131
Avitzur, Susan and Boaz   126

Baby M case   75-76
Ballonoff, Nelly   99
baptism   91-93, 205, 210
Baptism of Christ   175
Bar/Bat Mitzvah   209; (definition) 205
BC (definition)   205
BCE/CE (definition)   205
Bell, William   59
Berlin, Irving   187
Bilhah   76
birth control   69-71, 158
Bloch, Henry   59
blood libel   150
B'nai B'rith Women   1, 45, 80
BOOKS & ARTICLES, list of recommended   212-213
Bordeaux, Little Sun   54
Breakfast Casserole (recipe)   203
Brenner, Reeve Robert   26
bris or Brit Milah (definition) 205 See also Circumcision
Buddhists   44
burial   133-136

CALENDAR OF HOLIDAYS   170
cancer, cervical   98
Candelmas   170, 175
Canon Law   107, 205

Catholic (definition)   205   *See also* Christianity, Roman Catholic
CE (definition)   205
Charlesworth, James H.   212
Chesler, Phyllis   82
Chocolate Cake, flourless (recipe)   203
chosenness   152
Christian Century, The   214
Christian Science   18
Christianity, Fundamentalist   3, 62, 69, 158, 192
Christianity, Orthodox   44, 155, 169, 175, 178, 182, 188, 194, 195, 198, 210
Christianity, Protestant   2, 44, 49, 56, 70, 124, 131, 140, 141, 144, 154, 155, 158, 172, 178, 181, 186, 191, 210
Christianity, Roman Catholic 2, 42-44, 49, 56, 70-73, 81, 91, 131, 134, 135, 140, 144, 155, 157, 178, 183, 188, 193, 194, 195, 199, 210
Christmas   163-166, 169, 171
Christmas Dinner (menu)   201
Christmas Eve   195
Christmas Tree Cookies (recipe)   203
Church of Christ Scientist *See* Christian Science
Church of Jesus Christ of Latter Day Saints *See* Mormons
circumcision   11, 97-100, 150
Circumcision, Feast of   174, 205
coffin   131-132
Columbus Day   171, 190
Commonweal   214
Communion   91, 210, 168, 178, 181
Confession   91, 130, 156, 179, 210
Confirmation   91, 210
Consecration   205
Conservative Rabbinical Assembly   140-141
conversion   8-9, 15, 16
Council of Jewish Federations   2
Counting the Omer   170, 180
Cowan, Paul and Rachel   8, 42, 160, 167, 212
Crab, mock (recipe)   203
cremation   131–132
Crohn, Joel   23, 27, 27-29, 40, 83, 111, 141
cross/crucifix   160, 180; (definition)   206
custody, of children   127-129

dancing   53
Daughter of Jephthah   78
Daughters of Sarah   214
David   77
Day of Atonement *See* Yom Kippur
Day, Thomas   212
Days of Awe   171, 189-191
Deborah   78
Deedy, John   212
DEFINITIONS   205–211
deicide   153
Dispensation from Canonical Form   44
divorce   78, 123-127
dogmas, Catholic   154-157

Easter   170, 182-183
Easter Morning (menu)   201
Eastern Orthodox *See* Christianity, Orthodox
embalming   131
Epiphany   170, 174
Esther   78, 179
Ethical Culture   18
ethical will   130

218

Eucharist *See* Communion
euthanasia 129, 214
Eve 77, 156, 209
Fall of Jerusalem 171, 187
Falwell, Jerry 65
Familial Dysautonomia 76
Faso, Charles N. 214
Father's Day 171, 187
Feast of Lights. *See* Hanukkah
Feast of Our Lady 184
Feast of St. Joseph the Worker 184
Feast of Unleavened Bread 168
Federation of Reconstructionist Congregations and Havurot 49
Fehren, Henry 42
Feingold, Dena 98
Flag Day 171, 186
Flusser, David 209
food, culture and 33
food laws 198-200 *See also* kosher/kashrut
Fourth of July *See* Independence Day
Freud, Sigmund 67, 121
Fridman, Edwin H. 212
Fundamentalists *See* Christianity, Fundamentalist

Gamblers Anonymous 35
Gaucher's Disease 76
Gazpacho, white (recipe) 202
Genetic engineering 76
Gentiles (definition) 206
Gershenfeld, Matti 106
gett 125–126; (definition) 206
Ghetto of Venice 142, 142-143
GLOSSARY OF USEFUL TERMS 205-211
godparents 95-96
Goldberg, Michael 212
Goldstein, Marie 145
Good Friday 168, 170, 181
Good Friday Seder (menu) 201
Goyim (definition) 206
Grace (definition) 206
Greek Orthodox Church *See* Christianity, Orthodox
Greenberg, Blu 80, 181, 182, 209, 213
Greenfield, Armalona 54
Greenspan, Mark 164
Gresham, Joy Davidman 106
Groundhog Day 170, 175
Gruzen, Lee 21
Gur, Mordechai 76

Hagar 75
hallah 173, 204 (recipe)
Hallowe'en 169, 171, 192
Hanukkah 163-166, 169, 171,195
Hardon, John A., 213
HaShana Rabba 171
Hasidism *See* Judaism, Orthodox
Havdalah 173
Hecht, Jacob 55
Heilman, Samuel 68
High Holydays 171, 189-191, 206; (definition) 211
Hindus 45
Hodgkins Disease 76
Hoffman, Mary 106

HOLIDAYS, TABLE OF 172–197
Holocaust, discussion of 65
Holocaust Remembrance Day 170, 182
Holy Orders 210
Holy Saturday 170, 182
Holy Thursday 19, 168, 170, 181
holy water (definition) 206
Holy Week 167-169, 170, 179, 181-182
Huldah 78, 147
humor, and culture 36
Hunt, Patricia 49
huppah 45, 46; (definition) 207

icon (definition) 207
idolatry, Christianity as 154
Immaculate Conception (dogma) 156; Feast of the, 171, 194
in vitro fertilization 75
Independence Day (American) 171, 205
infertility 75
Inquisition, The 19
intercourse 68-69
    anal 68
    during menstruation 69
    oral 68
Isaiah House 145
Israel, American Jews and 151-152
Israel Independence Day 170, 183

Jakobovits, Immanuel 74, 76
Jegen, Carol Frances, 213
Jehovah's Witnesses 138
Jerusalem Seige Fast 170, 175
Jesus 19, 81, 158, 168, 174, 178, 181, 182, 194, 196, 209, 210
Jewish (definition) 207
Jews for Jesus 18-19
Jezebel 78
John Paul II 68, 71
John XXIII 19
Judaism (definition) 207; Conservative 11, 12, 56, 72, 75, 123, 125, 140-141, 144, 207;
    Humanist 20, 48; Orthodox 11, 51, 55, 62, 68-69, 71, 75, 76, 78, 80, 101, 123, 125, 131,
    134, 140, 141, 152, 154, 192, 198, 207, 211; Reconstructionist 11, 49, 134, 207; Reform 11,
    45, 48, 76, 123, 134, 141, 143, 152, 164, 192, 207, 209

kaddish (definition) 207
Kahane, Meir 58, 65
Kaplan, Howard 75
kashrut (guidelines) 199-200 *See also* kosher/kashrut
ketuba 46, 126; (definition) 208
kiddushin (definition) 208
King, Martin Luther. *See* Martin Luther King Day
kipa (definition) 208
Kleiman, Nancy 133
Knights of Columbus 135, 190; (definition) 208
kosher/kashrut, food laws 198; (definition) 208
Kwanzaa 172

Labor Day 169, 171, 189
Lady Day 175
Lag b'Omer 167, 170, 184
Lambeth Conference of Anglican Churches 70
Lasagne alla Bolognese (recipe) 202
Last Supper 19, 168, 181 *See also* Holy Thursday; Communion

220

League of Women Voters 188
Leah 76
lector (definition) 208
Lehrman, Lew 58
Lent 120, 167-169, 170, 178-179, 198
Lerner, Michael 106
Lewis, C. S. 106
life support withdrawal 214
Lilith 78
Lilith (magazine) 214
Lincoln's Birthday 177
Lindblad, Samantha 134
living will 130
London, Trudie 99
Lord's Day 120, 172, 173
Lord's Supper 181 *See also* Communion
Lupercalia 176
Luther, Martin 191, 210

Machlin, Edna Servi 191
MAGAZINES, list of recommended 214
Magen David (definition) 208
Maimonides 78
Margulies, Myron 125
Martha 147
Martin Luther King Day 170, 175, 176
Martin, Judith *See* Miss Manners
Mary (mother of Jesus) 81, 156, 184, 188, 194, 209, 210
Mary (sister of Martha) 147
Maslin, Simeon J. 48
masturbation 70
Matrimony (as sacrament) 210
Maundy Thursday *See* Holy Thursday
May Day 171, 184
Mayer, Egon 13, 213
McCarthy, Edward A. 94
Meier, Levi 213
Meir, Aryeh 163
Memorial Day 171, 186
Mendelson, Ruth 136
Mennonites 185
menorah (definition) 208
MENUS 201
mezuzah (definition) 208
Michal 77
mikveh 11; (definition) 208
Miriam 78, 147
Miss Manners 53
mitzvah (definition) 209
modesty, religious 72
money, and culture 29-31
Mormons 44, 70, 134
Mortara, Edgardo 94
Moses 185, 199
Moslems 44
Mother's Day 171, 185
mourning rituals 135, 138
music, wedding 49

Naming, baby 101-103
National Conference of Catholic Bishops 8, 19
National Council of Christians and Jews 44, 163
Neusner, Jacob 45

New Year, Jewish. *See* Rosh Hashanah
New Year's Day   170, 174
New Year's Eve   174

Ogintz, Eileen   43, 108, 136
Onan   68, 70
onanism   70
organ donation   130; transplants   130
orgasm   77
Origen   157
Original Sin   93, 94, 156, 194, 209
Orthodox American Rabbinical Council   71
Orthodox Easter *See* Easter Sunday
Orthodox Christians *See* Christianity, Orthodox
Orthodox Judaism *See* Judaism, Orthodox
Our Lady, Feast of   184

Palm Sunday   170, 178, 210
papal infallibility   155-156
parochial schools   56
Passover   19, 141, 147, 150, 167-169, 170, 178, 180, 210
Passover Brunch (menu)   201
patriarchalism   78-80
patrilineal descent   209
patriotism, Catholics and   157; Jews and 151-152
Pearl Harbor Day   172
Pentecost, Christian   171, 186
Pentecost, Jewish   171, 185
Pesach *See* Passover
Petsonk, Judy   213
Pharisees (definition)   209
Phoebe   147
photographs, wedding   49
Phylacteries. *See* tefillin
pidyon ha-ben   101
Pius XI   70
pogrom   63, 142, 168
Pomona, feast of   192
post-fertilization implants   75
prayer shawl *See* Tallis
prenuptial agreement   126
Presidents Day   170, 177
Priscilla   147
Project Hope   145
Protestants *See* Christianity, Protestant
Prstowsky, Seymour   68
Purim   167, 170, 179

Rabbinic Center for Research and Counseling   98
Rabbinical Council of America   130
Rachel   75
Raphael, Sally Jessy   26
RECIPES   202-204
Reconciliation. *See* Confession
recreation, and culture   34-35
Reformation   78, 210
Reformation Sunday   171, 191
Reilly, Robert T.   92, 136
Remsen, Jim   213
residence, religion and places of   54-55
Reuben, Steven Carr   52, 105
ring, wedding   51
Ritual bath *See* Mikveh

Rivera, Geraldo 116
Roffman, Barry 94
Roman Catholic See Christianity, Roman Catholic
rosary (definition) 210
Rosh Hashanah 169, 171, 189
Rosh Hodesh 171, 197
Rosten, Leo 38
Rothenberg, Sam 58
Rothschild, Guy de 112
Rudavsky, Benjamin 98
Rudin, James 163
Rush, Benjamin 141

Sabbath, Christian See Lord's Day
Sabbath, Jewish 118-119, 173; sex on 78
Sabra Mousse (recipe) 202
sacrament (definition) 210
St. Basil's Day 174
St. Blaise's Day 176
St. David's Day 179
St. Hugh of Lincoln 63
St. Jerome 77
St. Joseph, Feast of 179
St. Joseph the Worker, Feast of 184
St. Lucia (Lucy) 164, 172
St. Mark's Basilica 145-146
St. Nicholas 172
St. Patrick's Day. 167, 170, 179
St. Paul 19, 67, 81, 97, 166
St. Peter 198
St. Swithin's Day 172
St. Thomas Aquinas 73, 97, 157
St. Valentine 176
St. Valentine's Day 170
St. Walburga 184
salvation, Catholic 157
salvation, Jewish 152
Samhain 192
Sarah 75, 147
Sarosky, Marlene 213
Schindler, Alexander 55
Schneider, Susan Weidman 46, 126, 214
Schulweis, Harold 47
seder 19, 141, 147, 168, 180-181; (definition) 210
Seder (menu) 201
Sephardi (definition) 210
Seventh Day Adventists 18
Shannon, Thomas A. 214
Shavuot 167, 171, 185, 202
shaygetz (definition) 210
Shea, James 43, 91, 108
Shemini Atzeret 171, 192
Sherwin, Byron L. 213
Shield of David (definition) 208
shiksah (definition) 210
shiva, sitting 135; 210 (definition)
shofar (definition) 210
Shrove Tuesday 167, 170
Sickle-Cell Anemia 76
Siegel, Seymour 75
Silver, Samuel 47, 105
Simkhat Torah 171, 192
Simms-Boeke case 127

Sol Invictus   164
Solemnity of Mary   170, 174
Star of David (definition)   208
sukkah   169, 191-192
Sukkot   165, 171, 191-192
Sunday *See* Lord's Day   171
surrogacy   75

TABLE OF HOLIDAYS AND THEIR CELEBRATIONS   172-177
tallis (definition)   210
Talmud (definition)   211
Tay-Sachs Disease   76
tefillin   68; (definition) 209, 211
Tendler, Moses   76
Thalassemia   76
Thanksgiving Day   171, 193
Tikkun   214
Tishe b'Av   171, 188
Tolkien, J. R. R.   118
Trinity, doctrine of the   154
Trinity Sunday   167, 170, 178, 183
Truth, Sojourner   81, 188
Tu b'Av   172

Union of Orthodox Rabbis of the US and Canada 72
Unitarians 17, 210

Vatican II   19, 25, 44, 93, 124, 155, 174, 198
Veterans Day   171, 193
viewing, of the dead   131
Virgin Birth   156, 194

wake   131
Waldoks, Moshe   38
Walpurgis Night   184
Washington's Birthday   177
WASP (definition)   211
Watson, Tom   59
weekends   171
Weingart, Irving A.   135
Wexler, Jacqueline Grennan   44
Whitsun *See* Pentecost, Christian
Willimon, William H.   140
Wohlberg, Jeffrey   45
Woman of Valor   80
Women's Equality Day   171, 188
work, ritual definition of   173
World Peace Sunday   193

Yael   78
yarmulke (definition)   211
Yid   211
Yiddish (definition)   211
Yom ha-Atzmaut See Israel Independence Day
Yom ha-Shoah See Holocaust Remembrance
Yom Kippur   143, 153, 169, 171, 190
Yom Kippur Katan   172

Zilpah   76
Zionism   151-152
Zionist Organization of America   58
Z"l   211